Evolution of Goods and Services Tax in India

The Goods and Services Tax (GST) was implemented in India on 1 July 2017, after four decades of protracted deliberations amid critical socio-economic and political challenges. It is a comprehensive multistage value-added tax on goods and services where both central and state governments share the same tax base. Finding a suitable design for GST that encompasses taxes from both the centre and the state tax baskets makes the Indian GST unique among GSTs implemented in other federal countries. This book tracks the debates around its evolution in India since the report of the Taxation Enquiry Commission (1953–54). It studies the following issues and debates inclusions and exclusions in GST, finding revenue neutrality of the tax reform, providing compensation to states for any possible loss of revenue due to its adoption, and possible scope for coordination in GST administration.

The book is divided into three sections. The first section studies the debate on fiscal autonomy versus tax harmonisation as an important issue for any tax reform that involves multiple layers of government with independent taxation power. The second section focuses on policy alternatives available to include items excluded from GST and shows that an element of tax cascading will be retained if energy sources are kept out of the GST system. The third section assesses the possible impact of GST on economic growth and inflation, and provides alternative ways of its administration.

R. Kavita Rao is Professor at the National Institute of Public Finance and Policy, New Delhi. She has been a member of various finance committees and commissions in India since 2001, and has been involved in a number of training programmes on VAT policy and administration for officials of sales tax departments of Indian states. Her research interests are design and implementation of GST, VAT, tax reforms, tax exemptions, and revenue mobilisation.

Sacchidananda Mukherjee is Associate Professor at the National Institute of Public Finance and Policy, New Delhi. He has worked on public finance, environmental economics and water resources management issues in India for more than a decade. His research interest includes public finance and fiscal policy in general and GST, VAT, performance assessment of tax administration, restructuring and reorganisation of tax administration, tax compliance behaviour, revenue potential estimation, tax and non-tax revenue mobilisation in particular.

Evolution of Goods and Services Tax in India

R. Kavita Rao

Sacchidananda Mukherjee

with contribution from **Amaresh Bagchi**

CAMBRIDGE
UNIVERSITY PRESS

CAMBRIDGE
UNIVERSITY PRESS

University Printing House, Cambridge CB2 8BS, United Kingdom

One Liberty Plaza, 20th Floor, New York, NY 10006, USA

477 Williamstown Road, Port Melbourne, vic 3207, Australia

314 to 321, 3rd Floor, Plot No.3, Splendor Forum, Jasola District Centre, New Delhi 110025, India

79 Anson Road, #06–04/06, Singapore 079906

Cambridge University Press is part of the University of Cambridge.

It furthers the University's mission by disseminating knowledge in the pursuit of education, learning and research at the highest international levels of excellence.

www.cambridge.org
Information on this title: www.cambridge.org/9781108473965

First published 2019

Printed in India by Nutech Print Services, New Delhi 110020

A catalogue record for this publication is available from the British Library

ISBN 978-1-108-47396-5 HB

Contents

∼

Part I Genesis and Evolution of GST in India

Part II Revenue Neutrality of GST

Figures

Tables

Acknowledgements

This book is the outcome of research carried out at the National Institute of Public Finance and Policy (NIPFP), New Delhi, on goods and services tax (GST). The enlightening discussions with our colleagues at NIPFP, often leading to fruitful outcomes, are gratefully acknowledged. We are also thankful to every individual who directly or indirectly have helped us through energised debates, dialogues and discussions in shaping our thought process on GST. We are truly grateful to Dr Rathin Roy, Director, NIPFP, for his constant encouragements and intellectual supports.

We are particularly thankful for the constant support from Ms Anwesha Rana of Cambridge University Press, who kept her faith in our efforts since the proposal stage. Special thanks go to Mr Aniruddha De and the editorial team of Cambridge University Press.

Finally we would like to thank our respective family members for bearing with us while we were working on the volume. Without that unending support, the volume would never have come out.

R. Kavita Rao
Sacchidananda Mukherjee

Abbreviations

ACTA	Agreement on Coordination of Tax Administration
AED	additional excise duty
ARA	Autonomous Revenue Agency
ATF	aviation turbine fuel
CBEC	Central Board of Customs and Central Excise
CE	central excise
CEA	Chief Economic Advisor
CENVAT	central value added tax
CFDA	Catalogue of Federal Domestic Assistance
CGST	central GST
CII	Confederation of Indian Industry
CIS	change in stock
CMIE	Centre for Monitoring Indian Economy
CRA	Canadian Revenue Agency
CSO	Central Statistics Office
CST	central sales tax
CVAT	central VAT
CVD	countervailing duty
DoR	Department of Revenue
DTI	direct tax incidence
EC	Empowered Committee of State Finance Ministers
ED	excise duty
ESL	European Community Sales List
ETR	effective tax rate
EU	European Union
FD	final demand
FICCI	Federation of Indian Chambers of Commerce and Industry
FISIM	Financial Intermediation Services Indirectly Measured
FRBM	Fiscal Responsibility and Budget Management
FTA	Forum on Tax Administration
GCF	gross capital formation
GDP	gross domestic product

GFCE	government final consumption expenditure
GFCF	gross fixed capital formation
GoI	Government of India
GSDP	gross state domestic product (GDP for state)
GST	goods and services tax
GSTC	GST Council
GSTN	GST Network
GVA	gross value added
HSD	high-speed diesel
HST	harmonised sales tax
IGST	integrated GST
IMF	International Monetary Fund
I-O	input–output
ITC	input tax credit
JITSIC	Joint Tax Shelter Information Centre
KTF	Kelkar Task Force
LPG	liquid petroleum gas
MANVAT	manufacturing level value added tax
MCA	Ministry of Corporate Affairs
MODVAT	modified value added tax
MoF	Ministry of Finance
NAS	National Academy of Sciences
NCCD	National Calamity Contingency Duty
NDC	National Development Council
NDP	net domestic product
NIC	national industries classification
NIC	National Informatics Centre
NIPFP	National Institute of Public Finance and Policy
NIT	net indirect taxes
OECD	Organisation for Economic Cooperation and Development
OMC	oil marketing company
PDS	public distribution system
PFCE	private final consumption expenditure
PFCL	Power Finance Corporation of Ltd.
PPAC	Petroleum Policy Analysis Cell
PSU	public sector undertaking
QST	Quebec sales tax
RBI	Reserve Bank of India
RNR	revenue neutral rate
SAD	special additional duty
SARA	Semi-Autonomous Revenue Agency
SEB	State Electricity Board
SGST	state GST
ST	service tax

TARC	Tax Administration Reform Commission
TBCS	Treasury Board of Canada Secretariat
TC	tax cascading
TFC	Thirteenth Finance Commission
THFC	Thirteenth Finance Commission
TIE	Tax Information Exchange
TINXSYS	Tax Information Exchange System
TO	total output
TRC	Tax Reforms Committee
TTI	total tax incidence
UFC	Union Finance Commission
UNEP	United Nations Environment Programme
UR	under recovery
VAT	value-added tax
VOP	value of output of petroleum products

Introduction

R. Kavita Rao *and* Sacchidananda Mukherjee

The objective of this book is to provide a comprehensive overview of the journey towards introduction of the goods and services tax (GST) in India. The book is based on research carried out at the National Institute of Public Finance and Policy (NIPFP), New Delhi, spanning over a decade. The basic objective of the volume is to highlight the contributions of the chapters in shaping the design and structure of the GST as well as capturing the evolution of the concept of GST in India since the late 1980s. The Indian GST is unique for its structure, design and administrative framework. The country-specific experience discussed in the chapters will help the readers to familiarise themselves with the alternative arrangements available with reference to design, structure and administration of GST from the perspective of a federal country. The concept of GST evolved over time in India and successive tax reform committees played an important role in shaping the Indian indirect tax system that finally culminated in the introduction of GST. Designing a destination-based dual value-added tax (VAT) system for a federal country like India was a challenge and from this perspective the Indian GST is unique. In this volume an attempt is made to capture the historical journey of policy research that was initiated since the inception of the government's interest in a national-level GST for India in the union budget speech of 2006–07. The introductory chapter of the book summarises the recommendations of successive tax reforms committees, constituted since Independence, with specific reference to the indirect tax regime. The recommendations contributed to a clear focus on the removal of the cascading of taxes (building up of taxes) and transition to a destination-based GST regime in India. This volume covers tax reforms carried out both in central and state indirect taxes during the last four decades and provides a background for the introduction of GST.

The chapters were written at different points in time spanning a decade and contributed to the then-ongoing discussion on GST. Each chapter of the book is based on rigorous theoretical as well as empirical research. In many countries, GST has been a tax levied by the national government. This has certain advantages. However, given the constitutional assignment of tax powers in India, with the states having a significant role in indirect taxes, that arrangement was not an option for India in its quest to introduce a regime with lower levels of cascading. The Indian experiment of an alternative model for GST is therefore interesting as a reference point for a discussion on a VAT for federal countries with strong sub-national governments.

The book is divided into three parts – *Genesis and Evolution of the Concept of GST in India, Revenue Neutrality of GST* and *GST Administration* and *the Possible Impact of GST on the Indian Economy.* The first part consists of four chapters and it aims to capture the genesis and evolution of the concept of GST in India.

The introductory chapter documents the evolution of the concept of GST in India by reviewing reports of successive tax reforms committees, constituted since Independence. Removal of cascading of taxes and designing destination-based VAT system are the major criteria adopted in the chapter to evaluate the recommendations of the tax reform committees. Following the recommendations of various tax reforms committees, introduction of reforms at different points in time helped in sequencing tax reforms and also paved the way for a 'big bang' tax reform such as GST in India. For a federal country like India, having a fairly decentralised system of fiscal arrangement, sequencing of tax reforms plays an important role in minimising the disruption from major tax reforms such as GST.

In the second chapter, Dr Amaresh Bagchi explores alternative designs of GST for India and, taking a cue from the Canadian QST-GST model, he recommends a dual VAT/GST. The chapter also explores possible arrangements for the administration of GST and opines that mutual trust and coordination between the centre and the states would be crucial for the smooth implementation of GST. Dr Bagchi makes the case for an 'independent quasi-judicial body to enforce agreements between the centre and the states and among the states.'

Chapter 3 is a criticism of the approach adopted by the Thirteenth Finance Commission (TFC) with reference to GST. Recommendations of the TFC are based on the findings of the study of the Task Force constituted by the TFC. The Thirteenth Finance Commission was required to look into the revenue impact of the introduction of the goods and services tax. Its report, based on the recommendations of a task force constituted to study the issue, recommends a highly uniform and centralised format that does not adequately recognise a tax reform exercise in a multi-level fiscal system that involves compromises and trade-offs. While several flaws can be pointed out in its design, developments that have taken place before and since the report was submitted have to a large extent rendered the commission's recommendations irrelevant. All this underlines the need for a model that goes beyond uniform rates of tax and allows states to vary beyond a floor, with a fixed classification of commodities and services, so that they can choose an appropriate rate to ensure that their revenue requirements are met.

Chapter 4 discusses the rationale behind moving towards the GST system and provides in-depth analysis of challenges before the introduction of GST. To remove the cascading effect of taxes and provide a common nation-wide market for goods and services, India is moving towards the introduction of GST. Under the proposed indirect tax reform both central and state governments will have concurrent taxation power to levy tax on supply of goods and services. It is expected that the proposed regime will improve tax collection and minimise leakage, as both central and state tax administrations will monitor and assess the same set of taxpayers. There are several challenges before the introduction of GST and these can be classified into two broad heads: (*a*) GST design and structure related and (*b*) GST administration and institutions. On design-related issues, a broad consensus on choice of revenue neutral rates (RNRs), harmonisation of GST rate(s) across states, harmonisation of list of exempted and excluded goods and services and thresholds for mandatory GST registration across states are yet to be reached. Similarly, there are several issues involved in tax administration (between central and state tax administrations and also across state tax administrations) that are yet to be resolved. Taking cognizance of the discussion available in the public domain, this chapter attempts to provide a broad contour of the proposed GST regime and highlights major challenges that require immediate attention of the governments.

The debate on fiscal autonomy versus tax harmonisation is an important issue for a tax reform like GST which involves multiple levels of government with independent taxation power. The evolution of GST in India has had to contend with this issue and therefrom emerge many of the features of the GST regime in place today. These issues are explored in some detail in the first part of the volume. Given that a number of very important taxes were to be subsumed into GST, it was important for all governments concerned that the GST regime be revenue neutral. Some of the issues that impacted the discussion on revenue neutrality are discussed in Part 2. There are three chapters in Part 2. The first two chapters focus on issues related to the revenue neutrality of the tax reform. The third chapter deals with policy alternatives available to include excluded items from GST and show the possible extent of tax cascading that will be retained if major energy sources (like electricity and petroleum products) are kept out of the GST system.

In the discussion on RNR, two alternative estimates are available. The first estimate was the result of the study carried out by the NIPFP. This estimate is presented in Chapter 5. The second estimate is the outcome of the Committee on the Revenue Neutral Rate (RNR) constituted by the Ministry of Finance and headed by the Chief Economic Adviser. This estimate is available in the public domain.

The two estimates differ in their assumptions and Chapter 6 carries out an in-depth analysis of the two estimates and identifies reasons for differences.

The search for revenue neutrality became a contentious issue and research carried out at NIPFP played a pivotal role in shaping a contour for the GST rate. Chapter 7 analyses the impact of keeping crude petroleum, natural gas, motor spirit (gasoline/petrol), high-speed diesel (diesel), aviation turbine fuel and electricity out of the VAT scheme. Specifically, the chapter finds that keeping these items out of the input tax credit mechanism (either partially or fully) would result in cascading. Through an input–output framework, this study proposes some alternatives to the proposed design of the GST and assesses the implications for cascading and prices. It captures the degree of cascading across 48 sectors under different scenarios and explores alternative policy options to phase out under-recoveries of oil marketing companies on account of sales of diesel and petrol under the administered pricing mechanism.

The third part consists of two chapters. The first chapter explores alternative options for GST administration while the second chapter and the Conclusion provide assessment of the possible impact of GST on the Indian economy and also provide a critical view of the present structure of the GST.

There are uncertainties associated with investment, economic growth and inflation in the post-GST regime and, based on international experiences, possible impacts are highlighted in this book. A simple tax system is desirable from both tax compliance and administration points of view. However, the final design of the GST retains complexities of the previous tax regime and it may raise compliance cost as well as tax evasion.

I

Genesis and Evolution of GST in India

1

Decades of Indirect Tax Reforms in India

A Journey towards Goods and Services Tax (GST)

Sacchidananda Mukherjee *and* R. Kavita Rao

Introduction

The quest for a suitable indirect tax framework in India encompassing goods as well as services started a long time back. The constitutional assignment of powers for taxation in India included a number of stand-alone taxes on goods and services in addition to a few relatively more broad-based taxes, none of which were comprehensive in covering both goods and services. Further, this assignment divided the powers between the union and the state governments, thereby requiring a considerable degree of cooperation and coordination between the union and the state governments in order to initiate and establish a new indirect tax regime which addressed some of the concerns emanating from the old regime. Given the constitutional assignment of taxation power to different governments, fiscal autonomy enjoyed by the subnational governments, and complexities involved in bringing consensus among the subnational governments, the evolution of the Indian goods and services tax (GST) provides an interesting example of reforms in indirect taxes for scholars interested in public finance, especially in the case of federal countries.

Reforms in indirect taxes initiated since 1986–87 helped in sequencing big tax reform such as GST in India. It helped to accommodate the political-economy dimensions as well as the acceptability aspects of the tax reform. What is significant about the Indian GST is that each and every aspect of design, structure and administration of the GST has evolved on the basis of political consensus between the union and provincial governments. For a federal country like India where subnational governments enjoy more or less a power structure similar to that of the union government and where there is considerable diversity among provincial (subnational) governments, building consensus for a destination-based dual GST system is a great achievement in the history of fiscal federalism. The role played by different institutions/committees in achieving the Indian GST requires special mention here. The present chapter is an attempt to provide readers an overview into the evolution of the concept of GST in India.

India introduced GST from 1 July 2017. It is a comprehensive multistage value-added tax (VAT) on goods as well as services and it provides concurrent taxation powers to the centre (federal) and state (provincial) governments to collect tax on every stage of value addition.

The objective of this chapter is to study the evolution of the concept of GST in India by reviewing reports of successive tax reforms committees. Removal of cascading of taxes and designing destination-based VAT system are the major criteria adopted in this chapter to evaluate the recommendations of the tax reform committees. Following the recommendations of various tax reforms committees, introduction of reforms at different points in time helped in sequencing tax reforms and also paved the way for a 'big bang' tax reform such as the GST in India. For a federal country like India, having a fairly decentralised system of fiscal arrangement, sequencing of tax reforms plays an important role in minimising the disruption from major tax reforms like the GST.

In the next section, titled 'Indirect Tax Reforms in Central Taxes', we provide a comprehensive overview of reforms carried out in indirect taxes for the central government since Independence. In the following section ('State Taxes'), we evaluate state VAT system (mostly introduced in April 2005 by states) and drivers for GST. Removing central sales tax (CST) was the major challenge to enshrine destination principle in GST design. In a subsection of the section, we provide discussion on challenges associated with cutting CST rate and eliminating CST. In the last section ('Casting of the Structure of GST'), we discuss the evolution of the design and structural aspects of the Indian GST. The challenges related to revenue neutrality and administration of GST are also discussed in the last section.

Indirect Tax Reforms in Central Taxes

The central excise duty, customs duty and service tax were the major indirect taxes of the central government. Central excise duty (along with additional excise duties, special additional excise duty (AED), cesses and surcharges) is a tax on the manufacturing of goods and the Indian Constitution assigns power to tax manufacturing (except alcoholic beverages for human consumption and opium, Indian hemp and other narcotic drugs and narcotics) to the central government. Following recommendation of the Indirect Taxation Enquiry Committee (1977–78) (also known as the L. K. Jha Committee), the central excise duty was converted to a manufacturing stage

VAT for a limited number of goods in 1986–87 and renamed Modified VAT or MODVAT. Over the years more goods are brought under the MODVAT system to achieve comprehensive coverage of the manufacturing sector. This was followed by a phase of rationalisation of the rates of the tax which culminated in the introduction of a single-standard rate and a few special rates. This regime was referred to as the Central VAT (CENVAT) system. Even with all this rationalisation, however, some commodities remained outside coverage, for example, some petroleum products (gasoline, diesel and aviation turbine fuel [ATF]) and tobacco and tobacco products.

Service tax was the second important source of indirect tax revenue of the central government. The union government invoked residual power of taxation, as bestowed under article 97 in the union list (Rao 2004) and introduced a tax on the value of services supplied. In 1994–95, service tax was introduced selectively for three services – tax on telephone billing, tax on general insurance premium and tax on stock brokerage commission. Over the years, the domain of the service tax expanded by including more services under the service tax net. In 2012, the base for taxation of services was changed from a well-defined and identified set of services to one demarcated through a list of exclusions. In other words, from 2012, there was a list of services which were not subject to tax, while all other services were to be taxed. Following the recommendation of the Expert Group on Taxation of Services (2001) (chaired by M. Govinda Rao) backed by the Kelkar Task Force (KTF) Report on Indirect Taxation, input tax credit (ITC) against service tax liability was introduced for a limited number of services in 2002–03. The scheme was extended further in 2003–04 by covering all services. Cross-utilisation of credit between CENVAT and service tax was introduced in 2004–05. With this step, while the base for taxation under central tax remained patchy – though manufacturing and supply of services were taxable, sale of goods was not taxable under this regime – the ITC mechanism was reasonably comprehensive. The introduction of ITC adjustment system between CENVAT and service tax helped in reducing the cascading of taxes and paved the way for the introduction of GST in India.

Customs duty (including additional duty of customs and special countervailing duty [CVD]) is a tax on import of commodities. In addition to basic customs duty (also known as Customs or trade tariff), imports also used to attract an additional duty of customs (also known as CVD) in lieu of CENVAT and Special CVD or (special additional duty or SAD) in lieu of state taxes.[1] Customs duty was the third-largest source of indirect taxes for the central government. In 2004–05, harmonisation in CVD rates at the level equivalent to excise duty was achieved. Further, importers were allowed to claim ITC of CVD against subsequent central taxes payable. However, given that central taxes did not extend to sale of goods, at least a part of

---

[1] In 2005–06, CVD was introduced at the rate of 4 per cent to compensate state-level taxes on Information Technology Agreement (ITA)-bound (except IT software) items and their imports. Full credit of this duty is allowed to manufacturers of excisable goods.

the ITC might not have been claimed. The tax rate of SAD was 4 per cent whereas standard state sales tax rate was higher at 12.5 per cent since the introduction of state VAT. The changes in customs duty were once again a change in the direction of rationalisation of the indirect tax regime towards a level playing field.

In the following discussion, we will study the recommendations of various tax reforms committees in removing cascading of taxes and achieving destination-based VAT system in India. Indian indirect tax environment has gone through major reforms and these reforms helped in achieving comprehensive GST.

Taxation Enquiry Commission (1953–54)

The indirect tax regime at the time of adoption of the Constitution of India was a destination-based regime. However, the regime lacked the necessary structure to appropriately deal with interstate transactions while at the same time maintaining the destination principle. This caused some problems of compliance for the sellers and problems of administering the tax for the tax departments. In light of this and other issues that arose from the Constitutional assignment of tax powers, the Taxation Enquiry Commission (1953–54) was set up, headed by John Matthai (Government of India 1955). Two major recommendations of the commission were implemented and had considerable implications for the indirect tax regime in India.

First, on the recommendation of the commission, CST was introduced on interstate sales of goods in 1957 (under the Central Sales Tax Act, 1956). Though the CST Act is a central legislation, the power to collect and retain the taxes on interstate trade was vested in the states. The tax was applicable only on sales but not on consignment transfers or branch transfers across state borders.

The main objective behind the introduction of CST was to reduce compliance burden of taxpayers dealing in interstate trade. The obligation to file returns in both origin and destination states resulted in considerable compliance burden for dealers dealing in interstate trade.

The commission recommended:

> *Considerations of future policy regarding sales tax.* – In essence, the sales tax must continue to be a state tax. However, power and responsibility of the State must end and that of the Union begin when the sales tax of one State impinges administratively on the dealers and fiscally on the consumers of another State. Inter-State sales should be the concern of the Union. The Union should also have power to control the taxation of sales of raw materials which figure significantly in inter-state commerce. Except in these cases, Parliament should not exercise current power in regard to the levy of sales tax. (Government of India 1955, vol. III, ch. 4, para 14)

> *Main features of Central legislation* – Parliamentary legislation will provide for the level of sales tax on inter-State transactions. It will provide for delegating

to the States the powers of the Central Government in respect of assessment, collection, etc. It will also provide that receives will be distributed to the States on the basis of collection. (Ibid., para 16)

Initially, CST was introduced with a tax rate of 1 per cent on interstate sales of goods between registered dealers. The suggested CST rate for transactions between registered dealers in origin state and unregistered dealers or consumers in destination state was the prevailing tax rate in the origin state. The commission also recommended the transfer of tax proceeds to the destination state for any tax collection 'in excess of the receipts from the rate normally leviable on inter-State trade between registered dealers'. Though in principle the recommendation supports the destination principle of the VAT system, in practice states retained the entire CST proceeds.

> Rate of tax on interstate transaction (other than those relating to 'goods of special importance in the inter-State trade'). The rate of the Central tax should be low. It may be one per cent when the inter-State transaction takes place between a registered dealer in one state and a registered dealer in another. As for transactions between registered dealers in one state and unregistered dealers or consumers in another the rate of tax should be the same as the exporting state imposes on similar transaction in its own territory. The proceeds in excess of the receipts from the rate normally leviable on inter-State trade between registered dealers should be made available to the state where goods are delivered. The Central legislation should make no distinction between ordinary goods and luxury goods for the purposes of the rate of tax on inter-State transactions. (Ibid., paras 17–19)

At the time of introduction of CST, the rate was 1 per cent, which was increased first to 2 per cent, then to 3 per cent and effective from 1 July 1975 it was 4 per cent. Though ITC against CST sales was allowed, withholding of ITC for various reasons was common in many states (for example, in case of consignment/branch transfers). The introduction of CST increased the cost of doing business for manufacturers who were sourcing their inputs from multiple states and/or selling their outputs to other states. The system provided incentive to manufacturers to either locate their branch offices and/or set up their own distribution networks across all the states they operated in so that they could send the goods as branch/consignment transfers and avoid paying CST. Transaction costs associated with the setting up of branch offices or own distribution networks and compliance costs of dealing with multiple tax jurisdictions (with varying rules and regulations) were important factors determining expansion plans of businesses. The introduction of CST resulted in division of the single Indian market into several state markets. The system was not conducive for encouraging market efficiency, which in turn constrained the ability to improve efficiency and productivity of Indian business.

After the introduction of VAT, the CST rate was reduced from 4 per cent to 3 per cent with effect from 1 April 2007 and it was reduced further to 2 per cent with effect from 1 June 2008. Gradual reduction of the CST rate paved the way for the introduction of a destination-based VAT system in India.

Second, the commission suggested special tax treatment of certain 'goods of special importance in inter-State trade'. The recommendation is as follows:

> Central regulation of the states' sales taxes on goods of special importance in inter-State trade. The main condition will be that no state shall have a system of levy other than a single point tax on such goods. The tax maybe either on sales or purchases but will be recoverable only at the last stage of sale or purchase. We recommend that the rate of such tax should be three pies per rupee. No purchase tax will be levied by a state on these goods if a Central tax on inter-State trade has already been levied at the rate three pies in the rupee. The goods to be specified as goods of special importance in inter-State trade are coal, iron and steel, cotton, hides and skins, oilseeds and jute. (Ibid., paras 21–22)

Following the recommendation of the commission, the central government backed by Article 286(3)(a) of the Constitution of India – which authorises Parliament to declare some goods to be of 'special importance' and to impose restrictions and conditions in regard to the power of the states to levy, decide rates and other incidence of tax on such goods – declared some goods to be of special importance under under section 14 of the CST Act 1956 and placed restrictions under section 15 of the CST Act. The list of declared goods was not restricted to only those goods suggested by the commission but rather included a large number of goods (listed under section 14 of the CST Act 1956).[2]

Under section 15 of the CST Act, the centre placed the following restrictions and conditions on the powers of state governments to tax declared goods inside the state.[3]

1. Tax on declared goods not to exceed 4 per cent.
2. Reimbursement of local tax if declared goods sold interstate.
3. Goods must be sold in same form to obtain reimbursement – declared goods purchased must be sold in same form, that is, identical goods must be sold. Thus, if goods sold after processing are a different commodity, reimbursement of local sales tax is not available.
4. Special provisions about paddy and pulses
   i. If paddy is taxed within state and rice (which is produced from paddy) is also taxed, tax paid on paddy should be given setoff while levying tax on rice.
   ii. Each of the pulses, whether whole or separated and whether with or without husk, shall be treated as a single commodity for the purpose of levying tax

---

[2] See http://www.charteredonline.in/2012/01/declared-goods-under-cst-act-writeup.html (last accessed on 17 June 2018).

[3] Read more at https://www.caclubindia.com/articles/declared-goods-as-per-cst-act-279.asp (last accessed on 17 June 2018).

under state tax law, that is, if tax is paid on raw pulses, no further tax is payable after it is processed.

iii. If paddy is purchased on payment of sales tax and rice procured out of such paddy is exported, the paddy and rice will be treated as 'same goods' for the purpose of section 5(3) of the CST Act.

5. Sales tax rates applicable for sale of declared goods – state governments cannot charge sales tax for sale within the state at a rate that is more than 4 per cent.

The commission did not accept the view of levying AED in lieu of sales tax. However, this question was again examined by the National Development Council (NDC) in January 1956. The proposal to levy AED in lieu of sales tax on sugar, tobacco and textiles came into force after a decision was taken by the NDC. It was decided that the net proceeds of AED would be distributed among the states in accordance with the principles laid down by successive Finance Commissions. Through the Additional Duties of Excise (Goods of Special Importance) Act, 1957, the centre started collection of AED on these three items. The objective behind the AED was to 'achieve uniformity in the sales tax systems of the different States and sought to reduce collection costs, tax-evasion and hardship to the business community which was obliged to maintain elaborate accounts for sales tax purposes' (Singh 1964). However, the system resulted in revenue loss to states (Rao 2003; Singh 1964). The KTF report on indirect taxation recommended dispensing with the AED on sugar, textiles and tobacco imposed in lieu of sales tax. As part of the centre's compensation package to states for revenue loss on account of reduction of the CST rate to 2 per cent and implementation of state VAT, the power to levy tax on tobacco, textiles and sugar was transferred to the states from 1 April 2003. The abolition of AED on these three items happened subsequently.

The commission also recommended setting up an Inter-State Taxation Council to harmonise the sales tax system across states. The Empowered Committee of State Finance Ministers, which played an important role in rolling out VAT and GST, could be seen as an institution that performed this function though it came into existence much later in time.

Indirect Taxation Enquiry Committee (1977–78)

The report of the Indirect Taxation Enquiry Committee (1977–78), chaired by L. K. Jha, is the first report that articulated the need for a comprehensive VAT system for every stage of value addition – 'from the stage of production to the retail stage'.

> Essentially, VAT in its comprehensive form is a tax on all goods and services (except exports and Government services), its special characteristics being that it falls on the value added at each stage – from the stage of production to the retail stage .... producers are in effect freed from the taxation of inputs at every stage. Thus, a distinctive merit of the VAT is that it enables a country to have an

extended system of commodity taxation and yet avoid the problems of cascading and escalation of costs that are concomitants of general sales and excise taxes. It is relatively easy under the VAT system to completely free exports of internal commodity taxation. (Government of India 1977, para 104)

To reduce the cascading of taxes, the committee recommended a manufacturing-level VAT (named MANVAT):

> We consider that it would be premature now to think in terms of comprehensive system of VAT extending down to the retail level. But in order to put Central taxation on a rational basis we would urge that serious consideration be given for moving over to a VAT system at the manufacturing level – the so-called MANVAT. It is our view that in the ultimate analysis a satisfactory solution to the various distortions and problems that arise from an extended system of excise taxation lies in the adoption of MANVAT. The main advantage of MANVAT would be that it would altogether eliminate cascading on account of taxation of raw materials and other inputs. The tax levied on a final product would be the total tax on it and tax on inputs at earliest stages will not affect its cost or price…. MANVAT may also minimize the requirement of physical checks to ensure that there is not much evasion. Besides, the competitiveness of our products in the export markets will get a major thrust. (Ibid., para 10.9)

However, the committee was well aware of the political and administrative constraints to the introduction of a comprehensive VAT in India and they stated that

> [t]here could be two major arguments against the introduction of comprehensive VAT in India – one is political and the other is administrative. The political argument is the obvious one that the loss of power to levy sales taxes would seriously erode the fiscal autonomy of the State Governments and weaken the federal principle that each subordinate level of Government should have the discretion to raise more or less revenue as the people of the State concerned desire. The administrative argument is that the enforcement of VAT in relation to wholesalers and retailers is likely to create serious problems due to the need for dealing with a larger number of tax-payers and the difficulties likely to be faced by a majority of the traders to cope up with the accounting requirements. (Ibid., para 18.11)

> Given our federal system and the administrative problems of enforcing VAT at the post-manufacturing stages, the right course of action is not to pursue the theoretical best solution, namely, one integrated system based on the VAT principle but to adopt the second best solution of VAT applied to the manufacturing stage (to begin with) combined with a reformed system of sales taxation. (Ibid., para 18.13)

At the same time, the committee was also quite aware of the challenges associated with tax administration and the interjurisdictional nature of taxes, and therefore perceived that extending the VAT system up to the retail stage might be difficult during that time. Therefore, as an interim measure, they suggested that

> [t]o put Central taxation on a rational basis, we would urge that serious consideration be given for moving over to a VAT system at the manufacturing level – the so-called MANVAT. It is our view that in the ultimate analysis a satisfactory solution to the various distortions and problems that arise from an extended system of excise taxation lies in the adoption of MANVAT. (Government of India 1978)

However, it is to be noted that the suggested MANVAT system was not the first system to allow ITC in India. Prior to MODVAT, the then excise duty had provision under Rule 56-A (Proforma Credit) for setting off tax paid on inputs against the tax payable on the output. The system used to be based on physical verification instead of an invoice- or account-based method of tax credit. Moreover, the proforma credit scheme used to operate on a case-by-case basis where the decision on allowance of credit was subject to the satisfaction of the deciding authority. Possibilities of discretionary practices under the system cannot be ruled out. The MODVAT scheme was a rule-based system and the problem of classification disputes was expected to be minimum (Singh 1991). In the proforma credit system, availing credit was contingent upon the input and output of the manufacturer falling under the same or particular tariff items or sub-items. Under MODVAT, on the other hand, input fell only under tariff items or sub-items. Under the MODVAT system, the concept of input had a much wider connotation than under Rule 56-A. However, the regulations corresponding to the availing of benefits of Rule 56-A were cumbersome and Rule 56-A has been omitted since 20 May 1994.

The introduction of MODVAT in 1986–87 could be seen as the achievement of the committee. Though MODVAT was not free from shortcomings in structure, it could be seen as the first step towards the introduction of a modern VAT system in India which eventually helped to achieve GST.

The Tax Reforms Committee (1991–93) headed by Raja J. Chelliah provided a concise criticism of the MODVAT scheme:

> Under the Modvat scheme, as noted earlier, only taxes levied on inputs that go into production or get used up in the process are eligible for set-off. This means that excise taxes that fall on machinery, accessories, fittings, tools, office equipment and vehicles continue to cause cascading. There is no economic, technical or administrative justification for keeping these goods used in production out of the Modvat credit scheme except the argument that in a developing country, capital goods should be subject to tax in order to discourage the use of capital. On the other hand, in many countries, capital goods have been treated like other inputs precisely to concentrate the tax on consumption and to encourage saving. Also it is wrong to classify all non-incorporated 'inputs' along with machinery proper as capital goods. (Government of India 1991)

It is worthwhile to present the view of the Indirect Taxation Enquiry Committee on taxation of services. This was the first structured articulation of a tax on services. The committee suggested that the central government levy and administer the service tax, and the reason for such recommendation was the interstate character of services. The committee suggested the exemption of input services from the service tax.

> In the absence of adequate data we are unable to make an estimate of potential revenue from a service tax. We suggest that if the Government consider it desirable to tax services, the revenue potential as well as practical problems of such taxation should be thoroughly examined. We are inclined to the view that if such a tax were to be introduced it should be under Central legislation and administration, even if the proceeds from the tax go to States. One reason for this is that the sales of services often have an inter-state character. Further any such taxation will have to take into account its effect on the national economy as a whole. In particular, it should be important to ensure that services sold to producers are not made subject to taxation because they are in the nature of inputs otherwise the same problem of cascading and distortions that have arisen now in respect of taxation of sales of goods will arise in respect of taxation of services. (Government of India 1978, para 14.41, p. 246)

Tax Reform Committee (1991–93)

The Tax Reforms Committee (1991–93), headed by Raja J. Chelliah (Government of India 1991, 1992, 1993), was constituted in the context of the crisis faced by the Indian economy in 1991. The committee recommended major changes in the regimes of direct and indirect taxes. Within indirect taxes, the recommendations included rationalisation of the tax rate structure, minimisation of tax exemptions and simplification of procedures of the central indirect tax system.

The specific recommendations of the committee are summarised as follows:

- The indirect tax at the central level should be broadly neutral in relation to production and consumption and should, in course of time, cover commodities and services. This means that we should move towards VAT covering services and commodities. To make the VAT scheme simple and easily administrable, it should be levied at two or three rates, say, at 10 per cent, 15 per cent or 20 per cent. The selected excise duty on non-essential consumption could be levied at 30 per cent, 40 per cent or 50 per cent (this means that the maximum rate on a commodity will not exceed 50 per cent with a few exceptions like cigarettes) (Government of India, para 9.2).
- There is a need to widen the tax base and extend the coverage of excise duties (ibid., paras 9.6 and 9.29).
- All end-used-based exemptions for inputs should be withdrawn and the minimum duty rate of 10 per cent ad valorem should be levied on such inputs. If it is not possible to withdraw all such exemptions immediately, this should be done gradually over a period of time when inputs and finished products will bear duty with the benefit of MODVAT credit for inputs (ibid., para 9.7).

- The subsidy in the form of notional higher credit available to industries using inputs covered under the general scheme should be withdrawn (ibid., para 9.19).
- All exemption notifications should be subjected to a close scrutiny with a view to ascertaining whether these can be withdrawn (ibid., para 9.21).
- The power of granting exemptions from excise duty should be withdrawn. However, government may retain the power of adjusting rates of duty under very exceptional circumstances (ibid., para 9.22).
- In a system of commodity taxation, ad valorem duties are preferable to specific duties, particularly under the MODVAT regime. Switching over to ad valorem rates in respect of a number of commodities is, therefore, recommended. Simultaneously, rationalisation of the existing rates has also been suggested with a view to reducing multiplicity of rates. The ad valorem rates suggested for various items broadly conform to the duty slots in which the tariff is required to be structured in the long run. For administrative considerations, however, some commodities like petroleum products, tobacco products and textiles, coffee, tea, marble, and so on, may continue to have specific rates (ibid., para 9.29).
- Where specific rates are retained, there should be a system of revising the rates every year to take into account price increases as represented by the relevant sectoral wholesale price index. While fixing ad valorem rates, goods falling within the same class should as far as possible be made to be at the same rate (ibid., para 9.31).
- As the MODVAT or the VAT system gets extended and becomes the main plank for raising revenue from domestically produced goods and services, it would be necessary to move over to a system of assessment on the basis of invoice value. However, for this to be possible and easily administrable, it would be desirable to fulfil two conditions. First, there should be an extension of VAT from the manufacturing to the wholesale stage; this would considerably reduce attempts at undervaluation of products. Second, it would be necessary to give up the traditional method of administering excises on the basis of clearance of goods from the factory and move over to a system of assessment on the basis of periodic returns to be submitted by manufacturers. These are important changes and their feasibility would have to be studied in greater detail (ibid., para 9.40).
- The committee envisages that as the union exercise on commodities gets gradually transformed into a VAT at the manufacturing level, the services tax will get woven into the system and, therefore, tax could be levied also on services that enter into the productive processes (ibid., para 9.49).
- The harmful effects of the interstate sales tax-cum-consignment tax can be avoided or minimised in two different ways. The first and the more satisfactory arrangement would be as follows: (*a*) the interstate sales tax or CST or the consignment tax imposed by the exporting state will be given credit by the importing state against the sales tax payable to it by the 'importer', (*b*) the exporting state will credit the interstate sales tax and consignment tax collections to a central pool, (*c*) thus, all collections of these two taxes will be deposited in the central pool and will then be shared among the states on the basis of an agreed formula, and the formula should be so devised as to give even treatment to the producing and consuming

states and (*d*) the rate of interstate sales and consignment taxes would be 2 per cent. The second-best arrangement could be that the consignment tax would be imposed at 1 per cent after the ceiling rate of the CST has been reduced to 1 per cent (ibid., paras 9.58 and 9.59).

Introduction of Service Tax

Although there is no explicit mention of services either in the central list or state list in the seventh schedule, entry 97 under the central list empowers the central government to levy taxes on all items not mentioned in either the central or the state list, and the central government has been levying taxes on services under this entry.

On 1 July 1994, service tax was introduced for three services and at a tax rate of 5 per cent. Over the years, more and more services were included under the service tax net. The total number of services reached 119 in 2012 and from 1 July 2012 negative-list-based taxation of services was introduced.[4] Following the recommendation of the Expert Group on Taxation of Services (2001) (Government of India 2001), ITC against service tax was introduced for select services in 2002–03 and the scheme was extended to cover all services from 2003–04. With the introduction of the ITC system, the service tax rate was increased from 5 per cent to 8 per cent from 14 May 2003 and the rate was further increased to 10.20 per cent from 10 September 2004. Backed by high economic growth, the tax rate on services was further increased to 12.24 per cent from 14 April 2006 and 12.36 per cent from 11 May 2007. However, in the face of global recession and to provide stimulus to the Indian economy, the service tax rate was reduced from 12.36 per cent to 10.30 per cent from 24 February 2009. With the recovery of the Indian economy from recession, the service tax rate was again reverted to 12.36 per cent from 1 April 2012 and it was further increased to 14 per cent from 1 June 2015. The basic rationale for increasing the tax rate on services was to harmonise the tax rate of services with the CENVAT rate. This was followed by a further increase of 0.50 per cent on account of the Swachh Bharat cess. From 1 June 2016 to 1 July 2017, the service tax rate was 15 per cent. Integration of ITC between service tax and CENVAT was introduced from 2004–05, which paved the way for the introduction of GST.

On 15 January 2004, the Constitution (Eighty-Eighth Amendment) Act, 2003, inserted a new article, 268A, after article 268 and amended the Seventh Schedule

---

[4] In June 2000, an Expert Group headed by Dr M. Govinda Rao observed that 'selective approach to taxation of services is undesirable for this violates neutrality in taxation, leads to inadequate coverage in addition to raising several avoidable procedural and legal complications'. The group recommended that the centre should move towards a 'general and comprehensive extension of the tax to cover all services with a small and clearly-defined exemption list'. The group identified six categories of services that may be put in the negative list, and that included all public services of governments, all public utility services of essential nature and all school education.

to the Constitution by inserting an entry, '92C. Taxes on services', after the entry 92B of the List I – Union List.

> 268A. Service tax levied by Union and collected and appropriated by the Union and the States. – (1) Taxes on services shall be levied by the Government of India and such tax shall be collected and appropriated by the Government of India and the States in the manner provided in clause (2).
>
> (2) The proceeds in any financial year of any such tax levied in accordance with the provisions of clause (1) shall be –
>
> (a) collected by the Government of India and the States;
>
> (b) appropriated by the Government of India and the States,
>
> in accordance with such principles of collection and appropriation as may be formulated by Parliament by law.

The amendment assigns the power to levy a service tax to the central government, with the proceeds being collected and appropriated by the central and state governments in accordance with principles formulated by the Parliament.

States also collect service tax on a few stand-alone services, for example, taxes on goods and passengers carried by road or on inland waterways (entry 56 of the state list) and taxes on luxuries, including taxes on entertainment, amusement, betting and gambling (entry 62).

KTF Report on Indirect Taxation (2002)

The Ministry of Finance and Company Affairs constituted a task force for indirect taxes, headed by Vijay L. Kelkar, with the objective to bring indirect tax systems and procedures at par with the best international practices, encourage compliance and ensure transparency in administration. The terms of reference of the task force was 'simplification of laws and procedures, reducing cost of compliance, facilitating voluntary compliance, increased use of automation for a user-friendly and transparent tax administration, review of the statutorily prescribed records and returns (including their periodicity) and suggestions on their utility and simplification, time-bound disposal of cases, etc.' (Godbole 2002).

'The Consultation Paper of Task Force' (popularly known as KTF) (Government of India 2002) recommended various measures to reform the indirect tax environment. Some of the recommendations of the task force are summarised in the following subsection.

Select Recommendations of the KTF on Service Tax (excerpted from the KTF Consultation Paper)

- To the extent possible, service tax should be levied in a comprehensive manner leaving out only a few services by including them in a negative list.

- There should be complete integration of the CENVAT credit and service tax credit schemes with effect from 1 April 2003.
- Credit of central duties (on goods and services) should be utilised for payment of service tax collected and appropriated by the central government.
- Along with integration of the goods and services credit schemes from 1 April 2003, the rate of service tax should be suitably enhanced so as to achieve parity with the CENVAT rate by 2006–07. However, there should be two rates, one for service providers who avail credit and another, a lower rate, for those who do not.
- The service providers who provide services up to a value of INR 10 lakh (INR 1 million) in a financial year should be subjected to a total tax of 1 per cent on the value of the services annually on the basis of simple declaration. Such service providers would be exempt from the normal procedures of returns and documentation. This scheme does not envisage availing the credit of the duty paid on the input goods and services.
- There should be a separate legislation for levying service tax, which should eventually be integrated with the central excise law.
- The services should be classified on the basis of World Trade Organization (WTO) classification, which should be made a part of the service tax legislation.

The recommendations of the KTF played an important role to (*a*) shift taxation of services from selective-list-based to negative-list-based approach (implemented from 1 July 2012), (*b*) integrate CENVAT and service tax credits (2004–05), (*c*) reduce the difference between the service tax rate and CENVAT rate, (*d*) adopt the 88th amendment to the Constitution (see earlier) and (*e*) adopt a classification system for services (in 2003, section 65A was inserted in Chapter V of the Finance Act, 1994).

Select Recommendations of the KTF on Central Excise

- As a policy, we should review all levies and have only one levy, that is, the CENVAT. Some exceptions, however, have been suggested for the textile and petroleum sectors.
- Till such time as there are multiple levies, there should be a working schedule indicating the total tax payable on a particular product and the system should internally segregate the same into the respective levies.
- The following recommendations are made for the central excise duty structure:
    i. 0 per cent – for life-saving drugs and equipment, security items, food items, necessities and the like, and agricultural products.
    ii. 6 per cent – for processed food products and matches.
    iii. 14 per cent – standard rate for all items not mentioned against other rates.
    iv. 20 per cent – for motor vehicles, air conditioners and aerated water.
    v. Separate rates for tobacco products and their substitutes (like *pan masala*).

vi. The specific rate of excise duty of INR 1 per kilogram on bulk tea today translates to about 1 per cent in ad valorem terms. Raising it to 6 per cent may not be desirable, more so when coffee is already exempt from excise duty. Thus, bulk tea may also be exempted from duty. This is anyway a plantation product.

vii. Specific duty on cement may continue as most of the clearances are to the depots where the prices vary from day to day and ad valorem levy would necessitate provisional assessments, and may result in uncertainty.

In 2000–01, MODVAT was renamed as CENVAT with a single CENVAT rate (standard rate) of 16 per cent. In addition, there was a non-rebatable special duty at the rates of 8 per cent, 16 per cent or 24 per cent. At the same time, MODVAT credit was extended to all inputs except high-speed diesel (HSD) oil and motor spirit (petrol). The extension of MODVAT credit to all finished goods (except matches) and all capital goods (subject to availing of capital goods credit being spread over two years) helped to clean up the central excise duty system in India.

The KTF recommended the restructuring of the central excise rates into three rates (6 per cent, 14 per cent and 20 per cent) (except for the zero rating of life-saving drugs and equipment, and so on). However, the government aimed to converge multiple rates into a single CENVAT rate of 16 per cent over successive union budgets since 2000–01.

Select Recommendations of the KTF on Customs Duty

- As a policy, the multiplicity of levies must be reduced. Accordingly, it is recommended that there should be only three types of duties, namely basic customs duty, additional duty of customs (or CVD) and antidumping/safeguard duties. All other duties should be removed. However, the removal of SAD should be linked to the implementation of state-level VAT, where SAD would get replaced by the state VAT to be levied on imports.

Select Recommendations of the KTF on State VAT

- Attempt should be made towards uniformity of all state legislations, procedures and documentation relating to VAT.
- Issue of compensation, if it arises, must be primarily tackled through a mutually acceptable mechanism of additional resource mobilisation through service tax and not through budgetary support.
- With the introduction of VAT, all other local taxes (for example, entry tax, luxury tax, *mandi* cess and octroi) be discontinued, and the same should be taken into account in determining the revenue neutral rate (RNR).
- Whereas AED may continue for textiles up to 2005, it may continue even thereafter for cigarettes, which should not be subjected to VAT.
- The VAT scheme should provide for grant of credit of duty by the importing state for the duty paid in the exporting state, in the course of interstate movement of goods.

- For the stability and continuity of VAT, a VAT Council or a permanent suitable alternative vested with adequate powers to take steps against discriminatory taxes and practices and eliminate barriers to free flow of trade and commerce across the country should be explored.

State Taxes

Prior to the introduction of VAT at the state level, there was tax competition between states (Rao and Vaillancourt 1994) and disharmony in tax rates, number of tax schedules and exempted items, and so on. Table 1.1 provides a comprehensive overview of the sales tax system prevalent across states during 1989–90, much before the process of harmonisation was initiated. There was wide variation in the number of rate categories, with some states having 7 rate categories (Odisha and West Bengal) and others as high as 25 rate categories (for example, Gujarat). The general rate of sales tax varied from 4 per cent to 12 per cent. In addition, a wide variation in sales tax rate around the general rate was also reported across the states (Aggarwal 1995). Under the sales tax system, variations in the point of taxation (single point, double points and multiple points) across states resulted in major roadblocks for the introduction of state VAT. Inability to raise tax beyond first-point sales led states to impose additional levies such as turnover tax, additional sales tax, surcharges, and so on. This led to a non-transparent tax system and a high incidence of arbitrary and unpredictable taxes.

Following up on the *Chelliah Committee Report* in 1991–93, the *Reform of Domestic Trade Taxes in India*, authored by Bagchi et al. (1994), played an important role in reforming the state sales tax system to the state VAT. The main recommendations of the study are presented as follows:

1. Convert sales taxes into VAT by moving over to a multistage system of sales taxation with rebate for tax on all purchases with only minimal exceptions.
2. Extend the tax base to include all goods sold or leased with minimal exceptions. Eventually the states should be given the power to tax services in general. A beginning can be made by bringing under the state VATs services that are ancillary or incidental to the production or supply of goods and also those that form a significant part of final consumption such as photo processing. VAT on such items of consumption need not be rebatable. The Parliament can pass a legislation empowering the states to levy the tax on services so selected. Pending a general extension of the tax base to services, the taxes on entertainment, electricity duty and passengers and goods carried on road may continue to be levied by the states. In other words, since this was proposed as a replacement for the state VAT, it was not yet proposed as a comprehensive VAT covering all goods and all services.
3. Allow ITCs for all raw materials and parts, consumables, goods for resale, and production machinery and equipment. No rebate will be allowed in respect of overhead expenses such as repairs, office equipment, construction materials and

Table 1.1   A Brief Description of the Rate Structure of Sales Tax: 1989–90

States	Mode of Levy	Treatment of Goods When Used as Raw Materials	Additional Tax	Tax Rates		
				No.	Range (%)	General Rate
Andhra Pradesh	SP	CR (≤4%)	TT, SC (10%)	8	1–25	6
Assam	SP	E (SED)	–	12	2–50	7
Bihar	SP	CR (≤3%)	TT, SC (10%)	17	2–25	8
Delhi	SP	E	–	9	1–12	7
Goa	SP	E (SRM)[1]	SC (10%)	10	1–15	7
Gujarat	SP, DP	SO (SRM)	TT, SC (20%)	25	0.5–54	4/8
Haryana	SP	SO	SC (10%)	10	0.5–20	10
Himachal Pradesh	SP	SO	SC (10%)	12	0.5–25	8
Karnataka	SP,DP,MP	CR (≤4%)	TT	14	1–150	7
Kerala	SP	CR (≤2%)[2]	TT, SC (25%)	16	2–75	5
Madhya Pradesh	SP	CR (≤4%)	–	18	0.5–50	8
Maharashtra	SP	SO (CR ≤4 OR 6%)[3]	TT, SC (12%)	12	1–50	–
Orissa	SP	CR (≤4%)	SC (10%)	7	2–16	12
Punjab	SP	E[4]	SC (10%)	12	1–12	7
Rajasthan	SP	CR (≤3%)	–	15	2–30	10
Tamil Nadu	SP,MP[5]	CR (≤3%)	TT, SC (15%)[6]	17	1–50	8
Uttar Pradesh	SP	E (SRM), CR (SRM)	SC (25%)	14	2–32.5	8
West Bengal	SP,MP	CR (≤2%)	TT, SC (15%)	7	1–20	8

Source: Aggarwal (1995: 17, Table 2.2).

Notes: SP: single point, DP: double points, MP: multi-points, TT: turnover tax, SC: surcharge, CR: concessional rate, E: exempt, SO: set off, SED: selected eligible dealers, SRM: selected raw materials.

[1]Raw materials and packing materials, that is, commodities subjected to last-point tax, to be used as inputs, can be purchased without payment of tax.

[2]The benefit of concessional rate is not available if the finished goods are exported or sent on consignment basis.

[3]6 per cent is applicable when the manufactured goods are sent on branch transfer outside Maharashtra. Set-off is given in respect of the rate, to the extent it exceeds the concessional rate.

[4]All transactions among the registered dealers are exempt.

[5]In Tamil Nadu, SP and MP up to 3 March 1990 and only SP with effect from 01 April 1990.

[6]An addition surcharge of 5 per cent is payable in the Madras area.

fixtures, and purchases in use for transportation and distribution of goods. Here, once again, there was a notion of direct relation to the taxable business being the basis of tax credit.

4. Replace the existing structure of tax rates with two or three rates within specified bands, applicable in all states and union territories. Once an agreement is reached on the rates and the bands, the taxation of textiles, tobacco and sugar

should revert to the state governments within the state VAT regime. It was suggested that the notion of declared goods be retained to ensure that the states adhered to the harmonised rate structure.

a. The rate bands proposed are 4–5 per cent for essential goods and 12–14 per cent for all other goods. Basic, unprocessed food items may be exempted while tobacco, alcohol, petroleum, aviation fuel and narcotics may be subjected to a non-rebatable VAT at a floor rate of 20 per cent. The tax on the high-rated items will not be rebatable although the tax paid on their inputs will be credited against the VAT payable on them. Resellers would, however, be entitled to deduct the tax paid on their purchases from the VAT payable on their sales.

5. Remove the exemptions except for a basic threshold limit and items such as unprocessed food and also withdraw other concessions such as tax holiday, and so on.

6. Zero-rate exports out of the country and also interstate sales and consignment transfers to registered traders with suitable safeguards against misuse.

7. Tax interstate sales to non-registered persons as local sales. There is a fairly long discussion on the alternative models to deal with interstate transactions between two registered entities. In talking about an overhaul of the system of indirect taxes in India, the study provides a design of destination-based VAT system by suggesting a tax system for interstate trade where rebatable CENVAT would be the only tax on interstate sales and all taxes levied by the origin state will be zero-rated. The importing state will levy taxes on imports and importers will pay the taxes in destination state and get credit against CENVAT paid in origin state. A similar system was also proposed by the Indirect Taxation Enquiry Committee. The continuation of the ITC chain was the major challenge and such designs are useful to remove such challenges.

8. Modernise tax administration, computerise operations and the information system, and simplify forms and procedures.

The other recommendations of the study were as follows:

1. The most convenient method of operating a destination-based system of state VATs is to zero-rate interstate sales between registered dealers. As a safeguard against misuse, a system of advance payment of tax by the importing dealer can be devised. Under this system, interstate movement of goods through consignment transfers should be treated on the same footing as interstate sale between registered dealers. As an interim system, exporting states may levy a tax on interstate sales at a low rate for which importing states would grant rebate and the revenue will be shared through a pooling arrangement.

Under the initiative of the NDC, harmonisation in sales tax rate was achieved in January 2000 and the Empowered Committee of State Finance Ministers was formed to hammer out a consensus on the design of a VAT at the state level to replace the existing state sales taxes. Difficulties in arriving at decisions through consensus resulted in a considerable delay in introducing state VAT regimes. The introduction of this regime was not simultaneous in all the states – Haryana was the first state to introduce the tax in 2003. The rest of the states introduced the regime either in 2004 or 2005 (Nepram 2011).

To an extent, the introduction of the state VAT system resulted in a harmonisation of rules and regulations, number of tax schedules, tax rates and methods of tax administration. The variations in standard rates across states was limited to 3 per cent, and the number of tax schedules or rate categories too was limited and uniform across the country. However, this state VAT was not a destination-based consumption tax, especially with CST on interstate sales (Das-Gupta 2005).

State VAT was the first coordinated tax reform in India at the subnational (state) level. Introduction of the state VAT resulted in a harmonisation of the sales tax structure (VAT design), rules, regulations and processes (more or less). It also helped to achieve uniform floor rates for different categories of commodities. Deviation from the agreed VAT rates has been contained to less than 3 per cent in the standard rate. It resulted in a minimisation of the cascading effect (allowance of ITC against VAT purchases). The introduction of VAT resulted in differential revenue impact across states (Das-Gupta 2012). The gain from VAT was not uniform across states. In working towards the introduction of VAT, we also got an institution – the Empowered Committee of State Finance Ministers – which helped to build consensus among states to overcome challenges in the introduction of VAT.

However, VAT was not free from shortcomings. It was characterised by a narrow base, a plethora of exemptions, a multiple-rate structure (at least four), and a cascading effect on account of the breakdown of the ITC chain due to interstate sales. Non-inclusion of certain indirect taxes on goods (for example, petroleum products) and services (such as luxury tax and entertainment tax) under VAT meant that some cascading of taxes remained. Further, state VAT was applied on a base inclusive of CENVAT, implying an additional element of cascading. The system of CST and entry tax also resulted in cascading of taxes and divided the Indian market into several tax jurisdictions.

The discussion on state taxes will be incomplete without discussing entry tax. There are two forms of entry tax – (*a*) entry tax in lieu of octroi and (*b*) tax on entry of goods into the local area. The first type of entry tax was introduced after phasing out octroi. Octroi used to be a tax on entry of goods into the administrative jurisdiction of urban local bodies/municipalities and it used to be collected after valuation of goods based on physical verification at the entry points. Since revenue from octroi was dependent on physical verification and it required intensive monitoring of inflow of goods, possibilities of leakage of revenue could not be ruled out. In view of the revenue leakage and requirement of intensive monitoring, account-based 'entry tax' was introduced as a replacement for octroi.[5] The second type of entry tax was more or less an equalisation levy imposed on entry of goods by a state. The difference in the tax rate, where the tax rate in the destination state is lower than the origin state for a specific good, was the genesis for the imposition of entry tax. In some states, entry tax was commodity-specific whereas in some other states it was a broad-based levy for all interstate imports. Some states used to provide ITC against entry tax whereas in some other states there was no provision for ITC. Tax competition among states prior to the agreement on harmonisation of rates of tax across states created opportunities for trade diversion as a result of the difference in tax rates. The second type of entry tax was introduced to address this concern. The system of levying central sales tax along with entry tax divided the Indian market into several islands of tax jurisdictions. Manufacturers located in a state, irrespective of their productivity and efficiency, might enjoy absolute advantage over manufacturers located in other states. For a long time, there were a number of lawsuits before the Supreme Court of India challenging the legal validity of imposing entry tax by states. The Supreme Court upheld the constitutional validity of the entry tax imposed by states on goods coming in from other states on 11 November 2016.[6]

Casting of the Structure of GST

In the budget speech of the 2006–07 union budget, the then finance minister announced that a national-level GST would be introduced from 1 April 2010.[7]

> 155. It is my sense that there is a large consensus that the country should move towards a national level Goods and Services Tax (GST) that should be shared between the Centre and the States. I propose that we set April 1, 2010 as the date for introducing GST. World over, goods and services attract the same rate of tax. That is the foundation of a GST. People must get used to the idea of a GST. Hence, we must progressively converge the service tax rate and the CENVAT rate. I propose to take one step this year and increase the service tax rate from 10 per cent to 12 per cent. Let me hasten to add that since service tax paid can be credited against service tax payable or excise duty payable, the net impact will be very small. (Government of India 2006)

---

[5] 'Unlike Octroi, entry tax is not collected at the time of entry of a commodity into the state. It is an account-based levy assessed and collected on the pattern of sales tax, generally from the same set of registered dealers. It is collected along with the sales tax liability of the dealers' (Purohit 2015).

[6] In the Supreme Court of India, Civil Appellate Jurisdiction, Civil Appeal No. 3453/2002 dated 11 November 2016.

[7] At that time, it was not what the finance minister actually meant by 'national level' GST (Bagchi et al. 2006).

On the request of the finance minister, the Empowered Committee of State Finance Ministers prepared a road map for the introduction of GST in India.[8] The committee came out with the 'First Discussion Paper on Goods and Services Tax in India' on 10 November 2009 (The Empowered Committee of State Finance Ministers 2009). The discussion paper provided a broad contour of the expected design of the GST and played an important role in initiating debates and discussion among stakeholders on the expected benefits and costs of moving towards a GST regime.

The proposals of the discussion paper were as follows:

1. Constitutional amendment for concurrent taxation power to the centre and the states for all goods and services and for all stages of value addition.
2. Phasing out of CST from the date of introduction of GST.
3. Compensation of losses to the states for permanent phasing out of CST.
4. A dual GST structure with defined functions and responsibilities of the centre and the states: central GST (CGST) and state GST (SGST). The former was to be the responsibility of the union government and the latter of the states, both in forming the laws and rules and administering the acts.
5. A harmonised rate structure of GST.
6. Harmonisation of basic features of law such as chargeability, definition of taxable event and taxable person, measure of levy including valuation provisions, basis of classification, tax credit rules, and so on, across these statutes as far as practicable between union and state taxes as well as across states. However, since the two levies would be two separate levies, cross-adjustment/utilisation of ITC between CGST and SGST was not proposed, except for interstate transactions that will attract integrated GST (IGST).
7. Interstate transactions (including branch/consignment transfers) will attract IGST. The interstate seller will pay IGST on value addition after adjusting available credit of IGST, CGST and SGST on his purchases. The exporting state will transfer to the centre the credit of SGST used in payment of IGST. The importing dealer will claim credit of IGST while discharging his output tax liability in his own state. The centre will transfer to the importing state the credit of IGST used in the payment of SGST.
8. In case of exports, refund of input taxes proposed. It also recognised that there could be instances of refunds in case of an inverted duty structure.
9. A uniform SGST exemption threshold across states was proposed as being desirable – it was proposed at INR 10 lakh both for goods and services for

---

[8] First, before the introduction of state-level VAT, the unhealthy sales tax 'rate war' among the states would have to end, and sales tax rates would need to be harmonised by implementing uniform floor rates of sales tax for different categories of commodities with effect from 1 January 2000. Second, on the basis of achievement of the first objective, steps would be taken by the states for the introduction of state-level VAT after adequate preparation. For implementing these decisions, a Standing Committee of State Finance Ministers was formed which was then made an Empowered Committee of State Finance Ministers.

all the states and union territories. For CGST, however, it was proposed that the threshold be kept higher following from the existing regime where the CENVAT threshold was INR 1.5 crore (INR 15 million). It was proposed that for states which might be left with a higher exemption threshold than they had prior to the introduction of GST, adequate compensation should be provided.

10. Composition/compounding scheme for the purpose of GST should have an upper ceiling on gross annual turnover (of INR 50 lakh) and a floor tax rate (of 0.5 per cent) with respect to gross annual turnover.

11. Submission of periodic returns, in common format as far as possible, to both the central GST authority and the concerned state GST authorities.

12. PAN-linked taxpayer identification number (or GST registration number) with a total of 13/15 digits.

13. Functions such as assessment, enforcement, scrutiny and audit would be undertaken by the authority that is collecting the tax, with information sharing between the centre and the states.

14. Two-rate structure – a lower rate for necessary items and goods of basic importance and a standard rate for goods in general. There will also be a special rate for precious metals and a list of exempted items. For taxation of services, there may be a single rate for both CGST and SGST.

15. After the introduction of GST, the tax exemptions, remissions, and so on, related to industrial incentives should be converted, if at all needed, into cash refund schemes after the collection of tax, so that the GST scheme on the basis of a continuous chain of set-offs is not disturbed.

16. Need for compensation during the implementation of GST.

17. Specific provisions would also be made to the issues of dispute resolution and advance ruling.

18. Tobacco products would be brought under GST with provision for ITC. The centre may consider levying excise duty on tobacco products over and above GST without ITC.

19. A basket of petroleum products, that is, crude, motor spirit (including ATF) and HSD would be kept outside GST.

20. Alcoholic beverages would be kept out of the purview of GST.

21. In case purchase tax has to be subsumed under GST, then adequate and continuing compensation has to be provided to the states where the tax is prevalent.

22. Under the GST system, CGST will subsume central excise duty, AED, the excise duty levied under the Medicinal and Toiletries Preparation Act, service tax, additional customs duty, commonly known as CVD, SAD of customs (4 per cent), surcharges and cesses.

23. SGST will subsume VAT/sales tax, entertainment tax (unless it is levied by the local bodies), luxury tax, taxes on lottery, betting and gambling, state cesses and surcharges insofar as they relate to the supply of goods and services, and entry tax not in lieu of octroi.

The terms of reference of the Thirteenth Finance Commission (TFC) also demanded an assessment of 'the impact of the proposed implementation of Goods and Services Tax with effect from 1st April, 2010, including its impact on the country's foreign trade'. With this objective, the TFC constituted a task force to examine (*a*) the GST model best suited for the country, (*b*) the modalities of the implementation of GST including threshold limits, composition limits, treatment of interstate transactions and place of supply rules, (*c*) the potential tax base of the GST as exhaustively as possible and determine an appropriate RNR for the centre and the states, (*d*) suggest ways to incentivise states to adopt a model GST and (*e*) recommend a framework for administering the GST, including payment of compensation, monitoring of compliance and the institutional mechanism for making any change in the initial design of the GST.

The task force submitted the report (*Report of the Task Force on Goods & Services Tax*) on 15 December 2009 (Thirteenth Finance Commission 2009a) and, based on the recommendations, the TFC provided recommendations on GST in Chapter 5 of the commission's report. Among the recommendations, the most contentious was the compensation mechanism and the conditionalities in the disbursement of GST compensation (for losses on account of rolling out of GST), which was subject to fulfilling the conditions listed under 'Grand Bargain'.

Rao (2010) carried out an in-depth assessment of the recommendations of the TFC on GST (Thirteenth Finance Commission 2009b, Chapter 5: 'Goods and Service Tax'). Because of space constraints, we are avoiding a discussion on the TFC recommendations here. However, it is to be mentioned that the TFC recommendation on the 'Grand Bargain' and the conditionalities for transferring GST compensation to states made the states reluctant, which undermined the trust required to push through a major reform such as GST (Rao 2011). For a federal country such as India, introduction of GST required understanding between the centre and the states, as mutual fiscal autonomy would be put at stake in the GST regime. The recommendations were against the grain of cooperative federalism and detrimental for taking further the discussion on GST.

Rao (2011) observed:

> Not surprisingly, the entire reform process that was progressing so well got stalled. The recommendation that the states should not be compensated for loss of revenue if they did not implement the 'model GST' did not go down well and the very low estimate of the revenue-neutral rates led the states into increasing the VAT rate from 12.5% to 13.5% to ensure adequate compensation in case of a shortfall.

The Department of Revenue (DoR) under the Ministry of Finance, Government of India, gave detailed 'Comments of the Department of Revenue (DoR) on the

First Discussion Paper on GST' (2010).[9] The DoR suggested a uniform threshold of INR 10 lakh for goods and services and for both CGST and SGST. It also recommended single registration by a single agency for both SGST and CGST, no physical verification of premises and no pre-deposit of security, a simplified return format, longer frequency for return filing, electronic return filing through certified service centres, chartered accountants (CAs), and so on, audit in 1–2 per cent cases based on risk parameters, and lenient penal provisions. The DoR also suggested a composition scheme for businesses that had a turnover of up to INR 50 lakh and a floor rate of 0.5 per cent for the composition scheme. It further suggested leaving the administration of the composition scheme to the state tax administration for both CGST and SGST.

The Constitution (One Hundred and Twenty-Second Amendment) Bill, 2014, was introduced in the Lok Sabha on 19 December 2014, and passed by the House on 6 May 2015. In the Rajya Sabha, the bill was referred to a Select Committee on 14 May 2015. The Select Committee of the Rajya Sabha submitted its report on the bill on 22 July 2015. The committee accepted the majority of the provisions of the bill and recommended a few changes (Government of India 2015). Certain official amendments were circulated to the 2014 bill on 1 August 2016.[10] The bill was passed by the Rajya Sabha on 3 August 2016, and the amended bill was passed by the Lok Sabha on 8 August 2016. The bill, after ratification by the states, received assent from the President on 8 September 2016, and was notified in the *Gazette of India* on the same date.

In the 2014 bill, there was a provision for an additional tax of up to 1 per cent on the supply of goods in the course of interstate trade or commerce. The tax was to be levied by the centre and directly assigned to the states from where the supply originated. This would be for two years or more, as recommended by the GST Council. On the recommendation of the Select Committee, the provision was deleted in the revised 2016 bill. The Select Committee also recommended that GST compensation should be provided for a period of five years. This recommendation was not addressed by the 2016 amendments. However, in the Constitution (One Hundred and First Amendment) Act, 2016 (8 September 2016), the recommendation was accepted.

In the 2014 bill, it was mentioned that '[t]he GST Council may decide upon the modalities to resolve disputes arising out of its recommendations'. The 2016 amended bill made it explicit and mentioned that '[t]he GST Council shall establish a mechanism to adjudicate any dispute arising out of its recommendations. Disputes

[9] Available at http://www.gstcouncil.gov.in/sites/default/files/Comments-DoR-1st-discn-paper-01012010.pdf (last accessed on 25 June 2018).
[10] Notice of Amendments, Rajya Sabha, The Constitution (122nd Amendment) Bill, 2014, 1 August 2016, http://www.prsindia.org/uploads/media/Constitution%20122nd/GST%20amendments-%201%20aug%202016.pdf (last accessed on 30 January 2019).

can be between: (a) the centre vs. one or more states; (b) the centre and states vs. one or more states; (c) state vs. state. This implies there will be a standing mechanism to resolve disputes'. In the final Act, it is mentioned that

'[t]he Goods and Services Tax Council shall establish a mechanism to adjudicate any dispute – (a) between the Government of India and one or more States; or (b) between the Government of India and any State or States on one side and one or more other States on the other side; or (c) between two or more States, arising out of the recommendations of the Council or implementation thereof. (Government of India 2016)

Under the 2014 bill, the GST Council would make recommendations on the apportionment of the IGST. However, the term 'IGST' was not defined. The 2016 amendments replaced this term with 'goods and services tax levied on supplies in the course of inter-state trade or commerce'. This was a technical change in relation to the apportionment of the IGST. It clarified that the states' share of the IGST should not form a part of the consolidated fund of India.

In the 2014 bill it was mentioned that the GST collected and levied by the centre, other than the states' share of IGST, would also be distributed between the centre and states. In the 2016 amendments, it was stated that the CGST and the centre's share of IGST would be distributed between the centre and the states. This was just a restatement of the provisions in the 2014 bill in clearer terms.

On the inclusion of petroleum products under GST, the earlier draft bill kept these products out of the ambit of the Constitution amendment. The revised bill included these products but the decision on inclusion under GST was left to the GST Council. In the final Act, it is mentioned that '[t]he Goods and Services Tax Council shall recommend the date on which the goods and services tax be levied on petroleum crude, high speed diesel, motor spirit (commonly known as petrol), natural gas and aviation turbine fuel'.

The report of the Rajya Sabha Select Committee suggested that GST rates would be levied with floor rates and with bands, where a band was defined as a

[r]ange of GST rates over the floor rate within which Central Goods and Service Tax (CGST) or State Goods and Services Tax (SGST) may be levied on any specified goods or services or any specified class of goods or services by the Central or a particular State Government as the case may be. (Government of India 2015a)

There were also discussions that a maximum of 1–2 per cent deviation from the floor rate should be allowed.

The committee also recommended the establishment of a Goods and Services Tax Compensation Fund under the administrative control of the GST Council into which the central government would deposit the GST compensation.

GST and Revenue Neutrality

Like every tax reform, it was envisaged that GST would be revenue neutral – that means revenue from GST would be equal to the present collection of revenue on account of taxes that would be subsumed under the GST. The TFC estimated the GST base for 2007–08 as INR 31,25,325 crore (INR 31,253.25 billion) and recommended that the GST rate of 12 per cent (that is, 5 per cent CGST and 7 per cent SGST) would be revenue neutral.

In December 2015, the committee headed by the Chief Economic Adviser (CEA), Ministry of Finance, brought out the *Report on the Revenue Neutral Rate and Structure of Rates for the Goods and Services Tax (GST)* (hereafter *CEA Report*) (Government of India 2015a). Earlier to the *CEA Report*, the Empowered Committee of State Finance Ministers had sponsored a study to the National Institute of Public Finance and Policy (NIPFP) for estimating the RNR and the same report was discussed in several meetings on GST. However, the report of the study was not put in the public domain.

The report submitted to the Empowered Committee is included in the present volume as Chapter 5.

Comparing the methodologies of both the studies (the *CEA Report* and the Empowered Committee Study), Rao (2016) carried out an in-depth comparative assessment of the reports and the suggested RNRs. For the benefit of the readers, the same result is presented in Table 1.2.

GST Administration

Unlike the design of GST, the administration of GST did not receive much focus in the recommendations of the committees/commissions on tax reforms.

Table 1.2   A Comparison of the Tax Rates Proposed

	NIPFP		CEA	
Single rate		17.69%		15.05%–15.5%
Multiple rate	Gold and other high-value items	2%	Gold, etc.	2%–6%
	Lower rate on 45% of GST base	12%	Lower rate (Not clear how much of the base is taxable at lower rate)	12%
	Standard rate for all other supplies	22.8%	High rate on luxuries	40%
			Standard rate on all other supplies	16.9%–18.9%

Source: Rao (2016).

The Indirect Taxation Enquiry Committee (1977–78) observed that

> [t]here is a more important problem to be faced, namely, the administrative problem of enforcing VAT at the wholesale and retail stages, because, firstly, the number of tax-payers to be dealt with gets larger as we move further down the line in the chain of transactions; and secondly, the smaller dealers in a developing country and even in developed countries, maintain only a primitive form of accounting and may find it extremely difficult to cope with the accounting requirements of VAT. There is also the further consideration that wholesalers, and even more the retailers, are likely to be dealing in variety of commodities so that the matching of output and input taxes becomes difficult. (Government of India 1977, para 18.11)

Bagchi et al. (1994) observed that

> [e]ffective administration of a concurrent system would call for a degree of coordination between the Centre and the States that is lacking at present and would be difficult to achieve even with the best of intentions. (Bagchi et al. 1994)

The 'Comments of the DoR on the First Discussion Paper on GST' are also worth mentioning here:

> Since the tax base is to be identical for the two components, viz., CGST and SGST, it is desirable that any dispute between a taxpayer and either of the tax administrations is settled in a uniform manner. The possibility of setting up a harmonized system for scrutiny, audit and dispute settlement may be developed.

> The provisions related to dispute resolution, advance rulings and other business processes need to be harmonised between Centre and States.

The introduction of GST has resulted in the harmonisation of tax policy across states. Though it has resulted in the centralisation of some functions of tax administration (such as registration, return filing and payment), other functions (such as assessment, audit and recovery) still remain within the domain of the respective tax administrations. The GST Network (GSTN) has helped in minimising the burden of tax administration for both the central and state tax administrations. The system of online registration, return filing and payment through GSTN has enabled a common harmonised system of tax administration across tax jurisdictions. The system of a harmonised tax base, tax rates and thresholds is a commendable achievement of the GST system. Among other functions of tax administration, the most important is scrutiny assessment/audit, and it has been decided that there will be a vertical assignment of taxpayers (depending on annual turnover) between the centre and state authorities. Ninety per cent of the registered entities (including service providers) having an annual turnover of up to INR 1.5 crore (INR 15 million) will be assessed by the state tax administration and the rest by the central tax administration. For taxpayers having an annual turnover above INR 1.5 crore, there will be an equal distribution of assessees between the state and the central tax administrations. The proposed system is expected to reduce compliance burden for small taxpayers and also encourage a cooperative environment in tax administration. However, there is no clarity on the criteria for selection of cases/ assessees for assessment under state or central tax administration. It has also not been discussed whether uniform criteria (risk parameters) will be applied across all states for selection of cases for scrutiny assessment. Some states have developed extensive methods for selection of cases for scrutiny assessment; it would be desirable that the states shared their expertise with others.

There is further scope for coordination in tax administrations for functions such as appeal, demand and recovery, and so on. With the unification of the tax base under GST, the possibility of the unification of the tax administration as well is explored in Chapter 8 of this volume.

References

Aggarwal, Pawan K. (1995). *Incidence of Major Indirect Taxes in India*. New Delhi: NIPFP.

Bagchi, Amaresh (2006). 'Towards GST: Choices and Trade-offs'. *Economic and Political Weekly* 41(14): 1314–17.

Bagchi, Amaresh, Mahesh C. Purohit, S. Ven katarama Iyer, O. P. Gahrotra, Pawan Aggarwal, and V. L. Narayana (1994). *Reform of Domestic Trade Taxes in India: Issues and Options*. New Delhi: National Institute of Public Finance and Policy (NIPFP).

Das-Gupta, Arindam (2005). 'Will State VAT Deliver?' *Economic and Political Weekly* 4(36): 3917–19.

——— (2012). 'An Assessment of the Revenue Impact of State-Level VAT in India'. *Economic and Political Weekly* 47(10): 55–64.

Government of India (1955). *Report of the India Taxation Enquiry Commission, 1953–54*, Vols I–III. New Delhi: Government of India, February 1955.

——— (1977). *Report of the Indirect Taxation Enquiry Committee*, Part I. New Delhi: Ministry of Finance, Government of India, October 1977.

——— (1978). *Report of the Indirect Taxation Enquiry Committee*, Part II. New Delhi: Ministry of Finance, Government of India, January 1978.

——— (1991). *Interim Report of the Tax Reforms Committee*. New Delhi: Ministry of Finance, Government of India, December 1991.

——— (1992). *Tax Reforms Committee: Final Report, Part I*. New Delhi: Ministry of Finance, Government of India, August 1992.

——— (1993). *Tax Reforms Committee: Final Report, Part II*. New Delhi: Ministry of Finance, Government of India, January 1993.

——— (2001). *Report of the Expert Group on Taxation of Services*. New Delhi: Ministry of Finance, Government of India.

——— (2002). *Report of the Task Force on Indirect Taxes*. New Delhi: Ministry of Finance, Government of India, December 2002.

——— (2006). 'Budget 2006–07 Speech', 28 February 2006, https://www.indiabudget.gov.in/ub2006-07/bs/speecha.htm (last accessed on 30 January 2019).

──────── (2015a). *Report of the Select Committee on the Constitution (One Hundred & Twenty-Second Amendment) Bill, 2014*. Presented to the Rajya Sabha on 22 July 2015, Rajya Sabha, Parliament of India, Government of India, New Delhi.

──────── (2015b). *Report on the Revenue Neutral Rate and Structure of Rates for the Goods and Services Tax (GST)*. New Delhi: Ministry of Finance, Government of India, December 2015.

──────── (2016). 'The Constitution (One Hundred and First Amendment) Act, 2016', 8 September 2016, http://gstcouncil.gov.in/sites/default/files/consti-amend-act.pdf (last accessed on 30 January 2019).

Nepram, Damodar (2011). 'State-Level Value Added Tax and Its Revenue Implications in India: A Panel Data Analysis'. *The Journal of Applied Economic Research* 5(2): 245–65.

Purohit, Mahesh (2015). 'Is There a Case for States Carrying On with Entry Tax?' *Financial Express*, 29 January 2015, https://www.financialexpress.com/opinion/is-there-a-case-for-states-carrying-on-with-entry-tax/36247/ (last accessed on 30 January 2019).

Rao, M. Govinda (2001). 'Taxing Services: Issues and Strategy'. *Economic and Political Weekly* 36(42): 3999–4006.

──────── (2004). 'Taxing Services: Strategy and Challenges'. In *Fiscal Policies and Sustainable Growth in India*, ed. Edgardo M. Favaro and Ashok K. Lahiri, 60–79. New Delhi: Oxford University Press.

──────── (2011). 'Goods and Services Tax: A Gorilla, Chimpanzee or a Genus Like "Primates"?' *Economics and Political Weekly* 46(07): 43–7.

──────── (2003). 'Reform in Central Sales Tax in the Context of VAT'. *Economic and Political Weekly* 38(07): 627–36.

──────── (2010). 'The 13th Finance Commission's Report: Conundrum in Conditionalities'. *Economic and Political Weekly* 45(48): 46–55.

Rao, M. Govinda and François Vaillancourt (1994). 'Interstate Tax Disharmony in India: A Comparative Perspective'. *Publius* 24(4): 99–114.

Rao, R. Kavita (2010). 'Goods and Services Tax: The 13th Finance Commission and the Way Forward'. *Economic and Political Weekly* 45(48): 71–7.

──────── (2016). 'New Assumptions, New Estimates: Scrutinising a New Report on Revenue Neutral Rate'. *Economic and Political Weekly* 51(4): 63–6.

Singh, D. R. (1964). 'Substitution of Excise Duty for Sales Tax: Its Impact on State Revenues'. *Economic and Political Weekly* 11 (July): 1127–36.

Singh, B.N.P. (1991). *Programmes and Policies of Planning in India*. New Delhi: Deep & Deep Publications.

The Empowered Committee of State Finance Ministers (2009). 'First Discussion Paper on Goods and Services Tax in India', New Delhi, http://gstcouncil.gov.in/sites/default/files/First%20Discussion%20Paper%20on%20GST.pdf (last accessed on 30 January 2019).

Thirteenth Finance Commission (2009a). *Report of the Task Force on Goods & Services Tax*. New Delhi: Government of India, December 2009.

──────── (2009b). *Report of the Thirteenth Finance Commission*. New Delhi: Government of India, December 2009.

2

Towards GST
*Choices and Trade-offs**

Amaresh Bagchi

Why GST?

The announcement by union finance minister P.C. Chidambaram in this year's [2006–07] budget speech of his intent to introduce a national goods and services tax (GST) from 2010 has been enthusiastically welcomed by many, especially corporate businesses. This is understandable. For even after more than two decades of reforms, the task of reforming domestic trade taxes and moving towards a system of value added tax (VAT), which was considered necessary for the economy to function efficiently and smoothly, remains incomplete; a full-fledged VAT is still not in place. Neither CENVAT, the current name for excise duties levied by the union government, which is purportedly built on the VAT principle, nor the VATs that have come into operation in the majority of the states since April 2005 in replacement of their sales taxes bear all the attributes associated with a good VAT.[1] Excises are a tax on manufacturing and suffer all the limitations of a manufacturer-level tax (definitional, correct value determination, and so on), despite heroic efforts to get around them. While the rates have been compressed into a general rate of 16 per cent, selective exemptions/concessions continue resulting in effect in multiplicity of rates. Services are also being taxed by the centre but selectively and

---

* This chapter was originally published in the *Economic and Political Weekly* 41, no. 14 (8 April 2006): 1314–1317. Reprinted with permission.
[1] For a succinct description of these attributes, see Cnossen (1998).

not in an integrated fashion with goods. While cascading is sought to be alleviated by allowing credit for the tax paid on the purchase of services used as inputs against CENVAT payable on the manufactured product, the two taxes remain separate and administrated under different statutes. Crediting of service tax against CENVAT is riddled with rules that are far from simple. On the states' side, considerable progress has been made towards evolving a harmonised system of VAT. Even so, deficiencies and irritants remain. Efforts for harmonisation with the prescription of a uniform standard floor rate notwithstanding, the structure of the state VATs remains diverse and flawed, with many states deviating from the agreed rate scheme unilaterally. Their rate structure pays no heed to the basic tenet of VAT, viz., taxation of inputs and final products at the same rate. Industrial inputs are taxed at a lower rate than what is applicable generally and a large number of commodities are taxed at a rate much lower than the general rate. Besides, the base of state VATs suffers from a grave deficiency; it does not include services because of constitutional limitations. There are also sundry taxes like stamp duty on transfer of property and entry of goods in 'local areas' and on a few services like entertainment which ought to have been merged in VAT. Then there is the tax on interstate sales – the infamous central sales tax (CST). While several of these anachronisms are on their way to being phased out, it is widely felt that only a unified tax on all or nearly all goods and services based on the VAT principle can remove the infirmities of the tax system and enable Indian industry and the economy to flourish in a fast globalising world. Not surprisingly, the idea of a unified VAT on goods and services mooted by the Kelkar Task Force (KTF) on the implementation of the Fiscal Responsibility and Budget Management (FRBM) Act received widespread support and endorsement from the Twelfth Finance Commission. With the line between goods and services getting blurred, separate taxation of services has become untenable. The finance minister was not far from wrong when he said, 'It is my sense that there is a large consensus that the country should move towards a national level Goods and Services Tax (GST).'

But what kind of national VAT in the form of GST is under contemplation? Will it be in replacement of only CENVAT and the service taxes levied by the centre leaving the state VATs untouched? Or will it also displace the VATs now being levied by the states? The answers to these questions have a vital bearing not only on the shape of trade taxation in the country and how they impact on households and businesses, but also on the federal structure of the polity envisaged in the Constitution and call for a more careful consideration than has taken place so that choices are made with a clear-eyed view of the trade-offs. This chapter seeks to discuss briefly the merits and disadvantages of the alternatives and the trade-offs involved, and explore a workable alternative for India.

Options – A Single National VAT

While it is difficult to make out exactly what the finance minister had in mind while talking about a 'national level GST', the presumption (and wish) among businesses and even many economic journalists seems to be that what is being contemplated is a single, unified tax on goods and services levied and administered only at the central level. For them, VAT levied at the sub-national level with 29 states in the fray, each with its own laws and procedures is simply not on any more. A unified single market within the Indian economy cannot function smoothly, it is argued, unless the trade tax system is also unified at the national level. The question then boils down to this: should the contemplated national GST be the only tax on domestic trade in goods and services with arrangement for revenue sharing with the states? The finance minister's budget statement setting a target date for ushering in 'a national level GST that should be shared between the centre and the states' has raised expectations that this is the direction in which the reforms will be moving.

Apart from the obvious economic benefits from having a single VAT at the national level, for a long time it was believed even by experts that in a federal country VAT is best administered at the national level. Operating a destination-based VAT in a large federal country presents acute difficulty. In the absence of border controls, as is the case in federations, zero rating of interstate sales which is required to operate such a system opens up opportunities for fraud. Several federal countries (Germany, Austria, Switzerland, Belgium and since 2000, Australia) have their VAT levied nationally with arrangements for revenue sharing. A little reflection would, however, show that however neat and attractive each may seem, a VAT at the central level only is neither practicable nor desirable for India. It is not necessary either. First of all, it needs to be realised that the idea of an exclusively national VAT will be a non-starter in India as it would require the states' sales tax administration to be wound up or taken over by the centre. It is extremely doubtful if the states can be persuaded to accept such a proposal, even if they agree to the extension of union tax powers to enable the centre to tax sales through all stages under the 'Grand Bargain' proposed by the KTF. One also wonders whether it will be possible for a central tax agency, however well endowed, to administer a tax with 'such local moorings as sales tax' as the Taxation Enquiry Commission of 1953–54 said while turning down the demand for the centralisation of sales tax from trade and industry.[2] Reportedly, the number of taxpayers that the central excise (CE) department currently handles at present does not exceed one lakh and service tax assessees number about four lakhs. The number of registered dealers for state VATs/sales tax on the other hand would not be less than 35 lakhs, going by available figures. It is difficult to visualise the CE department handling such a large number of taxpayers spread across the country.

More importantly, taking away the powers of sales taxation, which is believed to be the dominant source of revenue for sub-national governments, from the states would be detrimental not only to their fiscal autonomy but also accountability as that would make the states merely spending agencies with little responsibility for the funds they spend. It cannot be gainsaid that the levy of GST in Australia

---

[2] *Report of the Taxation Enquiry Commission 1953–54*, Vol III.

only at the national level, however efficient from the economic angle, negates the rationale of federal governance marking the near elimination of 'the last vestiges of state fiscal autonomy in that country', as Richard Bird put it.[3] Even though the revenue is supposed to flow back to the states under the equalisation arrangements, it has greatly widened vertical fiscal imbalance in the Australian federation (Collins 2000). Revenues that flow from the centre cannot be regarded as something that the recipient governments are politically responsible for raising. Politicians and bureaucrats may find it convenient to avoid the onus of raising the monies they like to spend, but that way lies the road to fiscal irresponsibility.

Lastly, for the efficient implementation of a destination-based VAT, centralisation is not essential. While for a long time it was believed that VAT is a tax that is best administered at the national level, because of the problem of zero rating cross-border trade, recent discussion in the literature shows that expert opinion has veered away from this view and several models are now available that can make it possible to operate VAT at the sub-national level efficiently.[4]

For all these reasons the option of a single GST at the national level should be ruled out and alternatives looked for.

Alternatives – Dual VAT

The KTF, while putting forward the idea of a unified GST, also did not envisage the tax to be only a central levy. In their scheme, there would be a state component, presumably implying that it would partake of the character of what is called a 'dual VAT'. It is acknowledged that a well-designed and well-administered dual VAT can contribute to strengthening inter-governmental fiscal relations (World Bank 2004). If, however, the GST is to be levied at two levels, one at the centre and another at the states, there are several alternatives. Basically these are: (i) completely independent VATs at the two levels, (ii) a tax regime whereby each level of government sets its own rates independently but on a similar base and under close administrative cooperation, and (iii) a single 'joint' VAT with a state component in the rate and some of the revenue flowing to the states under an agreed arrangement or formula (Bird and Gendron 2001).[5]

The system of VAT in Brazil, the pioneer in having VAT as a major tax instrument, is of type (i). VAT is levied at the federal, state and also local level. Despite some central control over tax on interstate trade, under the Brazilian system the states have

---

[3] In a recent communication.

[4] See for a symposium on the models, articles in the *International Tax and Public Finance*, December 2000.

[5] Bird and Gendron (2001) add a fourth category whereby a compensating central VAT (CVAT) is levied along with the state VATs to help track interstate sales. For an elaboration of CVAT, see McLure (2000b).

considerable autonomy in running their VAT. Few, however, regard the Brazilian system as an example to emulate because of the many problems it has encountered. It is only categories (ii) and (iii) that seem to merit consideration.

In some respects the KTF model falls in category (ii) in that it envisions the GST to be levied at a rate made up of two components, one the central part (CGST) and the other, the states part (SGST). The key features of the dual VAT contemplated in the KTF report relevant in the present context are: there would be three rates apart from 'zero', viz., a standard rate of 20 per cent (12 per cent for the centre and 8 per cent for the states), a lower rate of 6 per cent and a maximum rate of 20 per cent. Exemptions would be few and limited mainly to food, medical care, education, residential housing and certain financial services. Central excises could be levied on products like petroleum, natural gas and tobacco.

Since the introduction of such a tax will require the centre to allow the states to tax services and the states to accept extension of the tax powers of the centre to tax sales at all stages, the task force proposed a 'grand bargain' between the two levels, referred to earlier, whereby

- Both levels will have concurrent but independent jurisdiction over a largely common tax base and the tax at both levels will extend to final consumers covering both goods and services.
- The existing octroi/entry tax, central sales tax, states sales tax, stamp duties, and other cascading taxes and fees will go.
- Both levels will have power to fix the rates but there would be one rate for all states and rate setting will be coordinated between the two levels.

Thus, clearly the KTF wanted the unified tax to be administered at two levels and not one at the national level. This is evidenced also by the suggestion in the KTF report for a clearing house mechanism to settle the dues of states arising from credit for tax allowed in the state of destination in interstate sales for the tax collected in the state of origin. (Whether such a mechanism can work in a country like India – it was considered unfeasible in the European Union [EU] – is another matter.)

However, the KTF has ignored the federalism angle in prescribing a uniform rate in all states and a rate scheme whereby the major part of GST revenue will go to the centre. Presumably, the SGST would be set on the basis of consultation or 'consensus' as has happened for state VATs but no state would be able to go beyond it if it so desires. While there is a strong case to harmonise the base and the procedures among the states, expert opinion is almost unanimous that the essence of a tax power lies in the power to fix the rates and so sub-national governments must have autonomy in the matter of rates subject only to a floor as in the EU. Unless this is allowed the 'grand bargain' contemplated by the KTF would operate to the disadvantage of the states. The vertical imbalance that marks the finances of the centre and the states will accentuate sharply under the KTF dispensation (Shah 2004). Rough computations indicate that the proportion of tax revenue raised by the states in the total tax revenue of the government (centre and states combined) which stands at around 33 per cent at present would come down to barely 15 per cent or so. That would grievously weaken the financial autonomy of the states and increase their dependence on the centre.

Hence while looking for a suitable dual VAT model for India one has to explore the feasibility of only alternative (ii). With a concurrent central GST it may not be necessary to go in for a compensating VAT or CVAT of the kind proposed by Varsano and McLure (2000a) as another model of a dual VAT. Thus one is left with only alternative (ii). But how feasible is it to operate a dual VAT of the kind envisaged in model (ii) in a federal polity as diverse as India?

Canadian Dual VAT[6]

Experience shows that it is perfectly possible to operate a dual VAT in a federation given some harmonisation (not total uniformity) and coordination between the two levels. Since 1991 Canada is having a federal level VAT in the form of GST while the provinces have their own sales tax or VAT. In fact, Canada runs more than one model of dual VAT/sales tax. Quebec has its own VAT, the Quebec sales tax (QST), levied at the rate of 7.5 per cent on the GST (7 per cent) inclusive of price. Ontario runs a retail sales tax at 8 per cent exclusive of the GST. The differences in the base that marked the QST and GST initially have now mostly gone. Thus a uniform VAT base is established for both federal and provincial VAT though differential treatment is allowed at the level of the final consumer. Initially, there were some differences in the input tax credits. These have been ironed out but some restrictions are still there in effect on input tax credits for large firms under QST. While such differences in the base are not desirable, the GST–QST model shows that these can be accommodated within limits under a dual VAT system.

The rates of the two taxes are set independently by the respective governments. The tax bases are also determined independently; however, they are essentially the same. Right from the beginning the two taxes are being collected by the revenue department of Quebec according to rules set by Ottawa. Taxes on interprovincial sales are dealt with on the 'deferred payment basis' as in the EU, that is, the sale from a registered vendor from Quebec to a registered counterpart in say Ontario is zero-rated for QST though not for GST. This in a way serves to maintain the VAT chain and helps enforcement. The overriding federal GST acts as an enforcement mechanism. Audit is conducted in consultation between the two authorities. The system is reported to be working fine at the technical level despite the political differences between the two governments. After reviewing the QST–GST system, Bird and Gendron (2001) conclude: 'Overall however the QST and GST, as they

---

[6] This section draws liberally on Bird and Gendron (2001).

exist, constitute an operational "dual" or "concurrent" VAT system – with essentially none of the problems usually associated with such systems'.

Proposals for reform of the Brazilian VATs also seek to replace the federal and state VATs by a dual VAT. The local level VAT which also operates in Brazil will be replaced by a retail sales tax at the municipal level. There will be uniform legal norms across the country; however, the states will have power to legislate on local 'specificities'. Tax rates both federal and state will be set by a federal law but states will have the power to vary the rate within a given band (15 to 20 per cent). The taxes will operate on the destination principle (Varsano 2004).

The idea of a parliamentary VAT law for the states may not be acceptable in India. However, harmonisation of the base and procedures can and should be established through a consultative body like the Empowered Committee. But the decisions reached at such a body should be enforceable with sanction which can be invoked not by going to the central government but by creating a separate judicial body as is done in the EU through the European Court of Justice.

Another model of 'dual' VAT operating in Canada since 1997 is the harmonised sales tax or HST. Under this system, operative in three maritime provinces the tax is levied on a harmonised base in place of the earlier federal and provincial sales taxes at a federal–provincial rate of 15 per cent. Of this 7 per cent is the federal GST and 8 per cent represents provincial sales tax. The tax is administered federally. Although the HST limits individual provincial autonomy any change in either the base or the rate of tax requires the unanimous agreement of the provinces.

Options for India

The HST no doubt serves to reduce the costs of both compliance and administration. However, the economic rationale for requiring uniform rates across provinces is questionable. For, as McLure puts it, '… tax harmonisation which may be needed to simplify compliance and administration, should not extend to the choice of tax rates' (Mclure 2000b). The QST–GST arrangement as it operates now seems superior providing almost an 'ideal solution'. The base should be harmonised but total rate uniformity need not be there across states. Only there should be just one rate in each jurisdiction. There should also be a mechanism (missing in the EU) to enable changes to be made in the consumer codes whenever required.

It is worth noting that the proposal for a national sales tax put forward by the federal authorities in Canada in 1991 to introduce a nationwide VAT in place of the sales taxes prevailing at the two levels fell through because of opposition from the provinces. The proposal for a common system of VAT for the EU proposed by the European Commission in 1996 also has not materialised since it was seen as curbing the fiscal sovereignty of the member states. No one can deny the need for harmony though, as argued in Cnossen (1990), there can be a case for some tax diversity as well. The advent of e-commerce and digital products is posing a threat to state or even national sovereignty in taxation. The challenge lies in reconciling the conflict between the need for harmony and preservation of federalism with its manifold advantages in its true spirit.

As and when its federal level GST comes into being, India should be in a position to replicate the QST–GST model. It needs to be considered, however, whether the two taxes should be administered by tax authorities at the two levels independently with concurrent jurisdictions as implied in the KTF report or whether it would be possible to have the two taxes administered by state governments as in Quebec. Implementation of the tax by two independent authorities running in parallel may be vexatious and troublesome. But the Quebec model of state governments administering both CGST and SGST would not seem to be feasible in India. In that case there seems to be no alternative but to have the CGST and SGST to be administered at two levels of government leaving the task of administration at the ground level to the states. With a harmonised base and procedures that may not be an impossible task.

One way to administer a dual VAT in India at two levels could be to require vendors to charge both the taxes on the invoice and remit the tax realised to the respective governments as is done for the federal GST and the provincial sales tax in the Canadian provinces having their own sales tax.[7] Of course there has to be nationwide agreement on the base and the procedures – like in the Sixth Directive of the European Commission – and coordinated audit. It may not be necessary for the central authorities to directly involve themselves in the administration of the tax in all stages or for all dealers. Every dealer liable to register for both CGST and SGST may be required to file a common return with the state tax authorities with an additional page for CGST. With a Tax Information Exchange (TIE) network now under construction the central tax agencies may be able to access any return whenever felt needed. If the SGST is levied on the CGST inclusive price, there will be an incentive for the states to see that the CGST is duly paid. Some states, if they so desire, should be given the option of harmonising their VAT and having it administered by the centre as in the maritime provinces of Canada.

Concluding Observations

To conclude, while there are significant advantages both economic and administrative in having only a single national VAT, it also involves costs that are both economic and political. Taking away the most important tax powers of the states goes against the tenets of decentralisation, which works best when the authorities that spend bear responsibility for raising the funds they spend. That impacts adversely on the efficient organisation of the public sector. Then there are political costs in weakening the sub-national governments. As Buchanan argues, efficiency should not be viewed

---

[7] This resembles the dual VAT scheme proposed in Poddar (1990).

only in the narrow economic sense. The imperatives of 'political efficiency' should not be lost sight of (Buchanan 1999). Trading off political efficiency against economic gains would be short-sighted.

Centralisation of sales taxation is not essential either. Central and state taxes can exist side by side as the experience of Canada with VAT and of the US with income taxes show. Given the limitations of resources of the central tax department and the experience of the states in implementing sales tax, however deficient, every effort should be made to get the best out of the two. A dual VAT – a variant of the QST–GST model of Canada – seems to be the most promising alternative with elbow room to the states in the matter of rates and to a limited extent in the base.

Administration at the field level is best left with the states. Audit has to be a joint endeavour but each authority should have the power to institute audit in cases selected by them. Trust and coordination between the centre and states tax authorities would, however, be essential for smooth implementation of a dual VAT. Given the experience with the working of the Empowered Committee, that should not be an impossible task. There should, however, be an independent quasi-judicial body to enforce agreements between the centre and the states and among the states. Thoughtfully, the Constitution provides for the creation of such a body under Article 307.

(Late) Amaresh Bagchi, one of the greatest economic policy reformers of India, is revered as the father of fiscal federalism in India. Dr Bagchi worked extensively on tax reforms, establishing the concept of value added tax. He served as the Director of the National Institute of Public Finance and Policy (NIPFP), New Delhi.

References

Bird, Richard and Pierre-Pascal Gendron (2001). 'VATs in Federal Countries: International Experience and Emerging Possibilities', Bulletin, International Bureau of Fiscal Documentation, July.

Buchanan, James (1999). *Public Finance and Public Choice*, MIT Press.

Cnossen, Sijbren (1990). 'The Case for Tax Diversity in the European Community', *European Economic Review*, 34(2–3): 471–479.

——— (1998). 'Global Trends and Issues in Value Added Taxation', *International Tax and Public Finance*, 5(3): 399–428.

Collins, D. J. (2000). 'The Impact of the GST Package on Commonwealth–State Financial Relations' (Australian Tax Foundation, Research Study No 34).

McLure, Charles (Jr) (2000a). 'Implementing Subnational Value Added Taxes on Internal Trade: The Compensating VAT', *International Tax and Public Finance*. 7(6): 723–740.

——— (2000b). 'Tax Assignment and Sub-national Fiscal Autonomy'. International Bureau of Fiscal Documentation, December.

Poddar, Satya N. (1990). 'Options for a VAT at the State Level'. In *Value Added Taxation in Developing Countries*, ed. Shoup Gillis and Sicat. World Bank.

Shah, Anwar (2004). 'Comments on KTF Proposals'. In World Bank (2004).

Varsano, Ricardo (2004). 'Brazil's Experience with an Interstate VAT'. In World Bank (2004).

World Bank (2004). 'Report to the Kelkar Task Force on a Proposed Dual VAT for India', October.

3

Goods and Services Tax

*The Thirteenth Finance Commission and the Way Forward**

R. Kavita Rao

Introduction

The introduction of the goods and services tax (GST) is expected to be a major reform in the arena of domestic indirect taxes in India. While this new regime will change the tax base of both central and state taxes, the extent of its impact on the economy as well as the finances of various levels of government was not clear. The Thirteenth Finance Commission (THFC) was assigned the task of incorporating the impact of the proposed implementation of the GST into its overall recommendations. To obtain an assessment of the GST's likely impact, the THFC constituted a task force. The task force submitted its report (Finance Commission 2009a) to the THFC on 15 December 2009 and its recommendations were endorsed in the final Report of the THFC (2010–2015) (Finance Commission 2009b, subsequently Report).

The recommendations of the THFC, which says that 'both the Centre and the States should conclude a Grand Bargain to implement the model GST', comprise five elements.

(1) There will be a prescribed design for the GST as a consumption-based tax subsuming the bulk of all indirect taxes, including stamp duty and state excises.

* This chapter was originally published in the *Economic and Political Weekly* 45, no. 48 (27 November 2010): 71–77. Reprinted with permission.

It will be a single rate regime with a few exemptions,[1] have a uniform threshold for the centre and all states, uniform rates of tax across all states, and include a proposed design for treatment of interstate transactions.

(2) There will be an emphasis on harmonised tax laws and procedures for administration, and common dispute resolution and advance ruling mechanisms, as well as simultaneous implementation by all the states.

(3) There will be a binding agreement between the centre and the states on the design as well as the rates of tax to be adopted, and the conditions under which the rates can be altered. The THFC's proposed scheme says that for decreasing the rates, all states will have to agree, but for increasing them, only two-thirds need agree. The power of veto will be vested in the centre.

(4) In the event of the agreement being violated, disincentives in the form of withholding state-specific grants and GST compensation grants will apply.

(5) There will be a phased implementation allowing for delayed incorporation of real estate transactions into the base and allowing for a two-rate tax in place of one in the initial years of implementation, with an agreement to move forward before 31 December 2014.

Any GST adopted, the THFC emphasises, has to be consistent with all the elements of the 'Grand Bargain' listed above. If not, the compensation package of Rs 50,000 crore proposed by it will not be disbursed.

There are three fundamental problems with the approach adopted by the THFC. First, since it was required to look into the revenue impact of the introduction of the GST, it had to work on the assumption of some design for the tax. It would have been prudent for the THFC to have explored alternative designs and assessed their corresponding revenue impact. Thus, it would have generated a bouquet of options for the policymakers, allowing them to evaluate the choices available. However, it preferred a route where it sought to identify and prescribe a model for the country. While this is a very meaningful academic exercise, it does not fit into the overall scheme of a union finance commission's (UFC) domain, especially because it is not the ultimate decision-maker in this policy reform exercise. By the time the THFC Report was submitted, it should be noted, the Empowered Committee of State Finance Ministers (EC) had already hammered out a consensus on some of the design issues and put out a discussion paper. Reopening these issues and suggesting a radically different view on some of them will not make the Report/design acceptable to the states, who are key partners in this tax reform. Further, the proposed design, by attempting to be comprehensive and complete, incorporates some difficult areas for taxation. It also proposes to radically alter the fiscal space, and the roles of the

---

[1] The prescribed list of exemptions are unprocessed food and public services provided by all governments, excluding railways, communications and public sector enterprises, service transactions between an employer and an employee, and health and education services.

centre and the states, in the country. The difficulties with the proposed design are discussed in the next section.

After this exercise, the THFC assumes that whichever be the design adopted, it will be revenue neutral to both the centre and the states. By making this assumption, however, it eliminated the need to incorporate the impact of the GST on the rest of its recommendations. In the same stroke, it also made its recommendations irrelevant to the debate on the GST in India. The extremely deterministic nature of the recommendations, along with the stipulation that the incentive grants for the GST will be accessible only if the entire model is accepted, allowed the centre to accept the Report and yet allow the GST debate to take a completely different course. As developments since the submission of the Report indicate, the evolving design of GST in India is somewhat removed from that recommended by the THFC.

Second, apart from recommendations on the design of the GST, the task force suggested rates for the centre and the state that would be adequate to raise the revenues required. The rate suggested in this exercise, 12 per cent for both levels of government put together, is substantially lower than the current rates of more than 20 per cent in the case of manufactured goods. By suggesting the feasibility of such a low rate, the task force built a case for a single-rate tax regime. It is quite commonly understood that at somewhat higher rates a single rate appears politically infeasible to policy-makers. It is therefore important to ask whether the methodology adopted by the task force provides a reliable estimate of the underlying base for the tax. The third section explores the methodology adopted and identifies some of its limitations. This is particularly important because in all subsequent discussions on the GST between policymakers and potential tax payers, this rate has become the benchmark for comparisons and both levels of government are hard-pressed to defend proposing distinctly higher rates. Third, the model GST of the THFC recommends a uniform rate across all states. While this approach is proposed on the grounds that it will aid in forming a common market across all the states in India, it is useful to understand what one means by a common market, what aids or hinders forming a common market, and what the downside is of such a recommendation. The fourth section explores these issues. Some concluding remarks on the way forward for the GST in India are presented in the last section.

Design Difficulties

The design of the GST proposed by the task force and adopted in the THFC Report is a classic comprehensive value added tax (VAT), which has a lot to commend it. As is well accepted, a comprehensive VAT is desirable to ensure that distortions to economic decision-making arising from cascading in the tax regime are minimised. While exempting final consumption does introduce some distortions, the effect is more damaging if an exemption is accorded to a sector that provides inputs to other taxable sectors. In the design proposed by the EC, electricity and transportation of goods are two important examples of input-providing sectors left out of GST coverage. If electricity is kept out of the GST structure, inputs used by this sector will be subject to GST, for which no mechanism of credit will be available – these taxes will be added to the cost of production. Further, there will be some other standalone taxes, for which credit will not be available within the GST. This will generate cascading, and result in distortions such as attempts by users of electricity to generate their own power instead of relying on supplies from the grid. In such cases, the sector and the economy do not reap any benefits from economies of scale. It is therefore desirable that all such sectors be incorporated into the GST design – an approach the task force and the THFC Report have taken, unlike the EC.

However, there are two sectors that pose some difficulties in being incorporated into a GST regime, financial services and real-estate-related transactions. Unlike in other supplies, the value addition in some financial services is embedded in a margin – the value addition by a bank through financial intermediation is captured in the interest margin that the bank earns. Taxing this margin is not difficult, but assigning the tax collected to the agents benefiting from these services so that they, in turn, can claim input tax credit for taxes paid on financial services is difficult. Therefore, in some countries, these services are exempt with limited tax credit for inputs purchased, while in others, the tax law mandates that where the charges for the services provided are in the form of a fee, a tax needs to be charged, but in the case of margin-based services, no taxes are payable. This is the case with the Indian service tax as well. The latter approach, however, encourages financial service providers to construct services where the charges are only implicit. The slew of bank accounts with a minimum balance that an account holder has to maintain in return for a wide spectrum of free services is an example of such financial engineering. Similarly, for incorporating non-life insurance services, it is important to identify the true value of the service supplied by the service provider.

Including financial services in the GST framework requires designing and adopting technical solutions. The task force report mentions three options, but leaves the choice to the policymakers. The need to bring financial services within the tax net conceptually relates to distortions introduced by exempting these services – since service providers will not have access to input tax credit for inputs purchased by them, they are likely to resort to self-supply or imports to avoid a tax liability. Further, some revenue could be lost because the services to final consumers will also escape taxation.

Here, it is useful to mention that from the input–output tables for 2006–7, more than 73 per cent of supplies of financial services are for business purposes. The loss of revenue from exemptions will therefore be from the remaining 27 per cent. To the extent there is some revenue captured through taxation of inputs, the revenue loss will be lower. To get a more precise idea, it will be useful to obtain alternative estimates of the extent to which these services are utilised by final consumers and the extent to which they support business enterprises. If business enterprises emerge as the more important and significant players, it will be adequate to find mechanisms to address the concerns of these segments and financial sector firms instead of attempting a more comprehensive taxation approach. A partial set-off, as proposed in Australia and Singapore, or a partial zero-rating, as proposed in New Zealand, are viable options to consider. The answers on how these services should be treated need to be ironed out before proposing a 'broad' base by incorporating these services into the GST base. The other sector which has received plenty of attention in the task force report as well as in the THFC recommendations is real estate. The task force argues for incorporating this sector – that is, all transactions related to sale and purchase as well as renting of commercial and non-commercial property – into the GST. Apart from arguments on equity, it asserts that this sector now faces very high tax liability in the form of sales taxes on the material used and a separate stamp duty on the sale and purchase of property. The high tax liability encourages undervaluation of property. Incorporation of these transactions into the GST regime will reduce cascading and diminish distortions in this sector. While this is the basic premise of any GST regime, implicitly, this argument presumes that the bulk of the distortions in the sector arises out of indirect taxes. However, income tax provisions and pre-existing valuation difficulties queer the pitch for such an argument. While the first sale of a new construction faces higher valuation, there is no incentive to record augmented values in any subsequent sale. Apart from a GST liability, such a valuation would trigger income tax liability as well. This can serve as a persistent disincentive to improved valuation. As long as this issue does not resolve itself, incorporating real-estate transactions into the GST will not be prudent.

One of the conditions under which some resolution is possible is the rapid expansion of the proportion of transactions that are financed through loans from formal financial institutions. Today, if one compares the value of transactions reported through purchase of non-judicial paper (assuming an average tax rate of 7 per cent) with the value of turnover reported in income tax returns by builders and developers, the latter accounts for 80 per cent of the former. While there is no information available on how many transactions these represent of the total, this fraction will account for the bulk of fair value transactions. Introducing GST in these cases will potentially reduce their tax liability as a result of input tax credit. For the others, the valuation issue remains. With the Direct Taxes Code proposing to harden its stance by allowing rollover of receipts into an alternative asset only in the case of the first house for an individual, any fair valuation would trigger capital gains tax, a potential liability which will neutralise any gains from the GST input tax credit.

Here, the Indian context provides an additional dimension of conflict. At present, the state governments have the right to levy and collect taxes on such transactions in the form of stamp duties. Incorporation of these transactions into the GST would require subsuming stamp duty into the basket of taxes to be replaced by the GST. Given the highly uniform and centralised format of the GST proposed in the THFC's Report, the states perceive this as a mechanism to reduce their fiscal autonomy. Given this, the states will endeavour to keep some other levies outside the purview of the GST to retain their sense of fiscal autonomy. Extension of the GST to include real estate will therefore have to be left to future reforms – a factor the task force as well as the THFC's Report does not recognise.

The task force report makes very heroic and often rosy assumptions while providing an assessment of the increments to tax base by incorporating real-estate transactions into it. It assumes that all household sector gross fixed capital formation is in housing. The household sector also comprises partnership firms, proprietary firms and self-employed individuals. All these units will be investing some amount on their business. For instance, if unregistered manufacturing accounts for almost a quarter of total manufacturing, it will be investing some amount towards capital formation. These amounts will be recorded as household investment. If all this investment is assumed to be investment in housing, and the land component of the GST base is assumed to be equally large, it will be an overestimate for these reasons alone. As a point of comparison, while the report assumes the land component of real-estate transactions to be Rs 4,29,260 crore, the total base for stamp duty at 7 per cent is barely Rs 4,02,179 crore – and this includes both land and buildings. Clearly, incorporating such a substantial estimate into the projected tax base will be way off the mark.

Apart from the specific coverage-based issues discussed, one distinct feature of the GST regime proposed is 'uniform rates, uniform procedures', with a significant lock-in to initial decisions taken. The model proposed suggests that all changes will require two-thirds of the states to agree and the centre will have veto power. While there is a broad consensus that GST is best levied and administered at the central level – most countries have such a system – it must be noted that a tax reform exercise in a multi-level fiscal system involves compromises and trade-offs. The main trade-off here is between tax harmonisation towards uniformity and fiscal autonomy of the states. The THFC's recommendations, however, represent a rather centralised model for India. The model, and its implementation, is in favour of a complete lock-in to uniformity and centralisation.

One pointer to uniformity and centralisation is the élan with which the Report proposes a model distinct from that proposed by the EC for dealing with interstate transactions. It suggests a 'modified bank model', which comes very close to having an autonomous tax administration that collects the tax and transfers the designated amount to respective levels of government. The modified bank model envisages that some nodal bank will be able to set up and run a comprehensive information system for the GST system. When compared to the Integrated GST (IGST) model, the modified bank model, as proposed in the Report, seems more restrictive, just as the overall design of the GST. The IGST model potentially allows the states to choose different rates of tax for local sales – a feature that makes it more flexible without losing any of the benefits of the 'modified bank model' proposed by the THFC.

The Report makes a very eloquent case for harmonisation of the law, rules, procedures, forms and rates across all states. While there is convenience in harmonisation, the decision to have uniform rates should be taken by the EC, and not be mandated by anyone else. The need to emphasise this point is the radical change in the fiscal space proposed by the Report and the EC's discussion paper. It is important to realise that the Report explicitly argues that the states give up the notion of autonomy in taxes and focus on the broader concept of autonomy in fiscal decisions. Whether this is an acceptable objective to the states needs to be widely debated; it cannot be considered a foregone conclusion.

Revenue Neutrality

For assessing the base of the tax, the Report provides five alternative estimates. Two are based on estimates of consumption expenditure, one based on information compiled from income tax returns of assessees, one based on the 'Shome Index' and, finally, one based on revenue collection by the union government, corrected for the incremental base that will result from moving to a comprehensive GST.

To begin with, let us look at the most conservative estimate in the Report, the one derived from the 'Shome Index'.[2] This index is basically a rule of thumb that says for a given rate of tax, the revenue (as a percentage of gross domestic product, GDP) a tax regime will generate varies between a third of that rate and half of that rate. In other words, if the rate of tax is 12 per cent, the revenue will vary between 4 per cent and 6 per cent of GDP. Regimes are expected to approximate 6 per cent if they have a broad base, good compliance and a transparent administration. From this, the task force presumes it appropriate to infer that the country will be at the upper end of the range suggested by the index and, correspondingly, the base for the tax will be half of GDP. After incorporating the effects of design, administrative effectiveness and degree of compliance into the Shome Index, which is basically a rule of thumb, it will be incorrect to consider the upper limit as an estimate or even an indicator of the size of the base. This appears more like wishful thinking and less like an estimator of any kind. Further, if India happens to lie closer to the lower end of the spectrum, and not the upper end as hypothesised, then the suggested tax base would be significantly smaller, a factor the Report does not want to consider. Following the format in the Report, if India is at the lower end, the base for the tax would be about Rs 15 lakh crore and not the Rs 21 lakh crore cited, and the corresponding revenue neutral rate will be more than 23 per cent.

Now let us look at the estimates based on income tax returns. This estimate is based on the profit and loss accounts filed by more than 28 lakh business entities for the financial year 2007–8. These accounts provide information on local supplies of goods and services, as well as on purchases of goods and services, including capital

---

[2] No reference to this index could be found in the literature.

goods, all of which entitle the firms to input tax credit. The difference between the value of supplies and the value of purchases would therefore be an estimate of the tax base. However, since the units would not have been entitled to tax credit on purchases from the informal sector, the Report makes some assumptions on the extent of such purchases. Further, corrections are made for sectors that are under-represented in the income tax data base, for instance, railway charges for transportation of goods.

A look at the data presented in this section suggests that there is a fundamental discrepancy between the income tax data and the Central Statistical Organisation (CSO) data on national income. The Report does mention that sales as reported in income tax data are higher than sales reported in the CSO data. However, the GDP estimates as per the CSO are significantly higher than those reported in the income tax data. In other words, the 'deductions' from gross output to derive the value added in the case of income tax data are substantially higher than those reported in the CSO data. As a result, the value added in the CSO data is significantly higher than that reported in the income tax figures – Rs 33,54,597 crore in the CSO figures against Rs 16,03,564 crore in the income tax figures. The income tax data therefore shows higher turnover but lower value added, but this feature is not explored or explained anywhere. It is not clear why the income tax data should be considered any more reliable than the CSO data.

Further, even if one takes the income tax figures at face value, it is important to point out that the ratio of intermediate inputs (B2) to sales (A1), as reported in Table 5 of the Report, suggest a margin of only 15.96 per cent to cover both profits and wages and salaries. Depending on the extent of specialisation in any industry, the ratio of profits to sales can vary. Information available from the Prowess database for 2007, however, suggests that the ratio of profits to sales for the manufacturing sector alone is 9 per cent of sales. Together with wages and salaries and depreciation deductions, it amounts to more than 18 per cent of sales. For other services, the ratios are significantly higher at 15.2 per cent for profit before tax and 36 per cent for profits, depreciation and wages as a proportion to total sales. These figures raise some questions about the usefulness of the database sourced from income tax returns for the estimation of the GST tax base.

Given the data, the Report makes corrections for purchases from the informal sector. It assumes that of the purchases reported in the profit and loss accounts, a fraction is from segments of the economy that are, and will continue to be, outside the tax net because of the exemption threshold. This approach assumes that there is a vibrant link between these two segments of the economy. While for sectors that are already in some form of a VAT system, it would not make sense to continue to purchase from units that cannot provide a VAT invoice for purchases, it is possible that there are hitherto untaxed sectors that have such a link. However, how large this link is, is an important question. The Report on average assumes that more than 20 per cent of total purchases are from the informal sector. While this number is as good or as bad as any other number, the derived tax base is quite sensitive to where the level is pegged. For instance, if the purchases from the informal sector are assumed to be 10 per cent, not 20 per cent, of total purchases, the total tax base would decrease from Rs 30 lakh crore to about Rs 20 lakh crore, and the revenue neutral rate of tax for the country would increase to more than 16 per cent.

Justifying these numbers in terms of the average size of the unorganised sector in the economy is rather arbitrary because, given the operation of various tax systems, there is an inherent interest in the unorganised sector to purchase from itself and hence become self-contained. Further, a chunk of the unorganised sector in India, as classified by the National Academy of Sciences (NAS), would comprise partnership and proprietary firms, which would be a part of the tax system as proposed by the GST design.

The third estimate presented is based on information from national income accounts. This alternative is based on the notion that the tax would apply on final consumption of goods and services by government and private individuals. Since this would include some exempted goods and/or purchases from the informal sector, some adjustments are made for it. A third component of the base in this approach is the gross domestic capital formation by the household sector, net of labour inputs in construction. The Report argues that all investment expenditure by the household sector should be included here because this segment has no scope for claiming any input to tax credit.[3] This approach then goes on to make an erroneous correction – as in the income tax approach, it assumes that purchases from the informal sector would add to the base. The approach based on the income tax data works through approximating the extent of value added, and if there are tax-free purchases by a firm, the way VAT operates, these purchases are added to the tax base and taxed as a part of the output of the firm. However, in the consumption approach, the estimates are figures for final consumption and not value added. So there is no additional liability on account of such purchases. But some other correction is definitely required – if there are purchases of organised sector output to be used as inputs in the unorganised sector/exempt sectors, then there will be tax payable on these purchases, which will not be reflected in the figures of final consumption from the organised sector.

Taking the figure for exempted sales/sales by the organised sector, applying the average ratio of purchases to sales, and assuming 18.8 per cent of total purchases to be from the informal sector (as assumed in the case of income tax data), or more conservatively, assuming half the purchases to be from the informal sector, it is possible to derive the value of purchases from the formal sector. With these revised numbers, the base for the tax is significantly lower at Rs 25 lakh crore against the estimate provided by the Report of Rs 37 lakh crore. If the second assumption is considered more appropriate, then the figure falls further to Rs 23 lakh crore.

---

[3] This would be an overestimate to the extent some household investment is in a business enterprise in the form of a partnership or proprietorship. While this would be called household or unorganised sector for other purposes, it could be a part of the tax net, given the manner in which the exemption threshold is defined.

Corresponding to these estimates, the revenue neutral rate for the country would be 13.4 per cent and 15 per cent, respectively.

The revenue method of the Report is also based on some optimistic assumptions. One such assumption is that all the revenue reported as forgone can actually be counted for determining the base or the potential for taxation. There are two qualifications that this number needs to be subjected to. The first, not all activity that exists under an exemption will survive if a tax is introduced on the activity. Some of the economic units will become unviable, and the scale of economic activity will be lower. This is a well-recognised issue when discussing interpretations of figures of revenue forgone. Studies on tax expenditures therefore make a distinction between revenue forgone and revenue earned (Villela et al. 2010).

Second, in the Indian context, the figures reported by the department of revenue are erroneous – while central VAT (CenVAT) reports figures for revenue collected net of input tax credit, the figures for revenue forgone are gross revenue. These figures are not comparable with the CenVAT figures, and cannot be added to CenVAT either. A similar difference exists between CenVAT and countervailing duties. The derived figures for output tax and input tax therefore need to be corrected. This approach also adds on potential revenue from services such as financial services and railways. The bulk of these services are used by the goods sector and hence taxes are here a contra entry, triggering a tax credit. To this extent, adding these services will be overestimating the base. Even assuming that only half the revenue forgone actually would accrue to the exchequer as additional revenue, and excluding additionalities from financial services and railways, the tax base will decline to Rs 25 lakh crore from Rs 29 lakh crore.

If the more conservative estimates suggested here are adopted, the average as computed in the task force report would drop to around Rs 23 lakh crore instead of the Rs 30 lakh crore in the Report. The corresponding rate of tax would be 15 per cent. However, when alternative estimates are provided in any context, it is appropriate to rank these estimates and choose from among them. The approach adopted by the Report of taking an average of these estimates as the base for the tax, especially when they are fairly divergent, beats reason. This approach does not provide any rationale for including widely different estimates in the pool, and does not attempt to assess the robustness of these estimates to changes in assumptions. A more pragmatic approach would have been to take the smallest estimate if no rational basis can be found to choose one of the estimates over the others.

Given the sensitivity of the numbers to underlying assumptions, and further, since the recommendation of a uniform rate of tax is closely dependent on the rate of tax emerging from this exercise, the recommendation needs to be reconsidered.

Common Markets and Uniform Rates

As mentioned above, one of the important arguments driving the reform towards a comprehensive GST in India is to remove all impediments to forming a single common market covering all the states. The present regime with incomplete coverage at the state level in VAT, along with limitations on input tax credit and source-based taxation of interstate transactions, has segmented the market, thereby denying the benefits of economies of scale to producers in the country. While the desirability of such a goal is not being disputed, it is important to understand what is absolutely essential for such a regime.

Most definitions of a common market refer to a group of entities, usually nations, which eliminate or reduce barriers on the movement of goods and services as well as productive inputs – capital and labour within the group. As the above suggests, a structure of taxes introduces some barriers to the movement of goods and services in a country. For instance, in India, since interstate sales are subject to central sales tax (CST), but consignment transfers were not subject to CST, it was optimal for firms to set up depots in all the states so as to convert all supplies to the state into consignment transfers and avoid CST. Similarly, with the introduction of state VAT with input tax credit limited to local purchases, every dealer likes to purchase locally, thereby discriminating between local purchases and interstate purchases. What these suggest is that these distortions to investment decisions can be avoided if taxes on purchases remain the same regardless of where the purchases are sourced from, and taxes on all sales in a jurisdiction remain the same regardless of the location of the supplier.

The above will imply that an investor will buy inputs from wherever they are best sourced, without consideration of tax costs. In the context of the GST or VAT, it will require that input tax credit is available for all input taxes, no matter where the taxes are paid. Further, an investor will choose a location for the enterprise based on economic parameters. There is no additional market access advantage any particular location provides. Wherever the enterprise is located, the tax costs of supplying to any given state will remain the same. These features are often referred to as a destination-based tax regime – where the tax on any transaction accrues to the place where the good or service is finally consumed, irrespective of where it is produced.

The IGST design provides a good mechanism for setting up a destination-based tax regime. While taxes are collected on inter-state sales by the exporting dealer, the revenue so collected is transferred to the importing state, where the importing dealer is allowed an input tax credit against subsequent sales/supplies, thus making them equivalent to local purchases in terms of tax treatment. For sales, all supplies made in a state will be taxed at the same rate.

It should be noted that while all sales in a state should be subject to the same taxes, so far, the argument does not require that the taxes be the same in all the states. As long as the integrity of the tax system in any given state can be maintained, the above system can allow the rates of tax to vary across states without compromising on the destination principle. A higher rate in one state when compared to another does not provide an opportunity for relocation because wherever the firm may be located, its sales in the two will face higher and lower taxes respectively. In other words, uniform rates are not necessary for the sustenance of a common market.

If there are differences in rates of tax between neighbouring states, it is possible that consumers may choose to travel to the low-tax jurisdiction and make purchases. This, in turn, could lead to rate wars among states. Most arguments for uniform rates arise from apprehensions of such an eventuality. It should be mentioned that while states in India did go through an extended period of rate wars and competition through tax-based industrial incentives, they could hammer out a solution to the problem in the form of the floor rates regime, first implemented in January 2000. While the regime was not completely foolproof and there were some violations by states, by and large, it is considered a fairly successful reform initiative, which resulted in improved revenue performance for states. These deviations, as well as deviations from the original design of state VATs through the adoption of higher rates of tax in the years beyond the compensation period, do suggest that while floor rates will be adequate to prevent rate wars, there is the need for some mechanism to ensure that the states conform to them.

While the above suggests that a common market does not require uniform rates of tax, it is quite commonly accepted that uniform rates are 'desirable'. Uniform rates and procedures would of course reduce compliance and administrative costs. However, imposing uniformity on the states would severely limit their fiscal capacities. The revenue base varies considerably across states. If one attempts to derive a revenue neutral rate for different states assuming that the present classification of goods remains unaltered, the lower rate for goods is 6 per cent and for services, 8 per cent. One would find considerable variation in the rates required to protect the revenues of individual states (Table 3.1). One primary feature that the table highlights is that while for more than half the states a rate of 9 per cent to 10 per cent does provide adequate revenue, there are at least five states that require rates higher than 12 per cent. Choosing a high rate will provide a bonus to the low-taxed states, while choosing a low rate will mean a revenue loss for some other states.

The central government as well as the THFC argue that adequate provisions will be made in the budget to compensate for any loss in revenue. However, it is important to emphasise that this revenue shortfall, if any, results from a structural deficit for the state and cannot be treated as a transitional issue. Compensation packages are short-term hand-holding exercises to provide comfort and confidence to the affected agent so that the reform process can be smooth. However, if there is an underlying structural deficit that a state faces, then adopting uniform rates of tax will be akin to suggesting that this state continue to remain dependent on transfers from various arms of the central government on a sustained basis. A state like Jharkhand, for instance, will lose more than Rs 500 crore if CST is eliminated. The bulk of this is derived from mineral exports from the state. Since compensating revenue is to come from services, if the services base is not large enough, Jharkhand will not be compensated in terms of its revenue potential. There are no answers available if one

Table 3.1 Revenue Neutral Rates for GST: A Comparison

	Scenario 1		Scenario 2	
	Single Rate	Two Rates	Single Rate	Two Rates
Andhra Pradesh	8.93	13.47	8.37	12.06
Arunachal Pradesh	7.17	8.69	6.21	5.23
Assam	7.29	9.05	6.39	5.95
Bihar	10.1	17.73	8.02	11.1
Chhattisgarh	10.51	17.75	9.46	15.36
Delhi	9.63	15.61	8.32	12.07
Goa	11.31	19.76	10.28	17.65
Gujarat	10.01	16.36	9.06	14.14
Haryana	10.72	18.22	9.72	16.04
Himachal Pradesh	9.12	14.13	7.99	10.97
Jharkhand	12	22.08	10.53	18.98
Jammu and Kashmir	8.27	11.73	7.5	9.56
Kerala	10.01	17.72	7.75	9.93
Karnataka	9.28	14.43	8.37	12.11
Madhya Pradesh	8.65	12.81	7.54	9.55
Maharashtra	8.79	13.23	7.64	9.87
Manipur	6.54	6.52	5.3	0.75
Meghalaya	7.87	10.63	6.52	5.68
Mizoram	5.98	4.16	4.58	−4.12
Nagaland	6.57	5.67	4.78	−5.52
Orissa	9.55	15.24	8.45	12.41
Punjab	10.02	16.6	8.79	13.51
Rajasthan	8.71	12.93	7.82	10.49
Sikkim	8.08	11.25	6.85	7.11
Tamil Nadu	9.81	15.88	8.79	13.4
Tripura	6.45	6.09	5.13	−0.47
Uttar Pradesh	9.3	14.64	8.12	11.4
Uttarakhand	7.53	9.75	6.74	7.21
West Bengal	8.96	13.97	7.28	8.31
Average Rate	9.34	14.71	8.23	12.1

Notes: Figures derived using finance account data on tax collections and estimates of service tax from Rao and Chakraborty (2010). Both scenarios assume that real-estate transactions remain outside the GST. Further, scenario I reflects no taxes from the IT sector and full credit for financial services. Scenario II has some local demand from IT yielding revenue and partial credit for financial services.

looks for them in a uniform rates regime. However, if the rates are allowed to vary beyond a floor, with a fixed classification of commodities and services, the states can be assigned the responsibility of choosing an appropriate rate to ensure their revenue requirements are met. In other words, states can be made more responsible for their finances.

Concluding Remarks

Given the approach adopted by the THFC and the developments that have taken place before and since its Report was submitted, its interventions in the GST arena have been rendered irrelevant. While the union government did initiate discussions on the lines suggested by the THFC, the discomfort voiced by states has changed the trajectory of the talks. In the dialogue until the second draft of the constitutional amendment bill, the centre has given up the veto power proposed for the union finance minister and also agreed to dilute the demand for uniformity. While what exactly this entails will be revealed in the days to come, what is apparent is that the highly centralised model of the THFC is not in play anymore.

While there is some open-endedness on what the GST regime will mandate as essential for all states, it is desirable to retain some commitment or conformity on the following issues.

- Classification of goods and services: While the states may be allowed to choose the rates associated with different categories of goods or services, the classification of goods and services into different categories should remain the same across all states and the central government.
- Homogenisation of forms and procedures: This would facilitate improved compliance and easy administration.
- Floor rates: These should be prescribed for all activities to minimise the damage from tax competition. International experience suggests that such regimes can be implemented, Canada and the European Union (EU) are two clear examples. The Canadian Harmonised Sales Tax (HST), initially introduced at a uniform rate in three provinces, now covers two more provinces and works with three rates of tax. While the rate in most of the provinces is 13 per cent, one chose to join the HST regime with a tax rate of 12 per cent and another to raise it to 15 per cent. All these taxes are implemented by a single agency. On the other hand, the EU experience is based on the floor rates principle. The Sixth Directive and its recast version of 2006 prescribe a floor on the rates of tax and on the classification of commodities into different categories. For instance, while these directives allow one or two lower rates to be in operation, the commodities or services on which they can be applied are listed.

References

Finance Commission (2009a). 'Report of the Task Force on Goods and Services Tax', Thirteenth Finance Commission, http://fincomindia.nic.in/writereadda- ta/html_en_files/Report291209.pdf.

——— (2009b). 'Report of the Thirteenth Finance Commission' (2010–2015), http://fincomindia.nic.in/TFC/13fcreng.pdf.

Rao, R. Kavita, and Pinaki Chakraborty (2010). 'Goods and Services Tax: An Assessment of the Base'. *Economic & Political Weekly*, 2 January, 49–63.

Villela, L., Andrea Lemgruber, and Michael Jorratt (2010). 'Tax Expenditure Budgets: Concepts and Challenges for Implementation', Inter-American Development Bank, Institutional Capacity and Finance Sector, Washington DC, http:// idbdocs.iadb.org/ wsdocs/getdocument.aspx?docnum=35170590.

4

Present State of Goods and Services Tax (GST) Reform in India*

Sacchidananda Mukherjee

Introduction

India is moving towards introduction of Goods and Services Tax (GST). The GST would be a multistage comprehensive value added tax encompassing both goods and services. In the federal structure of India and under the constitutionally assigned taxation powers to different governments, GST would be a major indirect tax reform, as both the Centre (the Union Government) and State Governments have concurrent rights to tax goods as well services at every stage of value addition in production and distribution.

The proposed GST builds on a series of reforms of indirect taxation. The introduction of Value Added Tax (VAT) at State level, mostly since April 2005, resulted in a first round of cleaning up of hidden indirect taxes which facilitated expansion of the tax base (Aggarwal 1995),[1] better tax compliance and higher tax buoyancy for the majority of Indian States. It is envisaged that the proposed GST will further clean up the indirect tax system by reducing cascading of taxes and facilitating a nation-wide market for goods and services. Under GST, it is expected that harmonisation of indirect tax structure (tax rates and tax base across States),

---

* This chapter was originally published as Working Paper No. 06/2015, Tax and Transfer Policy Institute, Crawford School of Public Policy, Australian National University, Canberra, Australia. Reprinted with permission.
[1] For majority of Indian States, sales tax was first point tax on sales which was not able to capture value addition in subsequent sales (Aggarwal 1995).

concurrent taxation power of Centre and States on consumption of goods and services and joint monitoring of same taxpayers would result in better tax compliance, reduce leakage of revenue and better coordination between Central and State tax administrations. The reduction of cascading of taxes and transaction costs associated with inter-State sales of goods could facilitate higher economic growth by attracting investment.[2] It is the expectation of the Central Government that introduction of GST will improve India's ranking in World Bank's ease of doing business as it will remove cascading of taxes as well as transaction costs involved in distribution of goods and provide services across States.[3]

Major fiscal motives behind the proposal to introduce GST include the expansion of fiscal space of the Central and State governments to address rising demands for public expenditure and revenue constraints; overcoming the Constitutional barriers relating to taxation by removing definitional differences between goods and services and the manufacturing and distribution of goods; and achieve greater fiscal prudence by aligning taxation powers to expenditure commitments/responsibilities under fiscal federalism.

The adoption of a rule-based fiscal management system in States under the Fiscal Responsibility and Budget Management (FRBM) Act has resulted in better fiscal management in the majority of Indian States. Under the Act, individual States are required to maintain zero revenue deficits and limit the fiscal deficit of maximum 3 per cent of Gross State Domestic Product (GSDP).[4] While most States meet their FRBM targets at least in revenue deficits, the Union Government is not able to contain its revenue as well as fiscal deficit to meet FRBM targets. The major reasons for low fiscal performance of the Union Government are its falling share of indirect tax in GDP since 1987–88 and low indirect tax buoyancy: the average buoyancy with reference to GDP is well below 1 per cent since the introduction of economic liberalisation in 1991, whereas indirect tax buoyancy of States is well above the Centre since 2008–09. It is expected that under the proposed GST system, the Union Government will share tax buoyancy of indirect taxes with States and vice versa. The resulting effect of this sharing could be a win–win situation for both stakeholders.[5]

---

[2] Underlying rationale behind attracting additional investment is that proposed GST will remove cascading of taxes (including transaction costs involved in interstate sales of goods) and release working capital which is currently blocked as unpaid input tax credit (ITC).

[3] India's rank in World Bank's ease of doing business is 130 out of 189 countries, as on June 2015 (Source: http://www.doingbusiness.org/rankings, last accessed on 12 November 2015).

[4] Revenue Deficit is defined as the difference between Revenue Expenditure and Total Revenue Receipts. Fiscal Deficit = Revenue Deficit + Capital Expenditure + Loans and Advances Disbursed (Expenditure) during the year – Loans and Advances (Receipts) – Miscellaneous Capital Receipts.

[5] Currently taxation power of services lies with Centre and under the GST, States will also have power to tax services and therefore will share tax buoyancy of services with Centre.

Stated objectives of proposed GST reform are – (a) widening the tax base by expanding the coverage of economic activities under GST and cutting down exemptions, (b) achieving better tax compliance through mitigation of tax cascading, double (multiple) taxation and by lowering tax burden under GST, (c) improving the competitiveness of domestic industries in international market by removing hidden and embedded taxes and (d) achieving common national market for goods and services by unifying the tax structure across States (Government of India 2015).

The present chapter attempts to review these objectives by considering the design and structure of GST, based on information available in the public domain. We briefly discuss the present system of indirect taxation of India in the next section and highlight the major drivers for introduction of GST in India. In the third section, we present the proposed structure and design features of GST. In the fourth section, we discuss the challenges in design and administration of GST and possible scope for tax coordination. We provide a brief discussion of GST institutions in the following section and draw our conclusions in the last section.

Present System of Taxation of Goods and Services in India

The indirect tax system in India has gone through several reforms in the last two decades (Rao and Rao 2005; Acharya 2005).[6] At the Central level, introduction of Central Value Added Tax (CENVAT) in 2000–01 and Service Tax in 1994 were the major reforms. Following the recommendations of the Tax Reform Committee,[7] CENVAT was introduced in India which gradually unified tax rates on manufacturing and gave greater importance on account-based administration in addition to allowing for input tax credit against inputs and capital goods up to the manufacturing stage. Before introduction of CENVAT, a manufacturing level VAT system (Modified Value Added Tax, MODVAT) had applied since 1986. The MODVAT had limited coverage and provision for input tax credits (Aggarwal 1995).[8] In 1994, the scheme was expanded and credit of duty paid on capital goods was also brought under the scheme. The MODVAT system was inspection-intensive

---

[6] Liberalisation of Indian economy in 1991 associated with major changes in the tax system and the recommendations of Tax Reforms Committee (TRC) played an important role in modernising the tax system. A comprehensive review of the present indirect taxation system is presented in Rao and Rao (2005). Also see Chapter 1 of this volume for a comprehensive review of recommendations of tax reform committees (with specific to indirect taxes), constituted since Independence.

[7] Tax Reform Committee was set up in 1991 under the Chairmanship of Dr Raja J. Chelliah and the Committee submitted three reports during 1991–93 (Bird 1993). Recommendations of the Committee helped to modernise Indian taxation system.

[8] MODVAT excluded textiles, petroleum and its products, tobacco and its products (Aggarwal 1995).

requiring physical verification of goods and the allowance of input tax credit based 'on a one-to-one correspondence between inputs and outputs' resulted in substantial administrative and compliance costs' (Rao and Rao 2005). Introduction of CENVAT widened the tax base and allowed input tax credits without physical verification.

At the Central Government level, service tax was introduced in 1994 with tax initially on three services.[9] Gradually, the number of services under service tax was expanded combined with rationalisation of tax rates (Rao and Chakraborty 2013). In 2004, the input tax credit scheme for CENVAT and service tax was merged to permit cross flow of credit across these taxes. In the Union Budget 2012–13, the concept of a 'negative list' for taxation of services was introduced with a list of 17 services excluded (as at 2013–14). Introduction of negative list based taxation of services resulted in transition from selective list based taxation of services to comprehensive approach where all services, except those are in the negative list, are brought under the service tax. However, a number of services which are in the negative list are either taxed by the State Governments (e.g., service of transportation of passengers, services by way of transportation of goods, betting, gambling or lottery, access to a road or a bridge on payment of toll charges, trading of goods) or by the Central Government through other taxes (e.g., processes amounting to manufacture or production of goods).[10]

Prior to introduction of VAT at State level, there was tax competition between States (Rao and Vaillancourt 1994) and disharmony in tax rates, number of tax schedules and exempted items.[11] VAT introduced since 2005 replaced the sales tax system[12] which encompassed sale of goods up to the retail stage. VAT is levied on intra-State sale of goods, but input tax credit on inputs and capital goods is available only for intra-State purchases of these goods. VAT credits are adjusted against VAT and/or CST liabilities.[13]

Introduction of VAT could be termed as the first coordinated tax reform initiative in India since independence and it achieved many milestones. First, an Empowered Committee of State Finance Ministers was formed to build a bridge across States as well as the Central Government. The Committee played a crucial role to build

---

[9] Tax on telephone billing, tax on general insurance premium and tax on stock brokerage commission.

[10] Public good nature of some services (e.g., services provided by government or local authority, services provided by Central Bank [Reserve Bank of India], services provided by a foreign diplomatic mission located in India) make difficult to tax.

[11] As for example, there were minimum 7 (in Odisha and West Bengal) to maximum 25 (in Gujarat) tax rates and sales tax general rate used to vary from 4 to 12 per cent. In addition, a wide variation in sales tax rate around the general rate was also reported across the States (Aggarwal 1995).

[12] Except for a few petroleum products (motor spirit/ gasoline, diesel, and aviation turbine fuel), crude petroleum, natural gas and alcohol.

[13] Central Sales Tax (CST) is a Central levy on inter-State sales of goods. However, it is collected and retained by the State Governments.

consensus among the States and the Central Government to roll out VAT. Second, the relatively harmonised tax structure, rates, tax schedules and tax base are achieved under VAT which resulted in cleaner tax system for State tax administration and harmonisation of rules and regulation created a favourable environment for economic activities. Third, introduction of pre-announced (informed) audit instead of surprise inspection of premises resulted in greater reliance on voluntary compliance by taxpayers. Fourth, by allowing input tax credit against inputs as well capital goods, the system facilitated State tax administrations to get familiar with processes of refunds which prepared the base for further tax reforms like GST. Fifth, adoption of information technology–intensive infrastructure empowered State tax administrations to sharpen their skills in more crucial parts of tax administration (e.g., scrutiny assessment, risk analysis, fraud detection). Sixth, by allowing input tax credits, the system unlocked substantial working capital previously locked in as unpaid credits, and provided incentives to taxpayers for voluntary compliance.

Taxation of Goods

There are four major taxes on domestically produced goods in India. First, CENVAT is a value added tax levied and collected by the Central Government on the manufacture of goods. CENVAT is uniform across States and input tax credits (CENVAT Credit) are allowed against central excise duty, service tax (since 2004), as well as Countervailing Duty and 'cesses' thereof (for imported goods/inputs) (since the era of MODVAT). Among the other three taxes, State sales tax or VAT and Entry Tax (in lieu of Octroi) are levied, collected and retained by the State Governments.[14] The Central Sales Tax (CST) is levied by the Central Government on inter-State sales of goods but it is collected and retained by the exporting States.

The rates of State taxes vary across States as do the rules and regulations to allow input tax credits. For example, the standard VAT rate varies from 12.5 per cent for the majority of States to 14.5 per cent (e.g., in Assam, West Bengal, Rajasthan). For goods which are under State VAT, input tax credits against in-State purchases are allowed. For the majority of States, Entry Tax (in lieu of Octroi) is commodity specific (e.g., Bihar, Himachal Pradesh, Gujarat) and some States do not allow an input tax credit against Entry Tax (e.g., Assam, Karnataka, Odisha). Entry tax rates vary across States and commodity. CST is levied on inter-State sales.[15] It is expected that under GST regime, the tax structure across States will be harmonised and multiple taxes will be subsumed under GST. The present system results in substantial transaction costs for businesses, as they have to comply with different State tax rules

---

[14] Also oblige to share with local bodies (Urban and Rural) as per the recommendation of State Finance Commission.

[15] A tax on inter-State sales of goods levied by the Central Government (the Central Sales Tax [CST] Act, 1956) but collected and retained by exporting States.

and regulations with different tax rates for same commodity, and it discourages voluntary compliance which leads to revenue leakage.[16]

The present system of taxation of goods can best be described as an origin-based tax system where the manufacturing (origin or exporting) State collects CST on goods being sold inter-State. Since it is a tax collected by the origin State, the destination (importing) State does not allow input tax credit against CST. Therefore, CST remains a stranded cost for inter-State dealers and manufacturers using goods procured from other States. Though input tax credit against CST sales is allowed, withholding of input tax credits for various reasons is common in many States (e.g., in case of consignment/branch transfers). The present rate of CST is 2 per cent (maximum limit). Many States, mostly special category States, do not levy CST. However, if the goods are sold from the origin State to final consumer (B2C transactions), the origin State levies CST at the rate equivalent to State VAT whereas the destination State does not get any tax on the transaction. However, if the incoming good is imported for trading (B2B transactions) through inter-State transactions, the import attracts full State VAT in the importing state in addition to Entry Tax depending on the type of the good and State of operation. In States where entry tax is collected on behalf of local governments and the revenue is passed on to them, Entry Tax remains a stranded cost for these States (e.g., Karnataka, Odisha) as no input tax credit against Entry Tax is allowed.[17] A few States provide input tax credits against Entry Tax provided the goods are meant for further value addition or trade in the State concerned (e.g., Bihar, Gujarat).

The present system of tax on inter-State movements of goods provides an incentive to manufacturers to either locate their branch offices and/or set up their own distribution networks across all the States of their operations so that they could send the goods as branch/consignment transfers and avoid paying CST and Entry Tax.[18] The present system does not allow the generation of a seamless common market for goods and services. In addition, business faces different tax rates across States and differing rules and regulations for input tax credits. Since legal trade attracts multiple taxes, the system also encourages illegal trades at least of high-value goods (e.g., tobacco products, alcohol). Therefore, the removal of CST and Entry Tax from inter-State movements of goods will help to shift indirect taxation system from origin-based to destination-based which is desired outcome of the proposed GST regime. At present, consumers in importing States pay taxes to exporting States where manufacturing is taking place. Since the manufacturing base in India is not evenly distributed across States, a few States gain from this distortionary tax system.

---

[16] It is expected that under GST, rules and regulations related to indirect taxes will be harmonised across States which will allow ease of doing business.
[17] In addition to central excise and VAT, Central Sales Tax (CST) is collected on inter-State sales of goods.
[18] Provided input tax credit is not allowed against entry tax.

Depending on the definitions of goods and services, and the stage of value addition (production or distribution), the Constitution of India assigns taxation power to the Centre as well as State Governments. The CENVAT is levied on manufactured goods at the factory gate whereas manufacturers also attract State sales tax or VAT on sale of the goods.[19,20] Since manufacturers are assessed on State sales tax/VAT, input tax credits are allowed on purchases of inputs (including capital goods) within the State adjusted against VAT or CST payable to State Government. Similarly, manufacturers adjust input taxes paid on input goods (CENVAT and/or CVD), plants and machinery, and services (service tax) against tax payable to the Central Government. Since traders (distributors) are not liable to tax under CENVAT, taxes paid by manufacturers (central excise duty) remain a stranded cost for traders. The service taxes paid on input services by traders are not adjusted against their tax liability to State Government. Similarly service providers are not liable to State VAT. So, any VAT paid on input goods remains a stranded cost for them.

The non-allowance of input tax credits breaks the chain, leading to cascading which is not conducive for businesses as it causes substantial locking up of working capital as unpaid credits. The system also does not provide enough incentives to businesses to take registration. Non-inclusion of a large section of businesses under the tax net is not conducive for the economy as well as taxation system. These features of the present indirect taxation system encourage a large part of economic activities to evade taxes and generate unaccounted income (NIPFP 2014). For the tax department, non-participation by a segment of the economy can induce lower confidence in the tax regime resulting in higher non-compliance even among segments which would normally pay taxes. In addition, input taxes are adjusted only against tax payable to output whereas duties, surcharges and cesses paid on input goods and services remain stranded costs for assessee.

Taxation of Services

Service tax is a Central Tax levied by the Central Government on all services, except a few services which are exempted (e.g., education, medical and health services) by keeping them under negative list in the Union Budget 2012–13. Since exempted services are not zero rated, these services cannot claim refund of CENVAT paid on purchase of goods and services and those remain stranded costs for them. The Central Government allows selective cross credits across CENVAT and service tax provided

---

[19] State sales tax is levied on some items which are not included under VAT, e.g., petrol (gasoline or motor spirit), diesel, aviation turbine fuel, natural gas, crude petroleum oil, and alcoholic beverages for human consumption.

[20] The Constitution assigns taxation of alcoholic beverages for human consumption to State Governments and taxation of tobacco products (including manufactured tobacco products) to Central Government. Under GST, taxes on tobacco and tobacco products will be subsumed under GST and States cannot levy additional tax over and above the SGST rate.

the assessee falls either under Central Excise and/or Service Tax assessment.[21] State Governments also levy stand-alone taxes on a few services (e.g., passenger and goods tax, luxury tax on hotels and lodging houses, entertainment and advertisement tax) but do not allow input tax credits against their VAT purchases. In addition, being assessee of the Central Government, service providers cannot claim ITC against VAT purchases of goods.

Proposed System of Goods and Services Tax (GST) in India

The key features of the proposed new GST regime are briefly summarised as follows:

1. The tax is to cover all goods and services; it is however, proposed that there would be a small negative list of goods and services which will not be taxed under GST. All other supplies of goods and services would be subject to tax.
2. Dual GST: there will be two taxes levied on each supply – one as a part of the Central GST (CGST) and the other as a part of the State GST (SGST).
3. It is proposed that the GST regime would have two rates of tax, a lower rate for supply of specially identified goods and services and the rest of the supplies would be taxable at a standard rate.
   a. Some supplies that are to remain outside the base for GST are petrol, diesel, aviation turbine fuel (ATF), crude petroleum, natural gas, alcoholic beverages for human consumption, real estate and electricity.
   b. The constitutional amendment allows for the incorporation of petrol, diesel, ATF and crude petroleum in the base at a subsequent date.
4. On interState supplies, it is proposed that the Centre will levy and collect Integrated GST (IGST) – the importing dealer can claim input tax credit for IGST paid on these goods against taxes payable on subsequent transactions.
   a. While in principle, all governments are in agreement that the Central Sales Tax regime would be removed when GST is introduced, this tax would remain on goods and services which are explicitly excluded from the GST regime.

---

[21] 'At the stage of determining eligibility for CENVAT credit, provisions of CENVAT Credit Rules, 2004 since its inception have contained requirement to establish nexus between the activity of manufacture/provision of service and goods/service in respect of which credit is being claimed. The nexus theory has been interwoven in the definitions of capital goods, inputs and input services providing that in order to be eligible for CENVAT credit, goods/ services should have been used "in the factory of manufacture of final goods" or "for providing output service" or "used in or in relation to manufacture of final products and clearance of final products up to the place of removal," etc.' (Source: http://www.taxindiaonline.com/RC2/print_story.php?newsid=16827, last accessed on 20 September 2015).

5. It is proposed that for the standard rate there would be a band which allows the States some flexibility in fixing rates.
6. In order to protect the States from any loss of revenue in the process of reform, the Central Government has proposed to compensate for any loss of revenue in the first five years of introduction of GST.
   a. Another measure which has been introduced in the same spirit is a temporary levy of 1 per cent on inter-State supply of goods to be collected and transferred to the exporting State. This levy is initially proposed for a period of two years, to be subsequently reviewed by the GST Council.
7. So as to put in place a mechanism which ensures the creation and sustenance of GST which is comprehensive and comparable across States, all policy decisions regarding GST are to be taken on the advice of the GST Council where the Central Government is to have a 33.33 per cent vote with the rest being assigned to the States.
8. GST is to be administered separately by the Central and State Tax Administrations. It is proposed that there would be common registration and common portal for filing of returns. There are no clear decisions available in the public domain on whether there would be further coordination between the two sets of tax administrations.

In the proposed system of GST, both Central and State Governments will have concurrent taxation power of goods and services at all stages of value addition (production and distribution or trade). The proposed system is an improvement over the present system. It will reduce the cascading of taxes arising due to non-allowance of input tax credits for input goods (or services) for production/distribution of services (or goods)[22] due to inter-jurisdiction (cross Tax Authority) nature of taxes, as well as differences of a non-overlapping nature in taxation power of goods and services. Second, it will reduce cascading from non-allowance of input tax credits against inter-State sales. However, inconvenience arising due to non-allowance of inter-jurisdiction (cross Tax Authority) input tax credits may not arise, even though under the proposed GST regime inter-jurisdiction ITC flow is not allowed.

Under the proposed system there will be parallel tax payment and credit systems – one for Central GST (CGST) and another one for State GST (SGST), where input tax credits for each tax will be adjusted before paying taxes to respective tax authorities. Since GST is a multistage value added tax, tax liability will depend on level of value add. Under the proposed system, continuation of input tax credit chain is ensured even for inter-State sales. For inter-State sales, the exporting dealers

---

[22] As under the present system, power of taxation of services goes with Central Government whereas the taxation of goods attracts both central excise duty (up to manufacturing stage) and State VAT/ Sales Tax (beyond manufacturing). Input tax credits against Central taxes (CENVAT and Service Tax) are not available to traders (distributors) similarly service providers are denied input tax credit against VAT/ Sales Tax.

will pay Integrated GST (IGST) to Central Tax Authority by adjusting input tax credits arising against IGST (if any), CGST and SGST. The IGST liability will comprise CGST, SGST (rate prevailing in destination State) and any other taxes imposed on inter-State sales of goods. Dealers in the destination State will pay CGST, SGST or IGST liabilities on subsequent sales by adjusting IGST credit pool. First, IGST will be utilised to pay IGST, then CGST and at last SGST.

The proposed system, although it seems complex, is an improvement from the present system. However, under the proposed system, there will be substantial compliance cost if SGST rates vary across States. In addition, the present discussion on levying 1 per cent additional CST type tax on inter-State sales (excluding Branch/Consignment Transfer) of goods for initial two years and subsequent to decision of the GST Council will break the input tax credit chain. This would be very much against the spirit of the tax reform.[23] It is prescribed that Government of India (Central Tax Authority in practice) will levy and collect the additional tax and pass on the net proceeds to the exporting (origin) State (Government of India 2015).[24] Though the interests of the manufacturing States will be protected through imposition of the additional tax, this will generate cascading of taxes.

In addition, non-inclusion of goods and services under GST will also generate cascading of taxes. Therefore the very purpose of having GST will be diluted. Non-inclusion of certain fossil fuels (e.g., petrol, diesel, ATF, natural gas and crude petroleum) and electricity which are directly and indirectly used as inputs for all goods and services, will result in cascading of taxes across all sectors and will hamper competitiveness of domestic industries in international market (Mukherjee and Rao 2015a). Given these various criticisms, it is worthwhile to raise the question whether it is desirable to introduce GST with so many structural defects.[25] Definitely it would provide relief to business community as they would not have to block substantial working capital as unpaid input tax credits.[26]

Challenges in Designing and Administration of GST

The benefits of the proposed GST system could only be reaped if certain challenges related to design and structure of GST are addressed by the governments. These can

---

[23] It is not clear what the purpose this additional levy would serve when full compensation of revenue to States for switching over to GST is assured by the Centre for first five years.

[24] This goes against the destination principle of GST.

[25] Several scholars criticised the proposed structure of GST for many reasons, for example see Shome (2015) and Vaitheeswaran and Datar (2015).

[26] It is argued that proposed GST will favour big manufacturing firms having pan India operations whereas small and medium businesses will be marginalised. Compliance burden is cited as one of the obstacles for small and medium businesses to take part in the GST.

be classified under two broad heads: GST design and structural issues; and GST administration and institutional issues.

Challenges in Designing GST

Learning from international experience, it is not expected that a faultless GST could be designed and rolled out in India as a single event, but some structural faults could easily be addressed and rectified without hampering basic spirit of the reform.

Limitations in Capturing GST Base and Estimation of Revenue Neutral Rates

Capturing GST base is important to understand the tax potential and estimation of tax rate(s) to achieve revenue neutrality. Successful capturing of GST base depends on several structural features of GST design. The most important are – (a) whether proposed GST would be origin (production) or destination (consumption) based, (b) whether income or consumption type, (c) whether implemented with credit (input tax) invoice based subtraction method or formula based (ad hoc) subtraction method for allowance of credit against input taxes and (d) having many or a few exemptions (Rao and Chakraborty 2013). The proposed GST will be a destination based, consumption type system and it would be implemented with credit invoice based method with a few exemptions. In addition to these, there are also issues related to turnover based threshold for mandatory GST registration, special scheme for small and medium enterprises (e.g., composition/compounding scheme) and exclusions of goods and services from GST system which all make the design complex.

Estimation of a revenue neutral rate for GST is a complex issue. Setting a perfect revenue neutral rate for GST cannot be a one-time event; the option should be kept open to adjust the rate in future, based on trial and error process and depending on revenue targets of the governments. Given the dual nature of GST, there will be two revenue neutral rates: one for the Central Government on which CGST will be levied and another one for State Governments. However, there is no consensus whether a single SGST rate will prevail across all States. It is also not clear whether within SGST it would be single rate or there will be two (or multiple) rates. The Rajya Sabha Select Committee suggested that GST rates will be levied with floor rates and with bands, where a band is defined as 'Range of GST rates over the floor rate within which Central Goods and Service Tax (CGST) or State Goods and Services Tax (SGST) may be levied on any specified goods or services or any specified class of goods or services by the Central or a particular State Government as the case may be' (Government of India 2015). There are also discussions that maximum 1 to 2 per cent deviation from the floor rate should be allowed. However, if the suggested deviation is not accepted it may hamper the fiscal autonomy of the States, as their freedom to set tax rate depending on revenue needs will be restricted. In the long run it will affect the fiscal relationship between the Centre and the States.

The revenue importance of the tax base on which GST would be levied is different for different States, and given the federal structure of India, protecting revenue is the foremost priority of the States. Therefore, any rule-based restriction on fiscal decisions of the State will go against the spirit of cooperative federalism. There is always a trade-off between harmonisation of tax system and fiscal autonomy of States. Given the federal structure of India, it is desirable that tax rates will be harmonised across States to minimise the compliance burden. Harmonisation of tax rates across States is expected to minimise rate wars across States and rein in revenue leakage due to cross-border tax shopping. Moreover, harmonisation of tax rules and regulations is more important than harmonisation of tax rate from a business perspective.

There have also been discussions on a legal restriction for the GST rate at maximum 18 per cent (Government of India 2015). However, any attempt to put a cap on the GST rate will restrict the fiscal freedom of governments as they cannot set their fiscal priorities depending on their revenue needs. Ideally, estimation of a revenue neutral rate should reflect behavioural responses to the tax rates also. The GST rate depends on dynamics of the economy and if introduction of GST improves economic efficiency, it will attract investment which would have multiplier impacts on the economy and may require lower rate to achieve revenue neutrality.

Revenue Consideration under GST

The proposed tax system will subsume both Central and State indirect taxes and levies. On the combined tax base a dual GST (CGST, SGST or IGST) will be levied. The details of State and Central taxes those will be subsumed under GST are presented below.

State Taxes	Central Taxes
• State Value Added Tax/Sales Tax	• Central excise duty
• Entertainment Tax (other than the tax levied by the local bodies)	• Additional excise duty
• Central sales tax (levied by the Centre and collected by the States)	• Excise duty levied under the Medicinal and Toilet Preparations (Excise Duties) Act, 1955
• Entry tax (in lieu of Octroi)	• Service Tax
• Purchase Tax	• Additional Customs Duty commonly known as Countervailing Duty
• Luxury Tax	
• Taxes on lottery, betting and gambling	• Special additional duty of customs
• State cesses and surcharges (related to supply of goods and services)	• Central surcharges and cesses (related to supply of goods and services)

Source: Government of India (2015).

Non-inclusion of a few petroleum products and alcohol for human consumption makes estimation of revenue baskets for Central and State Governments difficult, given the level of disaggregated data available in the public domain. State data presented by Rao and Chakraborty (2013) for 2009–10 on taxes that will be subsumed under GST are considered here for our analysis.[27] To clean out the Central Government tax collection from non-GST goods, we have used detailed tax collection data as available in the Receipt Budget of Union Government for the year 2009–10 (available in the Union Budget 2011–12) and commodity-wise Central Excise and Custom Duty collection from the Central Excise and Customs database for 2009–10 as available in the Annual Publication of Directorate of Data Management, Central Board of Customs and Central Excise (CBEC).

Table 4.1 shows that total revenue estimated under GST is only Rs 3,31,671 crore of which States' share is 53.2 per cent (Rs 1,76,419 Crore) and Central Government's share is 46.8 per cent (or Rs 1,55,252 Crore). The removal of cascading of taxes under GST will further shrink the revenue due to input tax credits to be adjusted against final tax payment. For State Governments, the revenue under consideration contributes only 22.3 per cent of revenue receipts, 32.5 per cent of total tax revenue and 46.7 per cent of own tax revenue. This could finance only 16.9 per cent of total expenditure (revenue and capital together).

For the Central Government, the revenue under consideration contributes only 27.1 per cent of revenue receipts, 24.9 per cent of gross tax revenue (or 34.01 per cent of net tax revenue – after deduction of States' and United Territories' share in Central Taxes). However, the entire revenue raised under GST for the Central Government will not be available to finance Central Government expenditures alone, as a part of net revenue from CGST (after deduction of cost of collection) must be shared with State Governments according to the recommendation of the Finance Commission.[28]

Non-inclusion of major revenue-earning goods under GST (like alcohol and petroleum products) reduces the revenue importance of GST and also renders the GST design as complex as the present system. However, through a gradual inclusion of excluded goods under the GST system, governments could clean up and broaden the indirect tax base. However, inclusions of these goods under GST will raise the standard GST rate. Therefore, the argument of an ideal model of broad-based low-rate consumption tax may not hold for the proposed GST. It is expected that the proposed GST system would be relatively cleaner and enhance the ease of doing business; this could not only reduce unwarranted workload of tax administrators but also improve tax compliance. A cleaner taxation system with clear rules and regulations (with little scope for alternative interpretations) is easy to administer and could reduce

---

[27] Rao and Chakraborty (2013) received the detailed information on State tax data of revenue collection (excluding non-GST goods) from the Empowered Committee of State Finance Ministers. The set of data for recent years is not available in the public domain. However, 2009–10 is a 'non-representative' year for Union Government since tax rates were below 'normal', due to stimulus packages announced by the Government in the aftermath of global recession.

[28] According to the recommendation of the Fourteenth Finance Commission 42 per cent of Net Tax collection needs to be shared with State Governments.

litigations/disputes. In a cleaner tax system, the tax administrator could devote more time to more sophisticated parts of tax administrations – scrutiny assessment, audit, risk analysis and fraud detection, etc. A cleaner tax system is likely to reduce both transaction and compliance costs and induce voluntary tax compliance.

We estimate that the inclusion of out-of-VAT items under GST could expand the combined (Centre and all States together) revenue under consideration by 1.4 times for 2009–10 or Rs 4,67,124 crore. The revised States' revenue under consideration under GST would be Rs 2,55,111crore, which will be 32.2 per cent of revenue receipts, 47 per cent of total tax revenue, 67.6 per cent of own tax revenue and 24.4 per cent of aggregate expenditure. For the Central Government, the revised revenue would have been Rs 2,12,013 crore, which will be 37 per cent of revenue receipts, 33.9 per cent of gross tax revenue and 20.7 per cent of aggregate expenditure. By excluding goods of major revenue importance (like petroleum products and alcohol) from the GST, both Central and State Governments protect their respective fiscal autonomy although this results in continuation of tax cascading and hamper export competitiveness of domestic industries: the cascading of taxes generates revenue for government though it goes against the interest of business. Removal of tax cascading would also affect different governments differently depending on their revenue importance of taxes subsumed under GST. In addition, a more harmonised taxation system (like GST) leads to little fiscal freedom for individual governments to deviate from the common harmonised tax structure. In the long run, it could erode fiscal autonomy of governments to protect revenue by changing tax rates or any other policy measures to generate revenue.[29]

Estimation of GST Rate: An Alternative Approach

In this part, we attempt to estimate the tax rate for the proposed GST in India drawing on a measure of efficiency and breadth of the GST base (or GST coverage of goods and services). This estimate is based on the average so-called 'C-efficiency' of lower middle income countries and that of Asia/Pacific region. The C-efficiency is a measure to assess the performance of VAT (Keen 2013).[30] Keen (2013) defines 'C-efficiency' as 'an indicator of the departure of the VAT from a perfectly enforced tax levied at a uniform rate on all consumption'. Apart from 'C-efficiency', depending on differentiation in tax rates across goods and services and exemptions, tax collection under VAT varies. 'C-efficiency' is defined as:

$$\text{C-efficiency} = (\text{VAT Revenue}) / (\text{Tax Rate} * \text{Consumption Expenditure}) \quad (1)$$

---

[29] It would be difficult for States to deviate from the common harmonised structure of GST. Therefore tax effort (e.g., strengthening tax administration) and non-tax revenue mobilisation would be playing important roles in mobilising additional revenue to keep the pace of rising demand for public expenditure.

[30] For other measures of VAT efficiency, see Martinez-Vazquez and Bird (2010).

Table 4.1 Revenue under GST for All States and Union Government: 2009–10 (Rs Crore)[31]

State Taxes	State Governments*	Central Taxes	Union Government**
VAT/sales tax[a]	138,655	Central Excise Duties[d]	46,730
Entertainment tax[b]	904	Service Tax[e]	58,422
Central Sales Tax[c]	23,255	Customs[f]	50,100
Luxury Tax	1,204		
Taxes on lottery, betting and gambling	531		
States cesses and surcharges in so far as they relate to supply of goods and services	1,971		
Entry tax not in lieu of octroi	8,381		
Purchase tax	1,518		
Total State Taxes	**176,419**	**Total Central Taxes**	**155,252**
Revenue Receipts	791,429		572,811
Total Tax Revenue	542,390		
Own Tax Revenue	377,377		624,528^
Aggregate Expenditure	1,043,860		1,024,487

Data Sources: Rao and Chakraborty (2013); Receipt Budget (Union Government): 2011–12, Customs and Central Excise 2009–10: Annual Publications of Directorate of Data Management, CBEC, New Delhi.

Notes: *Including NCT of Delhi and Puducherry

**Excluding United Territories

^Gross tax revenue (includes States' share in Central taxes and taxes collected from United Territories)

[a]Excluding tax on petroleum products and liquor

[b]Unless it is levied by the local bodies

[c]Includes ITC adjustment and excludes taxes collected from crude petroleum and petroleum products (petrol, diesel and ATF)

[d]Excludes basic excise duty, additional duties, cesses and surcharges on petrol, diesel, ATF and crude petroleum

[e]Includes education cesses

[f]Includes Additional Duty of Customs (CVD), Special CV Duty, NCCD, and Education Cesses and excludes all duties and cesses on petroleum products

---

[31] 1 crore = 10 million.

Therefore,

Tax Rate = (VAT Revenue) / (C-efficiency * Consumption Expenditure)   (2)

For a given C-efficiency and Consumption Expenditure, we have estimated the tax rate in Table 4.2. The estimated tax rates for the proposed GST system would vary from 23.5 to 19.2 per cent depending on average 'C-efficiency' targets that we would like to achieve. Table 4.2 also shows that with a more inclusive GST, tax rate will rise, given the target for C-efficiency. The estimated tax rates are not very different from the rates estimated for 2009–10 by Rao and Chakraborty (2013) for the proposed GST regime, if one combines revenue neutral rates for both Centre and States together.

Table 4.2   Estimation of GST Rates Based on C-Efficiency

Description	2009–10	
Private final consumption expenditure (A) (Rs Crore)	37,07,566	
Adjusted pvt. final consumption expenditure[1] (B) (Rs Crore)	2,969,040	
Adjusted pvt. final consumption expenditure[2] (C) (Rs Crore)	31,39,618	
Government final consumption expenditure – net purchase of commodities & services[3] (D) (Rs Crore)	1,68,717	
Total adjusted consumption expenditure (E=B+D) (Rs Crore)	31,37,757	
Total consumption expenditure (F=C+D) (Rs Crore)	33,08,335	
Revenue consideration under proposed GST[4] (F) (Rs Crore)	3,31,671	
Revenue consideration under all inclusive GST (G) (Rs Crore)	4,67,124	
GST rate estimation (%)	Proposed GST	All Inclusive GST
C-efficiency	Tax Rate	Tax Rate[5]
Average of lower middle income economies (2009): 45%	23.5	31.4
Average of Asia/Pacific (2009): 55%	19.2	25.7

Data Source: CSO (2014), Rao and Chakraborty (2013), and Keen (2013).

Notes: [1]Excludes consumption expenditures on electricity, other fuel (other than LPG & kerosene), beverages (alcohol), education, medical care & health services, and gross rent & water charges.
[2]Excludes consumption expenditures on education, medical care & health services, and gross rent & water charges.
[3]Excludes expenditures on compensation of employees and consumption of fixed capital from Government Final Consumption Expenditure.
[4]Excludes taxes on tobacco & tobacco products, alcoholic beverages, petroleum products.
[5]Under this scenario all excluded goods (alcoholic beverages and petroleum products) are taken under GST.

Non-inclusion of Goods under GST

The proposed design of GST does not include (a) alcoholic liquor for human consumptions, (b) electricity and (c) real estate. In addition, inclusions of petroleum products (petrol, diesel and ATF), crude petroleum and natural gas have been postponed to an unspecified future date that would be decided by the GST Council. Non-availability or partial availability of input tax credits will result in stranded costs for some sectors (where direct use of out-of-GST items are high) but the costs will be spread across all sectors of the economy, through sectoral interlinkages. By not including electricity and some other sources of fossil fuels (like petrol, diesel, ATF, natural gas and crude petroleum), the proposed GST system will retain substantial cascading of taxes which will be detrimental for achieving export competitiveness of Indian industries in the international markets (Mukherjee and Rao 2015a).

Mukherjee and Rao (2015a) suggest an alternative design of GST inclusive of petroleum products and electricity which would reduce tax cascading, lower inflationary pressure and protect tax revenue. Dismantling the administered pricing mechanism for diesel along with the introduction of comprehensive GST for petroleum products could benefit both upstream and downstream sectors. Being a final consumption good, excluding alcohol from GST does not result in cascading of taxes but some researchers argue that the present system of multiple taxes along with the lack of provision for input tax credit encourages illegal (tax avoided) sales and sales of counterfeit (spurious) alcohol (hooch) which is an important issue specially since the deaths of many people due to consumption of spurious alcohol. However, unpaid input tax credit may not be substantial for alcohol; therefore the benefits of unaccounted sales and the selling of spurious liquor will still remain substantial.

Under the present system, real estate transactions attract stamp duty and registration fees. In addition, some States have also brought real estate promoters under the preview of VAT registration where VAT is levied on job contracts. Non-inclusion of real estate under GST will mean input tax credits are not allowed and the sector cannot pass on the benefits to customers where property is purchased for commercial/business purposes, which constitutes 80 per cent of real estate transactions.

However, there is a common misconception that the inclusion of these excluded goods and services under GST could expand the GST base and therefore a lower GST rate would be needed to achieve revenue neutrality. In fact, goods which are presently kept out of GST (e.g., petroleum products) make up a substantial share of the total tax base of the Central and State Governments and attract tax rates which are substantially higher than standard CENVAT and/or VAT rates. For example, the effective tax rate on petroleum products (other than natural gas and crude petroleum) is 40 per cent (Mukherjee and Rao 2015a). Therefore, if these goods are included under GST, GST revenue neutral rate will go up. Table 4.2 supports this claim. For example, an additional 3 per cent tax, over and above the standard GST rate (i.e., 20 per cent, assumed), would be required to include all petroleum products and electricity under GST (Mukherjee and Rao 2015a).

There are some other misconceptions regarding GST which require clarification. First is the assumption that introduction of GST will broaden the tax base by expanding coverage of economic activities under the tax net and reducing the list of exemptions. This is not, on the whole, correct because most economic activities are presently taxed either by Central and/or State Governments. There is not much scope for further expanding the tax base by bringing more goods and services under the purview of GST unless we reduce the list of goods and services that are kept under the exemption list.[32] No consensus on thresholds and exemptions has been reached among the concerned governments yet, or the information is not available in the public domain. The only other possibility of expanding the GST base would be for services in the negative list for services tax to be brought under the GST. However, there are only a few services in the negative list that do not attract some other tax.

Second, it is a common view that mitigation of cascading and double (multiple) taxation and an overall lower tax burden under GST would induce better tax compliance. The problem is that under the proposed design of GST with exclusion of goods like electricity and petroleum products, cascading of taxes would remain (Mukherjee and Rao 2015a). Taxpayers who hitherto were faced with single tax administration (e.g. retailers, service providers) would face two tax administrations. Complying with different tax authorities for single transaction could enhance the compliance costs and this could work against voluntary compliance. Therefore, the argument on possibility of 'lowering of overall tax burden on goods and services' (Government of India 2015) does not have any basis.

Third, it is envisaged that competitiveness of domestic industries in the international market will improve as the system will remove latent and embedded taxes. However, by keeping major revenue earning as well as major energy sources like electricity, petroleum products (petrol, diesel and ATF), natural gas and crude petroleum out of the GST, the removal of cascading will be limited and therefore the impact on export competitiveness of Indian industries would be limited (Mukherjee and Rao 2015a).

Fourth, it is assumed that GST will provide a common national market for goods and services by unifying the tax structure across States. However, as explained, with the present discussion on additional 1 per cent tax on inter-State supplies of goods, and since there is no consensus on common GST rates, threshold and exemptions

---

[32] Being a consumption-based tax, if the proposed GST could induce behavioural changes in the consumption patterns of households and for that overall consumption expenditure increases, there might be a possibility of more revenue collection under GST. However, consumption pattern depends on income and prices, and if the proposed GST regime influences these factors in favour of consumers, a possibility of expansion of tax revenue under GST arises.

across States, providing common national market for goods and services is very much under question.

Consequences of GST on Inequality

The impact of GST on different strata of society will be different depending on the composition of their consumption basket. Under the present system different goods attract different tax rates (both CENVAT and VAT rates vary). The purpose of having multiple tax schedules is to minimise tax incidence on the poor section of society. If a single rate is proposed under GST (both for CGST and SGST) with a few exemptions, the resultant tax system could be regressive.[33] Therefore, it is expected that the introduction of GST would have an immediate impact on prices of goods and services and this will induce behavioural changes among consumers, provided the benefits of removal of cascading of taxes and/or costs of additional tax burden are passed on to consumers. Different group of consumers will have different responses to changes in prices. In the long run it is expected that inflationary pressure will subside due to removal of cascading of taxes under GST. However, given the criticism that VAT (or GST) is regressive (Emran and Stiglitz 2007), we suggest that a detailed tax incidence analysis should be carried out to understand the consequences of GST adoption on different strata of the society.

Consequences of GST on Informalisation

There is some suggestion in the literature that the introduction of a broad-based GST may induce informalisation of the economy for developing countries like India (Emran and Stiglitz 2005; Piggott and Whalley 2001). Given the large informal sector that escapes tax net and substantial cash transactions, the opportunity cost of being in the tax system will not always outweigh the benefits. The presence of informal credit and labour markets and large domestic demand for locally produced goods and services often lead to unaccounted incomes and avoidance of taxes. A recent paper by Mukherjee and Rao (2015b) shows that facilitating access to formal credits and government assistance in financial loan, subsidy, machinery/equipment, training, marketing and raw material could encourage enterprises to register under VAT.[34]

Challenges in GST Administration

With some progress in the design of Goods and Services Tax (GST), there is an emerging need to explore the options for administering the new tax regime. From the discussions and decisions taken so far, one of the important parameters of the new regime is the applicability of two taxes (Central GST, or CGST, and State GST, or SGST) on each and every transaction of supply of good and/or service in

---

[33] Unless commodity-wise impact analysis is carried out, it would be difficult to decide on tax rates for each commodity.

[34] Also see Mukherjee and Rao (2019).

the country. The central tax would accrue to the Central government and the state tax would accrue to the State governments.

Compared to the existing regime, the proposed tax represents a significant change in the tax administration. The proposed design is for a dual GST where CGST and IGST will be administered by the Central Board of Excise and Customs (CBEC) and the SGST will be administered by the State Commercial Tax Department of the respective State Governments. From available policy documents in the public domain it is not clear whether in the proposed system certain common administrative functions (e.g., taxpayer registration, return filing) will be undertaken jointly or independently by each of the administrations. Since both the tax administrations will deal with same set of taxpayers (ideally), separating common administrative functions will add compliance costs to taxpayers and additional burden on tax administration.

It is not clear whether there will be a common threshold for mandatory registration for all taxes under GST (CGST, IGST and SGST) or separate thresholds for Central and State taxes.[35] Harmonisation of thresholds across States for registration under SGST is another area of concern which requires broad consensus among States. The issue of single registration for all States or separate registration for each State of functions/operations for the multi-State nature of businesses/services requires clarity. For example, whether Commercial Banks require to register in each State of their operation and pay due taxes separately or a Single nation-wide registration and payment of due taxes under GST through Head Office will suffice is not clear yet. The issue of apportionment of revenue for multi-State nature of services (e.g., telecom) is an area which requires clarifications. The issue of point of taxation and place of supply rules for taxation of services are not available in the public domain yet.

The Central tax administration would need to deal with wholesale and retail traders in addition to its existing taxpayers (e.g., manufacturers, service providers). Similarly, the state tax departments would need to deal with service providers. The workload per employee as well as the skill set associated with tax administration would have to undergo a sharp change if the taxes are to be administered by maintaining a status quo on the forms of administration. In other words, grafting the new tax on to existing tax administrations would impose a significant cost of transition in addition to higher costs of collection.

---

[35] One option to overcome the differences in setting thresholds for CGST and SGST may be to allow uniform threshold where States will get additional power to administer CGST for those tax payers whose turnover falls below the desired turnover of the Central Tax Authority. Tax collected by the States on CGST part may be transferred to Centre after deducting the cost of collection. Alternatively, the same proceed could be utilised for making payment to States for GST compensation.

Some taxpayers will face a sharp change in the tax environment. All taxpayers other than manufacturers who had faced one tax and one tax department (e.g., wholesale and retail traders), under new regime potentially they will face two tax departments, and potentially an increase in the compliance cost associated with the new regime, thereby raising the opportunity cost of being in the tax system. The result could either be higher evasion or higher resistance to the new tax regime. Some segments of the taxpayers are already articulating a demand for addressing the sharp increase in the compliance requirements of the new regime.

Rao and Mukherjee (2010) explore various options for GST administration and one of their suggestions is joint administration for common functions (highlighted in the Figure 4.1).[36] In addition adoption of functional specialisation based scrutiny assessment of taxpayers could reduce compliance as well as administration costs. For example, the Central tax authority has long experience in dealing with service providers and they have a better understanding to deal with service taxpayers as compared to any State tax administration. Similarly, all State tax administrations are well conversant in dealing with traders/distributors. Therefore, coordination across tax authorities by assigning superiority of decisions taken by one tax authority over other could be mutually beneficial.

Figure 4.1   GST Administration: Possible Scope for Joint Administration

Identification				
Registration				
Tax Payer Services				
Advance Ruling				
Returns Filing	Payments	Assessment/ Reassessment	Revenue Accounting	Taxpayer Accounting
Arrears Collections				
Audit				
Appeals/Dispute Settlement				
Special Investigations				

Source: Rao and Mukherjee (2010).

---

[36] One of the suggestions of the paper was to set up Semi-Autonomous Revenue Agency (SARA) by comprising both Central and State tax administrators and delegating the task of GST collection to the agency.

Bringing the Informal Sector under GST

The proposed transition to the GST regime is expected to bring in a significant change in the economic environment of the country. With a reduction in the extent of cascading in the tax regime, it is argued by some that moving to GST would result in an expansion of economic activity. Since this new tax regime works through more integrated and redefined supply chains, for units to benefit from this new tax regime and for the success of the new regime, it is important that more and more firms find it useful to be a part of the GST regime. While firms and enterprises in the organised sector do participate in the GST regime, those in the unorganised sector may not be as well integrated. This poses a problem both for the units and the tax administration. For the former, apart from being unable to benefit from the growth enhancing processes in the economy, these units may also be subject to irregular visits by various authorities often associated with the payment of bribes (Rao et al. 2014). For the tax department, non-participation by a segment of the economy can induce lower confidence in the tax regime resulting in higher non-compliance even among segments which would normally pay taxes.

Depending on respective turnover based threshold set for VAT registration by State Governments, different State tax administrations face different levels of challenges of bringing unincorporated enterprises under the tax system. Since the exemption from registration under CENVAT is up to an annual turnover of Rs 1.5 crore, until now the challenge of bringing unincorporated enterprises under the tax system is not severe for the Central tax administration (Central Excise and Customs). If the threshold for registration for Central GST remains same under the forthcoming Goods and Services Tax (GST) regime, the challenge for Central tax administration will not be much different from the present.

However, to integrate the unincorporated enterprises with the rest of the economy, it is imperative to bring the enterprises under the tax system. Though there are costs associated with remaining outside the tax system, a number of enterprises and firms choose to do so. It appears that the self-policing dimension of the VAT regime does not provide adequate benefits. Even the presently existing tax compounding schemes do not seem to be attractive enough to bring the small dealers into the system. Mukherjee and Rao (2015b) based on NSS 67th round Enterprises Survey explore factors which influence decision of unincorporated enterprises to register under VAT. From the results in the study, it appears that facilitating access to formal sector credit might be one such instrument. The other can be a focus on expanding the consumer's incentives to ask for an invoice. If larger segments of the economy ask for invoices for the purchases made, the incentive and the option to remain out of the tax regime would be correspondingly reduced. Designing appropriate incentives structure for consumers to ask for invoice and setting up an information exchange between tax authorities and consumers could reduce the possibility of under-reporting of sales/income.

GST Institutions

For successful adoption of a GST framework in India, establishment of GST institutions is very important. Given the federal structure of India, the character of the institutions should be neutral and both the Centre and the State Governments should have equal space (opportunities) in these institutions to propagate the spirit of cooperative federalism.

GST Council

The GST Bill proposed establishment of a GST Council which will be the highest body to examine and make recommendations on issues related to GST to Central as well as State Governments. The broad contours of the structure and roles and responsibilities of the Council is available from the Bill (Government of India 2015) but the details on roles and responsibilities and Constitutional power of the Council are yet to be decided.

The Council will comprise the Union Finance Minister as Chairperson and a Vice Chairperson who will be selected among the members. The Union Minister of State in Charge of Revenue or Finance will be another representative from the Union Government to the Council. From each of the States, the Minister in charge of Finance or Taxation or any other minister as nominated by the State Government will be a member of the Council. Every decision of the Council shall be backed by a majority of the members and it cannot be less than three-fourths (75 per cent) of the weighted votes of the members present and voting. The weightage of vote of the Union Government will be one-third (33.33 per cent) of the total votes cast and that of State Governments taken together will be two-thirds (66.67 per cent).

From the broad design of the Council, it can be concluded that the Union Government will have veto power on each and every decisions of the Council and it could throw its weight for any decision that will be in line with revenue interest of the Centre. However, the proposed design will make it impossible for any individual State or group of States to change the decision in favour of its/their own interest. This disproportionate power relationship is not conducive for fiscal federalism for a federal country like India.

For example, if any State wants to deviate from a harmonised GST rate for revenue consideration, it cannot unless it is backed by all other States and the Centre. Even if all States come together, unless the Union Government supports the resolution, it cannot be passed; this is very unlikely. Therefore, the proposed design will hamper the fiscal autonomy of the States. However, harmonisation of tax rates is conducive to minimising tax competition across States and for the emergence of a common market across Indian States. It is also not clear whether the GST Council will act as a recommending body or as a decision-making body and what will be the dispute settlement mechanism for any dispute arising due to decisions taken by the Council. For example, if any State deviates from the harmonised structure of the GST what will be the mechanism to handle the deviation? It is also not clear what will be the degree of fiscal freedom (or limit of tolerance) at which individual States could take their decision to secure their respective revenue interests.

GST Network (GSTN)

Modern tax administration is very much dependent on IT infrastructure. The achievements of the coveted objectives of the proposed GST system depend on establishing an effective IT system and integrating the IT systems already prevailing across State and Central Governments. Integration of the IT system will provide smooth transfers of input tax credits across States and act as tax clearing house for inter-State transactions. The same platform could also provide seamless automatic transmission of information across governments.

To achieve the objectives, the GST Network (GSTN) has been formed as a Section 25 (not for profit), non-Government private limited company.[37] It was incorporated on 28 March 2013 and the Authorised Capital of the company is Rs 10 crore. The Government of India holds 24.5 per cent equity in GSTN and all States of the Indian Union, including NCT of Delhi and Puducherry, and the Empowered Committee of State Finance Ministers (EC), together hold another 24.5 per cent. Balance 51 per cent equity is with non-Government financial institutions. The Company has been set up primarily to provide IT infrastructure and services to the Central and State Governments, taxpayers and other stakeholders for implementation of the GST.

However, Public Sector Banks do not have an equity share in the GSTN, an issue which has been highlighted by the Rajya Sabha Select Committee. Being a major interface between governments and taxpayers in collection of taxes, it is desirable that public sector banks could be given opportunities to bring forward their views in designing the IT platform. Given the information available in the public domain, the present status of development of the IT platform is not clear. Simplification of the procedures and a common harmonised structure for return submission could induce voluntary compliance and therefore it is expected that minimum burden on taxpayers in terms of information sharing could induce them for better tax compliance.

Other GST Institutions

A GST Dispute Settlement Authority?

The GST Council will be established by the GST Act as a Constitutional Body, comprising Legislators only. The Council will make recommendations on GST related issues. However, no dispute settlement authority is established. Given the federal structure of India and constitutionally assigned fiscal powers, it would be detrimental for cooperative federalism if any entity tries to encroach upon other's freedom. On the

---

[37] http://www.gstn.org/Organization-Profile.html (last accessed on 10 September 2015).

one hand, there is the need for fiscal flexibility of each of the stakeholders and on the other hand, a failure to establish a dispute resolution authority which has a judicial character, above the GST Council, could lead to the complete failure of the Council which may go against the spirit of the taxation reform.

The GST Amendment Bill, as passed by the Lok Sabha, proposed that 'The Goods and Services Tax Council may decide about the modalities to resolve disputes arising out of its recommendations'. It is not clear how a recommending or decision-making body could act as a dispute settlement body also for disputes arising due its own decision. However, the earlier Amendment Bill (The Constitution [One Hundred Fifteenth Amendment] Bill, 2011) 'proposed to set up Goods & Services Tax Dispute Settlement Authority (Article 279B), which may be approached by the affected Government (whether the Centre or the States) seeking redressal for any loss caused by any action due to a deviation from the recommendations made by the Goods & Services Tax Council or for adversely affecting the harmonious structure and implementation of the GST.'

The main objection behind the setting up of the Authority was that '… this authority shall have powers of overriding the supremacy of the Parliament and the State Legislatures. It shall affect the fiscal autonomy of the States'[38] (Government of India 2013). By not having the dispute settlement authority, it is expected that both the Union and the State Governments would agree to follow all the recommendations or decisions taken at the GST Council and there will be no deviation from the common harmonised structure of GST, even in the event of revenue shortfall, which it quite unlikely for a federal country like India.

A GST Compensation Fund?

The GST Bill (The Constitution [122nd Amendment] Bill 2014) envisages that States will be fully compensated from the Central Government for any loss of revenue due to implementation of the Goods and Services Tax for a period of five years. The Rajya Sabha Select Committee on GST Bill recommends for establishment of a Goods and Services Compensation Fund under the administrative control of the GST Council into which the Central Government shall deposit the GST Compensation. It is expected that the establishment of such a fund will only build the credibility of the Central Government and regain the trust of the States where their past experience of getting compensation for loss of revenue in VAT implementation or phase-out of

---

[38] The Attorney General of India's comments on the objection was, 'The Dispute Settlement Authority is primarily with regard to the aspect of disputes in relation to deviation from any recommendation of the GSTC, and it is not just any deviation but a deviation which results in loss of revenue to a State Government or the Government of India, or affects the harmonised structure of the Goods and Service Tax. Notwithstanding the decision on the DSA, the ultimate control over finance will always be that of the legislatures' (Government of India 2013).

CST resulted in trust deficit. On the basis of the past experience of the States, timely payment of compensation in every financial year is a vital issue which is highlighted before and by the Rajya Sabha Select Committee.

Conclusions

The GST reform is important for the country, in spite of the criticisms made in this chapter. The Lok Sabha (Lower House of the Parliament) passed the Bill on 6 May 2015 and passed on the same to the Rajya Sabha (Upper House of the Parliament) for consideration. The Rajya Sabha referred the Bill to its Select Committee on 14 May 2015 and the Select Committee of the Rajya Sabha submitted their report on the Bill on 22 July 2015. The Committee accepted the majority of the provisions of the Bill and recommended a few changes. However, the Bill could not be taken up for voting in the monsoon session of the Parliament (21 July–13 August 2015). After passing the Bill in the Rajya Sabha, it will again come back to Lok Sabha for final approval and then it will be sent to the President of India for his final approval. After passing the Bill, it needs to be ratified at least half of the States to become a law. There are also three Bills that need to be passed – one by the Parliament and two by the State Legislative Assemblies – before GST is implemented.

Until recently, all decisions on GST have been taken without consultation with the major stakeholders like businesses and citizens (consumers). The decisions taken by the Empowered Committee of State Finance Ministers and the Central Government are not available in the public domain and therefore it is difficult to get clarity on the various aspects of GST. Since businesses are not consulted, their views on the present design and structure of GST are not clear. This may lead to resistance to the tax reform and/or negotiated tax environment which are not conducive for a modern rule-based tax system. Keeping major stakeholders out of the discussions on GST is not a good sign for any tax reform as decisions taken by the governments will influence their day-to-day decisions. It is desirable that a more transparent approach would be followed to disseminate the decisions among stakeholders and taking into account their views in policy designs.

This chapter argues that reform in tax administration is as important as tax policy for mobilisation of revenue. Given the present state of diversities in tax administration across governments, it is expected that tax administration reforms will be taken up sooner rather than later, to enable tax officials to administer the GST efficiently. By moving towards GST, it would be difficult for individual States to deviate from the harmonised structure of GST and it will further enhance the importance of tax administration to achieve revenue objectives of the State Governments. The present state of investment in tax administration is miniscule. Large scale vacancies in tax departments and limited availability of infrastructure are major constraints which influence tax efficiency. A large section of tax officials are engaged in carrying out routine works; there is hardly any scope for skill development and specialisation in tax administration. Modernisation of tax administrations by investing in manpower and infrastructure along with continuous research and training could inculcate the desires for specialisation in various aspects of tax administration.

Finally, the success of the proposed GST in terms of compliance and revenue mobilisation will largely depend on the provision of incentives for tax invoice based transactions and simplification of the tax administration. Based on the proposed design, a large part of transactions (both in goods and services) remain outside the tax net. Even there is no mechanism to verify the originality of the tax invoice issued by the vendors or service providers. The prevailing system of without-invoice transactions results in the generation of unaccounted income as it escapes tax nets of both direct and indirect taxes. The present system of separate tax administrations by the Centre and the States is not conducive for a GST-like tax system and it will increase both compliance and administrative costs. Therefore, options for a joint tax administration may be explored.

References

Acharya, Shankar. 2005. 'Thirty Years of Tax Reform in India'. *Economic and Political Weekly* 40(20): 2061–69.

Aggarwal, P. K.1995. *Incidence of Major Indirect Taxes in India*. New Delhi: NIPFP, 1995.

Bird, Richard. 1993. 'Tax Reform in India'. *Economic and Political Weekly* 28(50): 2721–26.

Central Statistics Office (CSO). 2014. 'National Account Statistics 2014'. Ministry of Statistics & Programme Implementation, Government of India, New Delhi.

Emran, S. M. and J. E. Stiglitz. 2007. 'Equity and Efficiency in Tax Reforms in Developing Countries'. SSRN No. 1001269. Social Science Research Networks Working Papers.

———. 2005. 'On Selective Indirect Tax Reform in Developing Countries'. *Journal of Public Economics* 89(4): 599–623.

Government of India. 2015. 'Report of the Select Committee on the Constitution (One Hundred & Twenty-Second Amendment) Bill, 2014'. Presented to the Rajya Sabha on 22 July, Rajya Sabha, Parliament of India, Government of India, New Delhi.

———. 2013. 'Seventy Third Report of the Standing Committee on Finance (2012–2013) (Fifteenth Lok Sabha) on the Constitution (One Hundred Fifteenth Amendment) Bill, 2011', Department of Revenue, Ministry of Finance, Government of India, New Delhi.

Keen, M. 2013. 'The Anatomy of the VAT'. No. WP/13/111. IMF Working Paper, International Monetary Fund (IMF), Washington, D.C.

Martinez-Vazquez, Jorge and Richard M. Bird. 2010. 'Value Added Tax: Onward and Upward?', International Studies Program Working Paper 10–26, Andrew Young School of Policy Studies, Georgia State University, Georgia, USA.

Mukherjee, S. and R. Kavita Rao. 2015a. 'Policy Options for Including Petroleum, Natural Gas and Electricity in the Goods and Services Tax'. *Economic and Political Weekly* 50(9): 98–107.

————. 2015b. 'Factors Influencing Unincorporated Enterprises to Register under Value Added Tax (VAT): An Analysis with Enterprises Survey Data'. Working Paper No. 145, National Institute of Public Finance and Policy (NIPFP), New Delhi.

————. 2019. 'Value Added Tax and Informality: Determinants of Registration of Enterprises under State VAT in India'. *Margin—The Journal of Applied Economic Research*, 13(1): 21–48.

NIPFP. 2014. 'Study on Unaccounted Incomes in India'. Project Report Submitted to Central Board of Direct Taxes, Department of Revenue, Ministry of Finance, Government of India, New Delhi.

Piggott, John and John Whalley. 2001. 'VAT Base Broadening, Self Supply and the Informal Sector'. *The American Economic Review* 91(4): 1084–94.

Rao, M. Govinda and François Vaillancourt. 1994. 'Interstate Tax Disharmony in India: A Comparative Perspective'. *Publius* 24(4): 99–114.

Rao, R. Kavita and P. Chakraborty. 2013. 'Revenue Implications of GST and Estimation of Revenue Neutral Rate: A State-wise Analysis'. Report submitted to the Empowered Committee of State Finance Ministers, New Delhi.

Rao, R. Kavita and Mukherjee, S. 2010. 'Administration of GST: Can We Continue with Present Structures?' Background Paper for the Workshop on GST, NIPFP, March.

Rao, R. Kavita, A. Mahanta and K. Bhadra. 2014. 'Tax Policy and Enterprise Development in South Asia: Country Study Report India'. Governance Institutes Network International (GINI), Islamabad, Pakistan.

Rao, M. Govinda and R. Kavita Rao. 2005. 'Trends and Issues in Tax Policy and Reform in India'. *India Policy Forum, Global Economy and Development Program, The Brookings Institution* 2(1): 55–122.

Shome, Parthasarathi. 2015. 'GST – Remains of a Decade', *Business Standard*, 15 September 2015.

Vaitheeswaran, K. and A. P. Datar. 2015. 'GST's Seven Deadly Defects', *The Indian Express*, 19 September 2015.

II

Revenue Neutrality of GST

5

Estimation of Revenue Neutral Rates for Goods and Services Tax in India*

R. Kavita Rao

Introduction

The purpose of this report is to generate Revenue Neutral Rates (RNR) for the Goods and Services Tax (GST) for both the Centre and each individual state using information on the contours of GST that have been decided so far in the discussions of the Union government and the Empowered Committee of State Finance Ministers. For this exercise, it is important to summarise the key features of the design of GST (section titled 'Key Features of GST Design'). Methodology adopted to estimate RNR is presented in the next section ('Methodology'). The section titled 'Results' provides the combined RNR followed by rates computed for each individual government including the Central government. In undertaking this exercise, two alternative estimates of base of services have been used – one using PROWESS data obtained from CMIE (Centre for Monitoring Indian Economy) and the other using turnover data from the Ministry of Corporate Affairs (MCA) provided by the Ministry of Finance, Government of India (GOI). It should be noted that the entire turnover of firms supplying services would not constitute additional base for GST. There are two possible reasons why the base can be different from the total turnover – one, if these firms purchase taxable goods which are used for providing these services, then they can avail of input tax credit. In other words, the turnover of these purchases needs to be deducted from the turnover of supply of services. Second, since these services

---

* This chapter was originally submitted as a research report to the Empowered Committee of State Finance Ministers, February 2014.

in turn can be used as inputs in the supply of presently taxable goods, they would already be a part of the base for taxation of goods at present. Hence, a correction on this count too would be required to identify the extent of turnover of supply of services for final consumption. The methodology used for deriving activity code wise turnover in each of these cases is discussed in the section titled 'Methodology'.

Key Features of GST Design

The key features on which decisions seem to have emerged on the design of GST can be summarised as follows:

1. Dual GST, a central GST and a state GST both levied on all goods and services.
   a. It is proposed that there would be a list of exemptions and exclusions from the regime, but the exact items on the list are yet to be decided.
   b. As per the GST bill passed in the Lok Sabha, petroleum products to remain outside the base for GST in the initial years of implementation: these can be brought into the base by the GST council in subsequent years.
   c. The Bill also kept alcoholic beverages outside the base for GST.
   d. Since there are no specific omissions in the bill, it would be appear that real estate transactions and electricity duty would continue to be taxed as per Stamps and Registration Duty and Electricity Duty respectively, without being integrated in GST.
   e. While there is no firm decision on the same, it has been difficult for governments to tax health and education as a part of the earlier regime. It is therefore not clear whether the new GST regime would extend to these services or not.
2. It is proposed that there would be two rates of tax, apart from a very low rate for gold and bullion.
      As per information obtained from the Empowered Committee of State Finance Ministers, taxes to be subsumed into GST are: VAT/Sales tax, entertainment tax, luxury tax, taxes on lottery, betting and gambling, states' cesses and surcharges relating to supply of goods and services. The GST bill passed in Lok Sabha deleted the Entry 52 in State list implying entry tax has been subsumed under GST. For the Union government, the taxes to be subsumed include union excise duty, service tax, countervailing duty and special additional duty components of customs duty.
3. Inter-state transactions would be subject to IGST – where the levy is to be collected by the central administration in the exporting state. The dealer in the importing state can claim input tax credit for such a tax paid against tax collected in the subsequent stage implying application of destination principle.
   a. It is proposed that while CST will be eliminated for these transactions, for the first two years to take into account the revenue concerns of exporting states, a 1 per cent tax on interstate sale of goods would be collected and retained by the exporting states.

Based on this design of GST, which is partly origin based (till the time 1 per cent CST continues), and largely destination based, we have estimated RNRs for the Central government and the individual state governments for the year 2013–14 keeping this design issue in mind. It should be mentioned here that RNR for the states under a potential GST regime has been worked out with this methodology using the PROWESS data for the 2007–08, 2009–10, 2011–12 and now for 2013–14. While the present exercise is primarily based on the same methodology, there are a few changes that were introduced.

- The number of taxes being subsumed into GST has been increased – the important new taxes proposed to be subsumed since the computations for 2011–12 are entry tax in lieu of octroi and purchase tax.
- In the earlier exercise, since all states were not taxing sugar and textiles, an attempt was made to correct the base for this omission. Since then, all states have started taxing these products and hence this correction was no longer necessary.
- While all the earlier exercises were based on PROWESS data augmented by information on service tax collections, it was suggested this time around that data on company-wise turnover can be taken from the MCA database as an alternative proxy for the size of the service sector, especially since the MCA database would have a larger number of companies than the PROWESS database.
- Further, since it has been decided that for a period of two years after the introduction of GST, there would be a 1 per cent levy on inter-state sale of goods, to be collected and retained by the exporting state, this feature too is being incorporated into the computation exercise.
- Finally, since petroleum products would remain outside the base for GST, CST would continue to apply for inter-state sale of these products. Hence, for the purposes of this exercise, CST revenues from non-petroleum products alone are being considered for arriving at figures for revenues to be compensated.

Further, in order to estimate RNR for the year 2013–14, the following decisions were taken in the meeting at the Ministry of Finance, GOI, chaired by the Revenue Secretary, GOI, on 9 June 2015:

- It was proposed that since the MCA data for the year 2012–13 covered a far more number of service providers, it may be more appropriate to use the MCA database for the year 2011–12 and 2012–13 to appropriately adjust the base for 2013–14.
- Some states had raised an issue that in the present regime, they collect some revenues on account of the fact that they deny input tax credit on some transactions. Such revenues would not be available in the new regime and hence this aspect too should be taken into account while estimating RNRs. In the above-mentioned meeting, it was decided that this aspect was not to be taken into account while calculating RNR. It was clarified that although this issue was raised by a few states in the Sub-Committee meetings, no decision has been taken by the EC in this regard. Moreover, the amount of input tax credit denied is already reflected in the total tax collection of States and is thus, being taken into account while

calculating the RNR. It would, therefore, not be appropriate to include it in the calculation of RNRs of the states.

Methodology

The approach adopted in this exercise is a combination of the 'tax turnover' method and data on service sector value added estimated from the PROWESS data set obtained from CMIE and MCA data provided by the Ministry of Finance, GOI. For the States, we have used data on taxes collected to derive the corresponding base for taxation corresponding to goods in the new regime. The sum total of base for all states is used as the base for the Centre. The advantage of the tax turnover method is that it is based on the data of taxable turnover of goods available with the respective tax departments of states and the Centre on goods and services.

For each state, taxes have been classified into two groups – taxes the base of which can be added to the taxable base in GST and taxes whose base might not add to the taxable base under GST. In the first category we have VAT, entry tax not in lieu of octroi, and entertainment tax. Rest of the levies are classified in the second category. This is because taxes such as entry tax in lieu of octroi would be levied over and above VAT or GST and hence would not provide additional base to the tax. Similar would be the case of purchase tax for instance. VAT revenue is further bifurcated into revenue from commodities which will be brought into tax under GST and those that would remain outside the base, i.e., liquor, diesel, petrol and aviation turbine fuel (ATF). We have used weighted average tax rates for the estimation of taxable turnover from the data on tax collected under entry tax not in lieu of octroi and VAT excluding those which would not form part of the GST, viz., liquor, diesel, petrol and ATF. To this is added an estimate of the likely base from entertainment tax assuming the tax rate is 30 per cent. This gives us the base corresponding to the taxation of goods under GST[1] (see Table 5.1 for summary and Appendix Table 5A.1 for details of state specific taxes to be subsumed in GST and the corresponding revenues to be compensated).

The revenue for the Centre was provided by the Central Board for Excise and Customs (see Table 5.2). As is evident, the reported revenue for the Centre includes the entire revenue from tobacco products. However, since a part of the revenue on tobacco products is to be realised through non-rebatable excises, for the purposes of the present exercise, it is assumed that one fourth of the revenue from tobacco products would be realised from GST.

For estimation of the base from taxation of services, two alternative approaches have been adopted. The first approach is based on the PROWESS data and the second approach is based on the turnover data from the MCA database. The methodology adopted in each of these cases is discussed below.

---

[1] Revenue for Chhattisgarh was not available for CST revenue from non-petroleum products. The average for major states for the share of CST derived from petroleum products and liquor was applied to derive the same.

Table 5.1   Summary of Revenue to Be Compensated for All States Combined (Rs Crore)

Tax Heads	Revenue to Be Compensated
Taxes contributing to base	
VAT & Sales Tax (excluding Non-VAT)	2,78,232
Entry Tax not in lieu of octroi	15,896
Entertainment Tax	2,138
Taxes not contributing to base	
CST (including ITC adjustment)	38,338
Lottery, Betting & Gambling	608
Luxury Tax	1,946
Non-VAT (collected on services/works contract)	1,047
Entry Tax in lieu of octroi	20,772
Toll tax not in lieu of service charges	552
Cesses & Surcharges	4,742
Advertisement Tax	1
Purchase Tax	4,559
ITC Reversal	11,677
TOTAL	**5,35,722**
Revenue to Be Compensated (4 per cent)	**4,07,167**
Revenue to Be Compensated (2 per cent)	**3,68,829**

Source: Compiled from State-wise Data Obtained from States (see Appendix Table 5A.1).

Table 5.2   Revenues of the Central Government: 2013–14 (Rs Crore)

Sl. No.	Type of Duty	Shared with States	Not Shared with States			Total
		Basic	NCCD*	Education Cess**	Others	
1	**Central duty (CE) duty**					
(a)	Non-Pol (excluding tobacco products) (Pol: petroleum products)	53,672	1,913	2,441	2,675	60,701
(b)	Tobacco products	14,855	1,319	528	1,153	17,855
	Total CE duty {Non-Pol} [(a)+(b)]	68,527	3,232	2,969	3,828	78,556
2	**CVD (Non-Pol)**	77,965	479	3,663	883	82,990
3	**SAD (Non-Pol)**	24,837	0	0	0	24,837
4	**Service Tax**	1,50,417	0	4,319	0	1,54,736
5	**TOTAL**	**3,21,746**	**3,711**	**10,951**	**4,711**	**3,41,119**
6	**Total revenue to be compensated***					**3,27,728**
6i	**Non-tobacco revenues to be compensated**					**3,23,264**
6ii	**Tobacco products revenue at 10 per cent**					**4,463.75**

Source: Provided by CBEC.
Notes: *NCCD: National Calamity Contingent Duty
**includes secondary and higher education cess.
***excluding 3/4th revenue from tobacco products.

PROWESS-Based Approach

To estimate the comprehensive base, we have started with the National Industries Classification (NIC) 2008 (NIC-2008) code to identify what constitutes service sector at the national level (Table 5.3). This is done to obtain the exhaustive list of services available for the purpose of taxation and to identify those services which are likely to be exempted from taxation. This comprehensive listing as per the NIC-2008 code eliminates subjectivity in the estimation of base.

Having obtained the NIC-2008 classification, we have used the CMIE's PROWESS database to obtain the value of sales for services for the purpose of taxation at the national level in each of these codes. It is to be noted that use of the PROWESS database would give a conservative estimate of the tax base, because it

Table 5.3   Service Sector as per NIC-2008 Classification

NIC-2008 Code	Activity Description	Likely to be Taxed or Exempt
19	Bottling of Liquefied Petroleum Gas (LPG)/Compressed Natural Gas (CNG)	Taxed
35	Power transmission line infrastructure	Exempt
46	Trade	Taxed
47	Commission agent services & retail outlets	Taxed
491	Rail transport	Taxed
492	Road transport	Taxed
493	Transport via pipeline	Taxed
50	Water transport	Taxed
51	Air transport	Taxed
521	Storage and warehousing	Taxed
522	Other transport service activities	Taxed
55	Hotel and restaurant	Taxed
61	Post & telecommunication	Taxed
62 & 63	Computer related activities	Taxed
64, 65 & 66	Banking and other financial services	Taxed
42, 68, 77	Real estate	Exempt
72 & 85	Research & development and education	Taxed but education might be exempt
70, 73, 74, 78, 79, 80 & 82	Business services	Taxed
84	Public administration	Exempt
86	Health	Likely to be exempt
93, 94	O.com, social & personal services	Taxed
	Others/Undifferentiated services	Taxed

Source: Computed by author.

does not include services provided by entities not registered in the stock exchange, whether they be provided by a corporate entity or by unincorporated entities. Some summary information on the PROWESS data is provided below.

What is available from the PROWESS data set?

PROWESS is a database of financial statements of large and medium Indian firms. It contains detailed information on over 26,000 firms. These comprise:

- All companies traded on India's major stock exchanges
- Several others including the central public sector enterprises
- The database covers most of the organised industrial activities
- Banking
- Organised financial and other services sectors in India.

The companies covered in PROWESS account for 76.51 per cent of all corporate taxes and over 84 per cent of excise duty plus service tax collected by GOI. PROWESS provides detailed information on each company. This includes a database of the financials covering 1,500 data items and ratios per company. The data extracted on the service sector sale at the all-India level is reported in Table 5.4.

Since the PROWESS data relates to only some of the companies, we have also made a partial correction for the informal sector, which is explained below. It is true that there is no clear idea about the size of the informal sector services that will be available for taxation under GST. Review of the literature on estimates and the size of the informal sector shows that the unorganised sector can be categorised into two components:

Table 5.4   The Estimate of Taxable Service Sector Base from PROWESS Data Set (Rs Crore)

Sales Data: As per NIC-2008 Code	2007–08	2009–10	2011–12	2013–14
Service sector sales (all India as per PROWESS data)	3,35,189	5,25,310	11,09,064	12,32,779
Revised sales figure/turnover	7,89,711	11,51,066	23,37,096	25,93,243
GDP at factor cost	43,20,892	60,91,485	79,31,381	1,01,81,611
Service sector GDP	23,39,468	33,32,976	42,20,369	59,72,287
Service sector sale as % of GDP	18.28	18.9	29.47	25.47
Service sector sale as % of service sector GDP	33.76	34.54	55.38	43.42
Service sector excluding exempt sectors	11,51,404	18,16,994	29,95,401	37,69,231
Service Sector sales as % of services excluding exempted services	68.59	63.35	78.02	68.80

Source: Economic Survey, National Accounts Statistics and CMIE's PROWESS Database.

(i) informal and (ii) others (Kannan et al., 2008).[2] For the purpose of estimation of GST base, we have considered the category called 'others' which comprises of enterprises:

a) registered under the Companies Act;
b) employing processes requiring high degree of technical knowhow;
c) franchises of formal sector units;
d) not covered under the production boundary; and
e) non-profit institutions.

As evident from Table 5.5, share of 'others' in total net domestic product (NDP) was around 10.7 per cent and if you take 'others' from the service sector alone, it works out to be 7.3 per cent of NDP. The ratio of NDP from 'others' in services to NDP from organised sector in services works out to 27 per cent. This ratio has been applied to estimate the base of informal sector services available for GST. While it is possible to argue that the informal sector can in fact be much larger, how much of it will be above an exemption threshold of Rs 25 lakh is not evident.

Correction Using Service Tax Collection

For a more realistic estimate of service sector base we have mapped service-wise tax collection data against the data on sales obtained as per the NIC code and adjusted the turnover/sales based on the tax collected from each category of services within the service tax regime. Service-wise tax collection data was provided by the Central

Table 5.5   Share of Informal Sector in Net Domestic Product (NDP): 2001–02 (Per Cent)

Industry Group	Informal	Others	Unorganised	Organised	Total
Agriculture, forestry and fishing	25.5		25.5	0.9	26.4
Mining and quarrying	0.2		0.2	1.8	2.0
Manufacturing	1.6	3.4	5.0	8.4	13.4
Electricity, gas and water supply	0.1		0.1	1.0	1.0
Construction	3.9		3.9	2.5	6.4
Trade, hotels, restaurants	9.3	2.5	11.9	3.8	15.6
Transport and communication	3.3	0.6	3.9	2.8	6.7
Real estate, financial services and ownership of dwellings	2.6	2.9	5.4	7.6	13.0
Community, social and personal services	1.3	1.3	2.6	12.8	15.4
Total	**47.7**	**10.7**	**58.5**	**41.5**	**100.0**

Source: Kannan et al. (2008).

---

[2] K. P. Kannan, N. S. Sastry, S. K. Nath, P. K. Ray, G. Raveendra, and S. V. Ramana Murthy. Contribution of the Unorganised Sector to GDP Report of the Sub Committee of a NCEUS Task Force, Working Paper No. 2, National Commission for Enterprises in the Unorganised Sector, 2008.

Board of Excise and Customs, Ministry of Finance, GOI.[3],[4] Having done this adjustment, we have obtained total turnover of service sector at Rs 3082422 crore for 2013–14. This is further adjusted for some of the important currently exempt services which would be part of the GST base, viz., railway passenger fares and railway freights on exempted commodities and air fares. For all the services, two kinds of adjustments have been made, viz., deduction for taxable inputs used for service provision and deduction of services provided when used as inputs into taxable activities. For these corrections, the input–output table for 2006–07 has been used to derive service specific input–output ratios (see Table 5.6).

In addition to the above, there are two sector specific corrections made in the data

1. For computer-related services, it has been argued that a sizeable part of the turnover is associated with exports – this component will not add to the taxable base for GST. Based on an IBEF study,[5] the domestic supply of computer services is 30 per cent of total sales value of computer-related activities and hence this 30 per cent is included in this study for arriving at the net additional base available for taxation.
2. For financial services, there are two difficulties. First, the coverage of financial services tends to be incomplete being largely limited to fee-based services. The present regime of taxation of financial services within Service Tax too is of this form. There is no clear indication to suggest that a radically new approach would be adopted in the proposed GST regime. Therefore, the base corresponding to the present service tax regime is considered a more appropriate base to incorporate into GST RNR estimation in both cases – PROWESS- and MCA-based estimates. Second, as per the input–output table, more than 80 per cent of total financial services are used as inputs. But since a significant part of financial services are in the form of embedded services, the possibility of taking input tax credit can be limited. So using the ratio of Financial Intermediation Services Indirectly Measured (FISIM) to total financial services, the extent of financial services used as inputs is reduced from 84 per cent to 54 per cent.

Approach Based on MCA Data

In this case, the activity codes assigned to companies was as per the 2004 NIC code. On examining the data it was found that some companies did not have a valid activity code as per the NIC classification. Further, as discussed earlier, it was

---

[3] The revenue collection data for service tax provided net collections by service categories. These were converted to gross collections using the overall ratio of PLA to credit in total collections of service tax. Further, the standard rate for service tax, i.e., 12.36 per cent was used to derive the corresponding turnover.

[4] For real-estate transactions, it has emerged from discussions that the present form of treatment for works contracts would continue in the GST regime. This is reflected in the treatment of real estate and the base corresponding to the present regime in service tax has been incorporated into the base.

[5] http://www.ibef.org/industry/indian-it-and-ites-industry-analysis-presentation.

Table 5.6 Input Coefficients and the Adjusted Base: PROWESS Database

NIC-2008	Activity	Taxable Inputs to Output Ratio	Sales Used as Inputs in Taxable Activities/ Output	Net Additional Base Available for Taxation
19	Bottling of LPG/CNG			0
35	Power transmission line infrastructure			0
46	Trade			0
47	Commission agent services & retail outlets			0
491	Rail transport	0.15815	0.65112	1,526
492	Road transport	0.11300	0.48822	24,979
493	Transport via pipeline	0.11300	0.48822	3,416
50	Water transport	0.18028	0.40803	4,647
51	Air transport	0.22652	0.41809	30,228
521	Storage and warehousing	0.07394	0.98869	1,520
522	Other transport service activities	0.06237	0.59899	11,989
55	Hotel and restaurant	0.18333	0.18695	16,327
61	Post & telecommunication	0.10196	0.74738	55,914
62 & 63	Computer-related activities	0.04255	0.12441	84,597
64, 65 & 66	Banking and other financial services	0.03605	0.84109	1,10,927
42, 68, 77	Real estate	0.55234	0.42024	1,26,995
72 & 85	Research & development and Education	0.00748	0.05712	47,961
70, 73, 74, 78, 79, 80 & 82	Business services	0.07883	0.98858	4,780
84	Public administration	0.00000	0.00000	15
86	Health	0.22556	0.21503	1,447
93, 94	O.com, social & personal services	0.11226	0.41409	37,132
	Others/undifferentiated services	0.07654	0.31880	1,34,542
Total unadjusted				**6,98,941**
Final base after all corrections				**8,27,549**

Source: Input–output table (2006–7) published by CSO and CMIE's PROWESS Database.

proposed to augment the data available for 2013–14 using information from 2011–12 and 2012–13. Before attempting these corrections, it would be useful to examine the data that is available for each of these years. The total number of firms reporting data in 2011–12 and 2012–13 appear to be much larger than those reporting for 2013–14. However, if one compares the number of firms with valid activity code and working in the supply of services, the differences are not that large – 3.56 lakh in 2012–13 as against 3.25 lakh in 2013–14. A comparison of turnovers suggests that while the overall turnovers in 2011–12 and 2012–13 are higher than those in 2013–14, the turnover of firms reporting to be service providers with a valid code is comparable to the turnover available for 2013–14 (Table 5.7).

Using the concordance tables, companies first are classified as per the NIC code for 2008. Further, since it was noted that a number of companies which filed returns in 2012–13 did not file returns in 2013–14, an attempt is made to undertake some corrections to get a more comprehensive base for 2013–14. These are discussed below.

> Step 1: For all companies reporting information in 2012–13 but not for 2013–14 and had a valid activity code, the data from 2012–13 has been extrapolated using the average growth rate for 2013–14 when compared to 2012–13.

Table 5.7   A Comparison of MCA Data (Rs Crore)

	2011–12	2012–13	2013–14
Number of firms			
1. Firms with no valid code	34,720	34,059	21,996
2. Firms not engaged in services	1,69,042	1,75,154	0
3. Firms in services	3,31,124	3,56,752	3,25,013
4. Firms in service but not included due to coverage[a]	71,813	76,128	0
Total	6,06,699	6,42,093	3,47,009
Turnover (Rs crore)			
1. Firms with no valid code	10,58,035	2,29,41,162	7,30,001
2. Firms not engaged in services	5,01,29,647	1,41,71,531	0
3. Firms in services	30,62,734	37,78,774[b]	34,12,732
4. Firms in service but not included due to coverage	10,43,559	11,61,634	0
Total	5,52,93,975	4,20,53,102	41,42,732

Source: Computed from data provided by Ministry of Corporate Affairs.
Notes: (a) Companies associated with electricity, gas and steam and construction for instance are excluded from the analysis.
(b) Data for one company appeared spurious it increased from Rs 89 crore in 2012–13 to Rs 115 lakh crore in 2013–14 and then dropped to Rs 180 crore in 2013–14. For purposes of comparison, this value was corrected.

Table 5.8   Computing Total Turnover for the Year 2013–14 (Rs crore)

Steps	Turnover
1. Data provided for 2013–14	**34,12,732**
2. Including companies for which data from 2012–13 was extrapolated for companies with valid activity code	**39,74,783**
3. Turnover without activity code in 2012–13	**15,11,747**
4. Turnover classified through assigning activity codes in 2012–13	**13,58,755**
5. Taxable turnover from step 4 (in 12–13 prices)	**3,77,204**
6. Taxable turnover in 13–14 prices	**4,05,707**
7. Total turnover from MCA after all corrections (2013–14)	**40,83,607**

Source: Computed from data provided by Ministry of Corporate Affairs.

Step 2: For all companies for which there was no description and/or no valid activity code, all companies with turnover above Rs 100 crore have been individually explored and classified into an appropriate activity code. These companies account for 89.88 per cent of the total turnover of uncoded companies.

Table 5.8 summarises the numbers after each of these steps and Table 5.9 provides estimates of the size of the additional base subsequent to all corrections using the MCA database. As in the case of PROWESS data, we have used the service tax collection to validate the turnover obtained from MCA – for any sector where the turnover corresponding to MCA is less than the turnover corresponding to service tax, the latter is incorporated as the relevant base. Further, all the corrections indicated in the case of PROWESS have also been undertaken here.[6]

After all these corrections, the services base and total base available for taxation by the two methods are summarised in Table 5.10. This table suggests that by both the methods, the net addition to taxable base from taxation of services is to the tune of 15–16 per cent of *Gross Value Added* (GVA) from services and the total GST base as a percentage of total GVA is in the range of 37–38 per cent.

Results

Using the revenue to be compensated and the base derived, we can arrive at the estimates of RNR for the Centre and the states under alternative assumptions. These are presented in Tables 5.11 and 5.12. The state-wise rates can be found in Tables 5.13–5.16. The alternative assumptions can be summarised as follows:

1. For arriving at the standard rate, it is assumed that 2 per cent of the original turnover of goods is taxed at 1 per cent, for taxation of gold and bullion. Fifty-six

---

[6] Since MCA represents a more comprehensive base when compared to PROWESS, we have not attempted to correct for informal sector in this case.

Table 5.9   Input Coefficients and the Adjusted Base: MCA Database

NIC 2008	Range	Taxable I–O Ratio	Share of Sales Used as Inputs	Net additional Base Available for Taxation
19	Bottling of LPG/CNG		1	0
35	Power transmission line infrastructure		1	0
46	Trade		1	0
47	Commission agent services & retail outlets		1	0
491	Rail transport	0.15815	0.65112	1,553
492	Road transport	0.11300	0.48822	24,979
493	Transport via pipeline	0.11300	0.48822	16,376
50	Water transport	0.18028	0.40803	5778
51	Air transport	0.22652	0.41809	24,462
521	Storage and warehousing	0.07394	0.98869	1397
522	Other transport service activities	0.06237	0.59899	4910
55	Hotel and restaurant	0.18333	0.18695	36,394
61	Post & telecommunication	0.10196	0.74738	49,069
62 & 63	Computer-related activities	0.04255	0.12441	1,16,242
64, 65 & 66	Banking and other financial services	0.03605	0.84109	1,10,927
42, 68, 77	Real estate	0.55234	0.42024	1,26,995
72 & 85	Research & development and Education	0.00748	0.05712	50,295
70, 73, 74, 78, 79, 80 & 82	Business services	0.07883	0.98858	7550
84	Public administration	0.00000	0.00000	3781
86	Health	0.22556	0.21503	2177
93, 94	O.com, social & personal services	0.11226	0.41409	43,668
	Others/undifferentiated services	0.07654	0.31880	1,18,838
Total				**7,45,390**
Total after all corrections				**8,53,235**

Source: Computed from data provided by Ministry of Corporate Affairs.

Table 5.10 Additional Base for GST: Alternative Estimates

	Value (Rs crore)	As % of Relevant GVA
Incremental services base (PROWESS)	8,27,549	15.39
Incremental services base (MCA)	8,53,235	15.87
Services GVA (2011–12 series)	53,76,045	
Total GST base (PROWESS)	39,11,056	37.33
Total GST base (MCA)	39,36,610	37.57
GVA total	1,04,77,140	

Source: Computed from data provided by Ministry of Corporate Affairs and CMIE's PROWESS Database.

Table 5.11 Comparative Table for 4 Per Cent CST Compensation

	MCA		PROWESS	
	Single Rate	Standard Rate	Single Rate	Standard Rate
Without 1 per cent levy				
State average	10.34	14.13	10.41	14.30
Centre	8.33	10.42	8.38	10.55
Total	18.67	24.55	18.79	24.85
With 1 per cent levy				
State average	9.86	13.23	9.87	13.30
Centre	8.33	10.42	8.38	10.55
Total	18.18	23.65	18.25	23.85

Source: Computed from data provided by Ministry of Corporate Affairs and CMIE's PROWESS Database.

Table 5.12 Comparative Table for 2 Per Cent CST Compensation

	MCA		PROWESS	
	Single Rate	Standard Rate	Single Rate	Standard Rate
Without 1 per cent levy				
State average	9.37	12.34	9.43	12.49
Centre	8.33	10.42	8.38	10.55
Total	17.69	22.76	17.81	23.03
With 1 per cent levy				
State average	8.88	11.44	8.89	11.49
Centre	8.33	10.42	8.38	10.55
Total	17.21	21.86	17.27	22.04

Source: Computed from data provided by Ministry of Corporate Affairs and CMIE's PROWESS Database.

Table 5.13 Scenario 1 (PROWESS Data): Without 1 Per Cent on Interstate Supplies

State/UT	4 Per Cent		2 Per Cent	
	RNR Single Rate	RNR Std. Rate	RNR Single Rate	RNR Std. Rate
Andhra Pradesh	10.4	14.9	9.6	13.4
Arunachal Pradesh	7.5	9.3	7.5	9.3
Assam	8.6	10.7	7.9	9.4
Bihar	7.0	7.8	6.9	7.8
Chhattisgarh	11.4	16.6	10.1	14.1
Delhi	11.2	15.2	9.0	11.4
Goa	9.1	12.1	8.8	11.4
Gujarat	11.8	17.6	10.2	14.5
Haryana	11.9	17.1	9.9	13.3
Himachal Pradesh	8.2	10.3	8.1	10.1
Jammu and Kashmir	13.6	20.6	13.5	20.5
Jharkhand	10.4	15.0	9.2	12.5
Karnataka	10.5	14.8	9.9	13.6
Kerala	8.2	10.1	8.0	9.8
Madhya Pradesh	11.7	16.3	10.6	14.5
Maharashtra	11.9	17.0	10.6	14.6
Manipur	6.5	7.0	6.4	6.9
Meghalaya	11.3	14.9	8.9	11.0
Mizoram	6.9	7.7	6.9	7.7
Nagaland	6.5	6.9	6.4	6.8
Odisha	11.5	16.0	10.3	13.8
Puducherry	15.6	23.9	11.8	16.8
Punjab	12.2	18.4	11.2	16.4
Rajasthan	8.7	11.2	8.4	10.5
Sikkim	13.4	20.9	12.6	19.2
Tamil Nadu	9.5	12.5	8.7	11.0
Tripura	12.9	18.6	9.9	13.2
Uttar Pradesh	8.9	11.7	8.4	10.7
Uttarakhand	10.1	13.4	8.7	10.9
West Bengal	8.7	10.7	8.1	9.7
All states	**10.4**	**14.3**	**9.4**	**12.5**
Centre	**8.4**	**10.6**	**8.4**	**10.6**

Source: Author's estimates.

Table 5.14 Scenario 2 (PROWESS Data): With 1 Per Cent on Interstate Supplies

State/UT	4 Per Cent		2 Per Cent	
	RNR Single Rate	RNR Std. Rate	RNR Single Rate	RNR Std. Rate
Andhra Pradesh	10.0	14.1	9.2	12.5
Arunachal Pradesh	7.5	9.3	7.5	9.3
Assam	8.2	10.0	7.5	8.7
Bihar	7.0	7.8	6.9	7.7
Chhattisgarh	10.7	15.2	9.4	12.6
Delhi	10.0	13.1	7.8	9.3
Goa	8.9	11.8	8.5	11.0
Gujarat	11.0	15.9	9.4	12.8
Haryana	10.8	15.0	8.8	11.2
Himachal Pradesh	8.1	10.2	8.0	10.0
Jammu and Kashmir	13.5	20.5	13.5	20.4
Jharkhand	9.7	13.6	8.5	11.1
Karnataka	10.2	14.2	9.5	12.9
Kerala	8.1	9.9	7.9	9.6
Madhya Pradesh	11.1	15.3	10.1	13.4
Maharashtra	11.2	15.7	9.9	13.3
Manipur	6.5	7.0	6.4	6.9
Meghalaya	10.0	12.8	7.6	8.8
Mizoram	6.9	7.7	6.9	7.7
Nagaland	6.4	6.8	6.3	6.7
Odisha	10.8	14.8	9.6	12.6
Puducherry	13.5	20.0	9.7	12.9
Punjab	11.6	17.3	10.6	15.2
Rajasthan	8.5	10.8	8.2	10.2
Sikkim	13.0	20.0	12.2	18.3
Tamil Nadu	9.1	11.7	8.2	10.1
Tripura	11.3	15.6	8.3	10.2
Uttar Pradesh	8.7	11.1	8.1	10.2
Uttarakhand	9.3	12.0	7.9	9.5
West Bengal	8.4	10.1	7.8	9.2
All states	**9.9**	**13.3**	**8.9**	**11.5**
Centre	**8.4**	**10.6**	**8.4**	**10.6**

Source: Author's estimates.

Table 5.15 Scenario 1 (MCA Data): Without 1 Per Cent on Interstate Supplies

State/UT	4 Per Cent		2 Per Cent	
	RNR Single Rate	RNR Std. Rate	RNR Single Rate	RNR Std. Rate
Andhra Pradesh	10.4	14.8	9.6	13.3
Arunachal Pradesh	7.5	9.2	7.5	9.2
Assam	8.5	10.5	7.8	9.3
Bihar	6.9	7.7	6.9	7.6
Chhattisgarh	11.4	16.5	10.0	13.9
Delhi	11.1	15.0	9.0	11.2
Goa	9.1	12.0	8.7	11.3
Gujarat	11.8	17.4	10.2	14.4
Haryana	11.8	16.9	9.8	13.1
Himachal Pradesh	8.2	10.2	8.0	10.0
Jammu and Kashmir	13.5	20.4	13.4	20.3
Jharkhand	10.4	14.8	9.1	12.3
Karnataka	10.5	14.7	9.8	13.5
Kerala	8.1	9.9	7.9	9.7
Madhya Pradesh	11.6	16.1	10.6	14.3
Maharashtra	11.8	16.8	10.5	14.4
Manipur	6.4	6.9	6.4	6.8
Meghalaya	11.2	14.7	8.8	10.8
Mizoram	6.8	7.6	6.8	7.6
Nagaland	6.4	6.8	6.3	6.6
Odisha	11.4	15.8	10.2	13.7
Puducherry	15.5	23.6	11.7	16.6
Punjab	12.2	18.2	11.1	16.2
Rajasthan	8.7	11.0	8.3	10.4
Sikkim	13.4	20.7	12.6	19.1
Tamil Nadu	9.5	12.4	8.6	10.8
Tripura	12.8	18.3	9.8	13.0
Uttar Pradesh	8.9	11.5	8.4	10.6
Uttarakhand	10.0	13.2	8.6	10.7
West Bengal	8.6	10.5	8.1	9.6
All states	**10.3**	**14.1**	**9.4**	**12.3**
Centre	**8.3**	**10.4**	**8.3**	**10.4**

Source: Author's estimates.

Table 5.16 Scenario 2 (MCA Data): With 1 Per Cent on Interstate Supplies

State/UT	4 Per Cent		2 Per Cent	
	RNR Single Rate	RNR Std. Rate	RNR Single Rate	RNR Std. Rate
Andhra Pradesh	10.0	14.0	9.2	12.5
Arunachal Pradesh	7.5	9.2	7.5	9.2
Assam	8.2	9.9	7.4	8.7
Bihar	6.9	7.7	6.9	7.6
Chhattisgarh	10.7	15.2	9.4	12.6
Delhi	10.1	13.1	7.9	9.4
Goa	8.9	11.7	8.5	11.0
Gujarat	11.0	15.9	9.4	12.8
Haryana	10.8	15.0	8.8	11.3
Himachal Pradesh	8.1	10.1	8.0	9.9
Jammu and Kashmir	13.5	20.3	13.4	20.2
Jharkhand	9.8	13.6	8.5	11.1
Karnataka	10.2	14.1	9.5	12.9
Kerala	8.0	9.8	7.9	9.5
Madhya Pradesh	11.1	15.2	10.0	13.3
Maharashtra	11.2	15.6	9.9	13.3
Manipur	6.4	6.9	6.4	6.8
Meghalaya	10.0	12.7	7.7	8.9
Mizoram	6.8	7.6	6.8	7.6
Nagaland	6.4	6.7	6.3	6.6
Odisha	10.8	14.7	9.6	12.6
Puducherry	13.6	20.1	9.8	13.1
Punjab	11.6	17.2	10.6	15.2
Rajasthan	8.5	10.7	8.2	10.1
Sikkim	13.0	19.9	12.2	18.3
Tamil Nadu	9.0	11.6	8.2	10.0
Tripura	11.3	15.7	8.4	10.3
Uttar Pradesh	8.6	11.1	8.1	10.1
Uttarakhand	9.3	12.0	7.9	9.5
West Bengal	8.3	10.0	7.8	9.1
All states	**9.9**	**13.2**	**8.9**	**11.4**
Centre	**8.3**	**10.4**	**8.3**	**10.4**

Source: Author's estimates.

per cent of the turnover of goods is taxed at the lower rate – this is equivalent to over 45 per cent of the gross GST base being taxed at the lower rate. The idea is that while some of the goods presently taxed at the lower rate would be moved to the standard rate, some services can be added to the list of supplies taxed at the lower rate. The standard rate is the rate that would apply to all other supplies of goods and services.

2. While the states collect CST at 2 per cent at present, they have been seeking compensation for the loss of revenue from abolition of CST at 4 per cent – the rate at which CST used to be collected when the discussion on GST was initiated and the phase-out of CST was started. So two scenarios have been considered – one with CST at 2 per cent and the other with CST at 4 per cent.

3. It was proposed that as a transition measure, the states would be allowed to collect 1 per cent on the interstate sale of goods for two years. Since there is some difference of view on whether such a levy should exist and whether it should be taken into account for determining RNR, two scenarios have been considered, with and without the levy.

These tables indicate the following interesting features

1. The tax rate if GST is implemented at a single rate is less than 20 per cent in all the scenarios considered.

2. Bringing down the CST to be compensated from 4 per cent to 2 per cent shaves off 1 per cent from the single rate and a little less than 2 per cent from the standard rate.

3. The difference between the PROWESS estimates and MCA estimates is less than quarter of a per cent in all cases.

It should be mentioned here that these rates do not incorporate any additional space for the Centre to meet its commitments to provide compensation to any states that face loss of revenue. Further, the results are crucially dependent on the ability of the Centre and the states to tax contracts such as works contracts on the same scale as at present, at the standard rate.

Appendix

Table 5A.1   Revenue Target for the Year 2013–14 under GST (as Obtained from the Empowered Committee of State Finance Ministers) (Rs Crore)

State/UT	CST (including ITC adjustment)	VAT & Sales Tax (excluding Non-VAT)	Non-VAT (collected on services/works contract)	Entertainment Tax	Lottery, Betting & Gambling	Luxury Tax	Entry Tax Not in Lieu of Octroi	Entry Tax in Lieu of Octroi	Toll Tax Not in Lieu of Service Charges	Cesses & Surcharges	Purchase Tax	ITC Reversal
Andhra Pradesh	1,961.29	21,132.9		118.86	66.95	92.56	14.99			633.88	38.08	1,166.05
Arunachal Pradesh	0	223.6					122.75					
Assam	443.37	3,966.09		38.93		8.67	404.69					
Bihar	60.38	4,443.78		39.31		10.01	4,282.84					
Chattisgarh	878.00	4,356.37		22.84		5.26	945.44				418.14	
Delhi	3,521.666	10,593.337		146.14	10.1	306.75						
Goa	80.77	1,238.52		109.59		127.19	366.43					
Gujarat	5,047.68	25,079.58		133.92		68.77	2,588.08					5,145.8
Haryana	3,272.36	11,408.2		61.85		60.59	30.58				1,000	165
Himachal Pradesh	39.48	2,311.33		0.82		38.49	156.19				1.86	117.82
J & K	13.67	2,223.3	1,046.79	0.52			142.53		551.99	133.17		
Jharkhand	1,006.66	6,276.8741		6.025	0.0507	12.0552	0			1.0621		
Karnataka	1,694.31	21,210.71		146.22	170.1	200		2,826.6			21.87	
Kerala	280.97	13,207.37		0	112.2	180.73				486.88	436.96	
Madhya Pradesh	1,285.98	8,640.07		54.16	0	33.49		2,578.74		0	159	328.91
Maharashtra	7,923.71	43,016		557	121	347	128	1,2477		0		2,007
Manipur	1.1	273.01		0.06		0.36						
Meghalaya	123.1081	341.31316		0.32127	1.305793	1.049586						
Mizoram	0	135.04		0.48								
Nagaland	2.77	176.52		1.92								
Odisha	1,152.99	6,880.64		12.81		0		1,613.45			0	732.98
Puducherry	296.23	608.08										
Punjab	1,775.36	12,214.56		34.56	73.91	35.15	2,198.19			1,048.48	1,758.72	
Rajasthan	606.92	12,928.5		13.89	0	54.57		287.92		336.5		
Sikkim	20.98	181.83		0.92	40					78.1		
Tamil Nadu	2,857.96	23,195.08		72.12	5.13	288.7	1,870.89			0	117.88	1,752.93
Tripura	291.53	669.22		0.63	0.46	1.01					574.76	
Uttar Pradesh	1,747.33	23,714.38		469.82		17.81	2,644.19					
Uttarakhand	613.21	3,074.54		23.44							28.78	
West Bengal	1,343.67	14,510.9		70.87	6.32	55.34		988.66		2,024.42		260.09
TOTAL	38,343.46	2,78,231.64	1,046.79	2,138.03	607.53	1,945.55	15,895.79	20,772.37	551.99	4,742.49	4,559.04	11,676.58

6

New Assumptions, New Estimates

Scrutinising a New Report on Revenue Neutral Rate*

R. Kavita Rao

Introduction

The report produced by the Ministry of Finance Committee on the Revenue Neutral Rate (RNR) and structure of rates for the Goods and Services Tax (GST) (which was headed by the Chief Economic Adviser – CEA) has given a new perspective to the discussion on the introduction of GST in India. At first glance the report suggests that GST can effectively be implemented at more reasonable rates when compared to rates being discussed in earlier press reports, without any loss of revenue to the centre or on average to the states. As is often argued, lower rates of tax are always more attractive since they would be compliance-friendly. The representatives of industry as well as the consultancy firms have pronounced that these are the correct estimates and provide a more reliable basis for introducing GST in India. Lower rates of tax are always attractive and it is the prerogative of the government to take a call on the appropriate rate at which to introduce GST. However, estimating a RNR should be viewed as an exercise to determine the rate of tax at which the government concerned can implement the new regime and obtain the same revenue as it currently does.

Any exercise to estimate the RNR would be based on assumptions other than on data which is available. There are two sets of estimates discussed in the public

* This chapter was originally published in the *Economic and Political Weekly* 51, no. 4 (23 January 2016): 63–66. Reprinted with permission.

domain, one by the National Institute of Public Finance and Policy (NIPFP) and the other by the committee headed by the CEA (these estimates will be referred to as NIPFP and CEA estimates respectively).

As discussed in the CEA's report, the Ministry of Finance Committee's estimates have been derived by making 'suitable corrections' to the NIPFP estimates or the indirect tax turnover estimates as they have been referred to in the report. These two sets of estimates vary considerably and there is a need to identify the sources of difference and the rationale for such a difference. In what follows, an attempt is made to assess each of the changes proposed by the CEA's study. To begin with, a brief summary of the overall approach adopted by both these studies.

Overview of Approach

The RNR is obtained by dividing the total revenue to be obtained by an estimate of the taxable base. While there exist alternative ways to estimate the base, the approach adopted here works for information available on tax collections by the union and state governments. Since the state governments tax all transactions of sale of goods through the Value-Added Tax (VAT) regimes, the base corresponding to goods is derived from the revenue collected by applying the average rate.

$$Goods\ base = \frac{VAT\ revenue}{Average\ rate\ of\ tax * (1 + CENVAT\ rate)}$$

Average rate of tax = $(\sum_i w_i t_i)$, where i refers to the different rate categories in the state, w is the share of each rate category in the total net taxable turnover and t is the corresponding tax rate. The denominator also has a term $(1 + CENVAT\ rate)$ since the tax base for the state VAT is currently the value of sales inclusive of Central Value Added Tax (CENVAT) paid. However, in the new regime, since both central GST and state GST would be on the same base, when deriving the goods base from VAT collections, the correction for inflation in the base on account of CENVAT needs to be done.

Since the tax would apply to both goods and services, for the services component of the base for each category of service in the National Informatics Centre (NIC) code, information from two sources was compared – total turnover from the Ministry of Company Affairs (MCA) data and total turnover as derived from service tax collections. The higher of the two was used as an estimate of total turnover. Since services would use goods as inputs and, in turn, be used as inputs by goods, using the input–output table, a correction was made for these two features.

$$Services\ base = \sum_j (1 - a_j)(1 - b_j)TT_j$$

where a_j is the ratio of value of taxable goods used for the supply of service j, b_j is the fraction of service j's output being used as an input to other taxable activities, TT_j is the total turnover of service j.

Total GST base is the sum of the goods base and the corrected services base. The total revenue that is to be subsumed into GST was provided by the central and state tax administrations.

In understanding the NIPFP and CEA estimates, it is important to know what is the difference between the two since the basic approach is the same for both. The differences can be summarised as follows:

i. The average rate of tax is different since the assumptions on the weights used are different.
ii. CENVAT rate for estimating goods base: statutory rate versus effective rate.
iii. The dimensions of a_j are different.
iv. The CEA estimates assume an addition to the base on account of improvements in the efficiency in the economy.

In what follows, an attempt is made to understand the basis and implications of these assumptions. Before embarking on this discussion, however, it would be useful to present the rates of tax as derived by the two alternative sets of assumptions.

From Table 6.1, it is evident that the estimates from the CEA's report are lower than those from the NIPFP report, though the differences are much smaller in the single rate scenarios. It is also clear that the multiple rate regimes are not comparable since one talks about three tax rates while the other considers a four-rate regime with a high rate of 40 per cent on some supplies such as luxury cars, aerated beverages, *paan masala*, and tobacco and tobacco products.

Table 6.1   A Comparison of the Tax Rates Proposed

	NIPFP		CEA	
Single rate		17.69%		15.05%–15.5%
Multiple rate	Gold and other high value items	2%	Gold, etc.	2%–6%
	Lower rate on 45% of GST base	12%	Lower rate (not clear how much of the base is taxable at lower rate)	12%
	Standard rate for all other supplies	22.8%	High rate on luxuries	40%
			Standard rate on all other supplies	16.9%–18.9%

The 'Corrected' Assumptions

Average Rate of Tax

The NIPFP study is based on figures derived from data of a few months for a study done for Karnataka in 2007. While the RNR analysis has been repeated a number of times since 2009–10, the Empowered Committee of State Finance Ministers and the member states have reiterated that the ratios derived from the 2007 study are acceptable. For 2013–14, data on the composition of revenue/turnover were sought from all states and only three states replied – Bihar, Maharashtra and Karnataka. Given the wide variation in the ratios across states and the paucity of data in the public domain, it was suggested by the empowered committee that the estimates for 2013–14 be determined on the basis of the earlier assumptions: 2 per cent of turnover is high value goods taxed at 1 per cent, 56.15 per cent is taxable at the lower rate and the balance is taxable at the standard rate.

The CEA Committee has based its analysis on the data it has been able to procure from 16 out of the 29 states in India. The share of gold and related high value transactions in this study is 11.6 per cent. The share of turnover taxable at the lower rate is 55.4 per cent, that taxable at the standard rate is 28.5 per cent and the balance 4 per cent is taxable at higher rates.

A higher share of commodities taxed at the lower rate would imply that the average tax rate for the NIPFP study would be higher than the CEA study and, correspondingly, the turnover associated with the NIPFP study will be lower than that arrived at in the CEA study. As the latter study points out, this makes a difference of Rs 3.12 lakh crore to the base. On the face of it, this would make it appear that since the data has been obtained from the states, this would be a more rational basis for working out the RNR. It would, however, be useful to validate the assumption and assess the impact of such an assumption on the overall RNR indicated in the CEA Committee report.

Before attempting to validate the information, it is important to mention that the report of the CEA Committee does not provide information on the state-wise turnover at different tax rates. While one does not question the methodology adopted to derive the average tax rates from the available information on 16 states, it is useful to remember that the share of gold and other high-value goods in total turnover varies substantially across states. It is 1.25 per cent in Bihar, 2.87 per cent in Odisha, 7 per cent in Rajasthan, 10 per cent in Karnataka and 19 per cent in Maharashtra. Clearly, demand for these products varies considerably across states. Low-income states have much lower shares than the high-income states. It is therefore important to know which 16 states were included in the analysis and whether the ratio would remain unaltered if the remaining 13 are also added to derive an overall average.

For validation, taking the turnover derived by NIPFP study, we can add the Rs 3.12 lakh crore for additional base as reported in the CEA Committee's report to get the new base for goods. Of this, 11.6 per cent is attributed to gold and other high-value transactions. Thus, the share of high-value transactions in India today would be Rs 3.94 lakh crore. The size of the gems and jewellery market in India as per a report of the Federation of Indian Chambers of Commerce and Industry in 2013 is Rs 3.54 lakh crore. Taking an alternative perspective, if one starts with the figures put out by the World Gold Council (2015) for supply in India multiplied by the average annual price of gold for 2013, we get Rs 2.57 lakh crore.[1] Adding another Rs 22,000 crore for demand for diamonds (De Beers 2015) with additional 15 per cent added on for making charges, and so on, still leaves the total market size for gems and jewellery sector in India at Rs 3.48 lakh crore. Even if we assume that this entire amount is tax paid, the total numbers fall short by more than 10 per cent. By common perception, it appears that gold purchases in India are by no means fully tax paid. This raises questions of whether there is overestimation of the share of gold and other high-value transactions in the total turnover.

What happens if the share of high-value goods in total turnover is overstated by taking the average of 16 states and applying that to all the states? The average tax rate would increase and the total net turnover estimated would decline. If the share of high-value goods is lower by 2 per cent, and the corresponding increase in share is in the goods taxed at the standard rate, the base would be lower by Rs 1 lakh crore. If, on the other hand, the share of goods taxable at the lower rate were to be higher, then the base would decrease by Rs 34,000 crore. These would, in turn, increase the RNR depending on which of the corrections is proposed. For instance, if we assume that the share of goods taxed at the standard rate is higher at 30.5 per cent, then the RNR increases from 15.05 per cent to 15.42 per cent by this correction alone. Looking at the same question from another angle, when a single rate RNR is proposed, it is assumed that all goods and services will be taxed at that rate. It is a matter of speculation whether the transactions in gold can withstand taxation of 15 per cent or a fraction would disappear from the formal segment. To consider an alternative, if these commodities remain taxable at 1 per cent and the RNR is applied to all the remaining goods and services, then the CEA Committee's RNR would go up from 15.05 per cent to 16.3 per cent.[2]

What follows from the above is that there could be reasons to believe that the turnover associated with gold and other high-value transactions is overstated which, in turn, leads to a reduction in the RNR. The sensitivity of the RNR to this assumption is quite significant and hence this assumption needs to be validated by taking the data for all states in India.

---

[1] Total supply of gold is 974.8 tonnes. The average price of gold for 2013 is Rs 264.4 crore per tonne.

[2] The NIPFP study too makes a similar assumption but since the share of gold assumed in that study was very small, segregating the turnover and taxes from gold and computing the RNR only increases the RNR by 0.25 per cent.

Assumptions Regarding the Effective Tax Rate for Central Excise

The second important assumption based on information that only the government departments have and are not usually shared with other agencies relates to the effective tax rate for central excise. The state VAT is applied on a base which is inclusive of CENVAT. In order to correct for this factor, the NIPFP study used the statutory rate of CENVAT, while the CEA Committee's estimate is based on the 'effective tax rate'. In principle, it would be correct to argue that the effective tax rate should be the factor of correction. However, there is not much information on the effective tax rate or even the average tax rate in the public domain since the turnovers subject to tax are not reported by the tax departments.

Usually, effective tax rates are defined as the ratio of tax collections to the corresponding tax base. In the present case, the effective tax rate can be taken as the ratio of CENVAT collected to value added in the manufacturing sector. Since the petroleum sector is to remain outside the base for GST, for this exercise it is important to keep petroleum products out from both the base and the tax collected. Since the data on value added is readily available for 2012–13, it can be used as a benchmark. The figures for 2012–13 suggest that the ratio of CENVAT collected to value added in registered manufacturing is 12.99 per cent.[3]

Even assuming value added in unregistered manufacturing to be part of the base brings the rate down only to 9.46 per cent. This is clearly higher than the rates referred to in the report. Perhaps, the report is referring to average tax rates and not effective tax rates! If so, we have no way of validating the same, since as mentioned earlier, information on the turnover subject to tax at different rates of tax is not available in the public domain. Thus, these could be credible or unrealistic, depending on what kind of data is put out in the public domain by the authorities who have access to the information.

Expansion in Base due to Efficiency Improvements

There is a lot of expectation from GST – it will lead to an expansion in economic activity. The possible sources for expansion in economic activity can be broadly identified as follows:

i. With the reduction in cascading of taxation in the economy, there is an overall decline in prices. As a result, demand increases, in turn, attracting more investment.

---

[3] Since some segments of manufacturing are not subject to the tax under CENVAT or part of the tax credit mechanism in CENVAT, the base for CENVAT has been taken excluding beverages (alcoholic beverages for human consumption are taxable by the state government), petroleum products (which will remain outside the base for GST and on which presently tax credit is not comprehensive) and spinning, weaving and finishing of textiles (since a sizeable part of this segment is not subject to tax in the present regime).

ii. With the abolition of Central Sales Tax (CST), the related need to have branches in all states so as to avoid payment of the tax disappears. The associated economies in costs as well as the need to design more suitable supply chains can bring more investment into the economy.

iii. The ease of compliance and/or the effectiveness of administration could encourage hitherto unaccounted transactions to move to the mainstream, thereby resulting in an expansion in the observed scale of economic activity.

It is often suggested that any gains in the form of lower tax liabilities from introduction of the new regime will be passed forward by the beneficiaries to the final consumer only gradually. In other words, the expansion in the demand component of the stimulus to the economy will take some time to play itself out. Turning to the second component, while there is ground to expect some movement on this front, if companies can get input tax credit for all interstate transactions, the costs associated with the old regime would be reduced. In this context, since the companies already have a system in place, there is no reason to believe that they would like to do a complete and comprehensive overhaul immediately upon the introduction of GST. Once again while these corrections would happen, they too may take time to play out. The third dimension depends on the design of the system of tax administration and the effectiveness of tax administration in identifying and penalising defaulters. More particularly, how effective are they now perceived to be?

It is not clear how any of these measures can be assumed to bring in instantaneous expansion in the tax base under GST to the tune of Rs 2 lakh crore or about 5 per cent of the estimated GST base. While a 5 per cent expansion in base may be considered a nominal increase, it should be noted that even the studies which quantified an expansion in the base on account of introduction of GST only postulated an increase to the tune of 1.5 per cent to 2 per cent and that too in the context of a move to a comprehensive GST from a regime which had more cascading than we presently witness.[4]

Purchases from Informal Sector

It is often argued that all purchases by registered dealers may not be from registered dealers. Since they can avail tax credit only for purchases from registered dealers, to the extent the purchases are from unregistered persons, the tax paid by the registered dealers will not be in proportion to the value added by them – it will in fact be higher. Using this argument, the CEA Committee's report has incorporated an additional base of Rs 45,000 crore. It is acceptable to make this argument for an economy where significant segments remain outside the purview of taxation by design. But once the

---

[4] The data referred to the year 2003–04, which was prior to the introduction of state VAT and prior to the introduction of cross-credit between CENVAT and service tax. These two measures of reform did contribute to reducing some of the cascading in the tax regime.

tax base has been expanded to include most economic activities, and there exists the possibility of claiming input tax credit if the purchases are from registered dealers, the registered tax payers would have less incentive to buy from unregistered dealers or alternatively to under-report corresponding sales if that were a possibility. Further, it is not clear from the report how this figure of an additional base has been arrived at.

It may be noted that the indirect tax system being designed for the GST regime proposes transaction-wise details of sales to be reported by dealers, with credit being available only for purchases where the corresponding seller has provided information on the sales. With this proposed model of seamless credit, the tax departments believe that there would be very little scope for unaccounted transactions. If, however, as the CEA Committee's report proposes, there could be some purchases from unregistered dealers, then the dimensions of such transactions as well as the effectiveness of the indirect tax system would both be under question. It should be mentioned here that the methodology used to estimate the base for goods already incorporates the impact of any purchases that the dealers might make from unregistered dealers since the methodology works backward from revenue collections and an average tax rate. Thus, the additionality being proposed is largely with respect to the services component of the base.

Sensitivity to Assumptions

A computed RNR is very sensitive to assumptions. As discussed, if the fraction of turnover coming from gold is lower by 2 percentage points, with a corresponding increase in the turnover of goods taxable at the standard rate, the RNR would increase from 15.05 per cent to 15.42 per cent. On the other hand, if the assumptions of incremental additions to the base on account of efficiency gains and purchases from unorganised sector are removed, the RNR would increase from 15.05 per cent to 15.89 per cent. The two together will lead to build-up in the computed RNR to 16.3 per cent. Recognising that it might be difficult to tax gold at 15 per cent, if the turnover corresponding to gold is kept outside the base for purposes of RNR calculation, then the RNR will increase to 17.1 per cent. In other words, with assumptions that are based on information which cannot be validated and with the resulting calculations of RNR being very volatile, the CEA Committee can be given credit for raising some pertinent issues but the resultant RNR needs to be treated as work in progress. Further, more importantly, the study once again establishes that identifying a 'suitable' rate for implementation of GST remains a political decision. The exercise to determine a RNR is always based on assumptions which can be contested and can only provide some inputs. Given the fact that very little data is in the public domain and the CEA Committee report too uses information that the general public is not and cannot hope to be privy to, such a report cannot be the basis of any informed debate. It only 'validates' or 'refutes' opinions and perhaps generates some more opinions.

In this context, it is important to also point out that the report does not take into account certain concerns of the states. Should states be compensated for loss of revenue from CST at 4 per cent or 2 per cent and should the exercise take into account the fact that the states have been denying input tax credit in certain cases of inter-state trade, thereby garnering more revenues in the present regime?

Taking the first issue, the ceiling imposed by the CST law on the rate of tax on interstate sales has been reduced over time from 4 per cent to 2 per cent, as a measure of preparation for introduction of GST. The states argue that while temporary compensation was provided for the interim, it was indicated by the union government that the long-term issues will be sorted out when GST is implemented. The states have been reading the same as an assurance that the revenue under CST will be protected as if the rate of tax were 4 per cent. The union government has been arguing that since the states are currently levying CST only at 2 per cent, they should be entitled to compensation only for these revenues.[5] While the views of both the centre and the states can be considered 'fair' in the CST compensation discussion, the report without explicitly addressing the issue takes the implicit view that CST compensation at 2 per cent alone needs to be built in. Providing for CST compensation at 4 per cent would raise the RNR.

The second issue discussed here relates to what states have been calling ITC denied. The states have been denying input tax credit (ITC) on some transactions. This results in additional revenue to the states. However, when the turnover for GST is derived from the revenues collected, this can result in an incorrect bloating of the base. Incorporating this correction too would result in an increase in the RNR. Once again the CEA's report has not explicitly dealt with this issue. While these issues are not game changers in the overall scheme of things, they can contribute to a perception that the concerns of the states are not adequately addressed. In other words, the debate the CEA Committee's report can stoke might be different from the one that it might have chosen to generate.

References

De Beers (2015). 'Diamond Insight Report 2015', https://www.debeersgroup.com/content/dam/de-beers/corporate/images/insight-re-port/pdf/DeBeers_Insight_Report_2015.pdf.

FICCI (2013). 'All That Glitters Is Gold: India Jewellery Review', http://www.ficci.com/spdocument/20332/India-Jewellery-Review-2013.pdf.

World Gold Council (2015). 'Gold Demand Trends Full Year 2015', https://www.gold.org/download/file/3262/GDT_Q4_2013.pdf.

---

[5] The union government has provided assurance of 100 per cent compensation for loss of revenue for five years from the date of introduction of GST. It is, however, not yet clear what the definition of loss for this purpose would be. Further, higher revenue needs would indicate a higher RNR or rate of tax of state GST. These two issues constitute the context for this discussion.

7

Exploring Policy Options to Include Petroleum, Natural Gas and Electricity under the Goods and Services Tax (GST) Regime in India*

Sacchidananda Mukherjee *and* R. Kavita Rao

Introduction

Various taxes, duties, levies and cesses on petroleum products and natural gas generate substantial revenues to the Central and State Governments.[1] The tax on petroleum products and corresponding change in prices generate both direct and indirect effects across the sectors. Petroleum products directly enter as an input into a large number of economic activities (e.g., transportation, electricity generation and fertiliser production). Apart from such direct uses, there are a number of indirect uses as well; for instance, since most commodities need to be transported for use by the final consumer, petroleum products enter into the picture. Therefore, changes in prices (or taxes) of petroleum products would have significant impact on the economy both through direct and indirect or cascading routes.

---

* This chapter was originally published as 'Policy Options for Including Petroleum, Natural Gas and Electricity in the Goods and Services Tax' in the *Economic and Political Weekly* 50, no. 9 (28 February 2018): 98–107. Reprinted with permission.

[1] If not specifically mentioned, by petroleum products we mean all petroleum products (Motor Spirit, High Speed Diesel, Aviation Turbine Fuel and other petroleum products), crude oil and natural gas.

The present regime of taxation of petroleum products and electricity results in cascading of taxes. Built-in invisible taxes are expected to increase prices in the domestic economy and adversely affect competitiveness of Indian exports as well. Given that the country is working towards the introduction of a comprehensive GST regime, it is an opportune moment to ask whether the proposed GST design is appropriate or whether significant degree of cascading remains. This chapter seeks to explore alternative configurations of the tax regime, with specific reference to petroleum products, and evaluate the extent of cascading under each. Given that these goods provide a major share of the revenues of the Central and State governments in indirect taxes, the comparison is attempted assuming revenue neutrality under all scenarios.

The other significant aspect of the petroleum sector is that the present administered pricing mechanism does not allow full price pass through for some refinery products (domestic LPG, PDS kerosene, diesel and petrol). This results in under-recoveries for oil marketing companies (OMCs). However, the government has not been providing full compensation to OMCs for such under-recoveries in sales of diesel and petrol. While part of the under-recovery is absorbed by the upstream oil companies, the rest remains stranded costs for the OMCs. The present system of disallowing compensation not only costs the Central Government exchequer (in terms of loss of dividend income), as most of the oil companies are under the Central Public Sector, but also provides a perverse incentive for not saving fossil fuels, thereby polluting the environment. The benefits of improving energy efficiency cannot be harvested without raising the prices of energy sources.[2] Therefore, the present study explores the configuration of revenues and prices resultant from alternative tax/subsidy regimes to understand whether elimination of price control in addition to streamlining the tax regime could be feasible, given the multiple objectives of reducing cascading, keeping a check on prices and protecting revenues.[3]

In the next section, a brief overview of the petroleum sector is presented. The section titled 'Structure of Taxes' provides an overview of the present structure of indirect taxes on petroleum products and the electricity sector. The section titled 'Methodology and Data Sources' describes the methodology and data sources for analysing the impact of the alternative tax and subsidy strategies, and the section titled 'Results and Analysis' summarises the results. This is followed by concluding remarks in the final section.

---

[2] With the improvement in energy efficiency, if energy prices (or energy taxes) are not increased, the demand for energy will go up and will offset the impact of the efficiency gain in fuel use. The underlying phenomenon is known as rebound effect (Greening et al. 2000).

[3] For India, price elasticity of demand for crude oil, diesel and petrol are –0.41, –0.56 and –0.85 respectively which implies that demands are not very elastic but decline to some extent with rising prices (Agrawal 2012).

Overview of Petroleum Sector

Petroleum products play an important role in India's energy security. While coal is predominantly used as input for thermal power plants, petroleum products are major inputs for the transport sector (including railway, water and air transport), apart from being feedstock for fertiliser industries. Of the total final consumption of energy (excluding consumption of biofuels and waste), the share of oil products and natural gas together contributes 52.38 per cent.[4]

In India, crude petroleum is predominantly imported, where import constitutes 81.3 per cent of total availability in 2010–11. In the absence of price control, it is expected that volatility in international crude oil prices would put pressure on domestic prices of refined petroleum products. This would have been further aggravated by exchange rate volatility. However, the present petroleum pricing system does not allow full price pass through for a few petroleum products (PDS kerosene, domestic LPG, diesel and petrol).[5] Due to the price control, the demand does not adjust to the changes in the prices and therefore the demand for import of crude oil remains unchanged even in the face of rising international prices.

Pricing of Petroleum Products

Prices of petrol, diesel, PDS kerosene and domestic LPG are administered in India.[6] The oil companies cannot freely change the market prices of these petroleum products in response to volatility of international crude oil prices, exchange rate volatility and/or their other costs of production. Therefore, domestic market prices of these petroleum products do not necessarily reflect either the international crude oil prices or other costs of production.[7] Whenever there is a need to adjust fuel prices (in response to international crude oil prices, exchange rate volatility or other costs of production) in the country, any government has the following options: (i) to transfer the entire burden of price hike to the consumers, (ii) to cut tax rates and share the burden in terms of tax revenue loss, or (iii) to finance the under-recoveries in prices of petroleum products through budgetary provisions. In India, for a few

---

[4] Energy Balance of India (2011), International Energy Agency (IEA). Available online at: http://www.iea.org/statistics/statisticssearch/report/?country=INDIA&product=balances&year=2011 (last accessed on 22 April 2014).

[5] High prices and/or rapid increases in the prices of these products, it is argued, would result in inflation and have adverse consequences for the quality of life of people in the country.

[6] Even though petrol price is decontrolled in India since June 2010, the price is neither entirely linked to international crude oil prices nor linked to domestic costs of production (including taxes). Periodic revision of petrol price depending on the under-recoveries of the oil companies is still in practice.

[7] Cost of production also includes refinery margin, taxes, levies, transportation costs and dealer's margin.

petroleum products governments have used both the second and third options, so as to reduce the extent of price increase. Under-recoveries of the OMCs are partly met out of budgetary or extra-budgetary transfers in the form of bonds from government or transfers from upstream oil companies,[8] or are partly reflected in lower profit margins of the OMCs (Table 7.1).[9] Therefore, any attempt to decontrol the prices of petroleum products could increase the retail prices.[10]

Revenue Generation from Petroleum Products

The contributions of petroleum products in the Central Government exchequer (indirect tax revenue) are through customs duties, cess on crude oil, excise duty and service tax charged on input of services. The contributions to the State Government exchequer (indirect tax revenue) are through sales tax/VAT and Central sales tax. In addition to Central and State taxes, Octroi and Entry tax are revenues that accrue to local bodies usually.

The estimated contribution of indirect tax revenue from the petroleum sector to the Central Government exchequer has gone up from Rs 46,533 crore in 2002–03 to Rs 99,928 crore in 2010–11 (Table 7.2).[11] For the State Government exchequer, the revenue collection from petroleum companies has gone up from Rs 30,493 crore in 2002–03 to Rs 1,05,384 crore in 2011–12. Of the total indirect tax collection of the Centre and the States put together, petroleum taxes account for 32.51 per cent.[12]

Structure of Taxes

The proposed regime of taxation under the GST system is to be a comprehensive VAT regime on goods and services with a few caveats. Some goods and services are proposed to be kept outside the base for GST. The proposed exclusions are

---

[8] Any absorption of under-recoveries by upstream oil companies causes revenue erosion for the government in the form of lower dividend receipts as most of the oil companies are Central PSUs.

[9] However, private sector OMCs are not entitled to claim any non-price compensation for under-recoveries which curtails their business prospects to invest in petroleum refineries unless they find international prices are remunerative to export refined petroleum products.

[10] The benefit of subsidy is also reaped by all downstream companies which use subsidised products/outputs as inputs for their production. The existing subsidy system reduces the unit price of input and therefore the final incidence of subsidy will be dispersed through several markets (Srivastava et al. 2003).

[11] The fall in revenue in 2011–12 on account of customs duty collection is mainly due to the complete exemption of crude oil from customs duty.

[12] In 2010–11, combined revenue receipts of the Centre and the States on account of customs duty, union excise duties and general sales tax is Rs 5,66,769.78 crore.

Table 7.1 Financing Pattern of Fuel Subsidy in India

Year	Sources of Under-Recoveries (Rs Crore)					Financing Pattern of Under-Recoveries (Rs Crore)			
	Domestic LPG	PDS Kerosene	Diesel	Petrol	Total	Upstream Companies	Oil Bonds/ Cash Subsidy	Borne by OMCs	Total
2005–06	10,246	14,384	12,647	2,723	40,000	14,000 (35)	11,500 (29)	14,500 (36)	40,000
2006–07	10,701	17,883	18,776	2,027	49,387	20,507 (42)	24,121 (49)	4,759 (10)	49,387
2007–08	15,523	19,102	35,166	7,332	77,123	25,708 (33)	35,290 (46)	16,125 (21)	77,123
2008–09	17,600	28,225	52,286	5,181	103,292	32,000 (31)	71,292 (69)	–	103,292
2009–10	14,257	17,364	9,279	5,151	46,051	14,430 (31)	26,000 (56)	5,621 (12)	46,051
2010–11	21,772	19,484	34,706	2,227	78,190	30,297 (39)	41,000 (52)	6,893 (9)	78,190

Source: Compiled from PPAC online resources.

Notes: Figures in the parentheses show the percentage share in total under-recoveries.

Table 7.2 MEstimated Contribution of Petroleum Companies to Central and State Government Exchequer through Indirect Taxes (in Rs Crore)*

	2002–03	2003–04	2004–05	2005–06	2006–07	2007–08	2008–09	2009–10	2010–11	2011–12
Central Exchequer										
Customs Duty	7,953	9,552	11,697	9,157	10,043	12,626	6,299	4,563	24,136	10,013
Cess on Crude Oil	5,213	4,766	4,891	4,884	6,899	6,924	6,758	6,559	6,810	7,108
Excise Duty	32,964	35,364	38,150	47,180	51,922	54,761	54,117	62,480	68,040	61,954
Others (includes Service Tax)	403	425	439	347	666	944	870	982	942	1,033
Sub total	**46,533**	**50,107**	**55,177**	**61,568**	**69,530**	**75,255**	**68,044**	**74,584**	**99,928**	**80,108**
State Exchequer										
Sales Tax	29,166	32,080	38,935	46,667	53,949	56,445	63,349	64,999	78,689	96,945
Octroi and Others (includes Entry Tax)	1,327	1,440	2,047	2,368	2,416	2,788	2,466	3,717	5,651	8,439
Sub total	**30,493**	**33,520**	**40,982**	**49,035**	**56,365**	**59,233**	**65,815**	**68,716**	**84,340**	**1,05,384**
Total Contribution	**77,026**	**83,627**	**96,159**	**1,10,603**	**1,25,895**	**1,34,488**	**1,33,859**	**1,43,300**	**1,84,268**	**1,85,492**

Data Source: PPAC (2012, 2010, 2009, 2008).

Notes: *royalties and direct taxes (corporate tax, tax on dividend) are excluded.

natural gas and crude petroleum, petrol, diesel and aviation turbine fuel (ATF), alcoholic beverages, and some essential goods and services for basic consumption. While the essential items are exempted in the proposed regime,[13] the other goods are subject to tax but are kept out of the purview of the tax credit mechanism. This would mean that there is no mechanism for input tax credit for taxes paid on the inputs used for producing these goods. Further, there is no option of input tax credit for taxes paid on these goods for activities which use them as inputs either. In other words, inputs going into the extraction of crude petroleum would remain embedded in the costs of exploration and production of crude and passed on to refineries. Similarly, when petrol, diesel and ATF are kept out of the VAT/GST system, the taxes associated with inputs used for production of these goods would remain embedded. This results in cascading. Since petroleum products are used as inputs in a large number of industries in the economy cascading would have wide spread impact.[14] Flow of uncredited input taxes in the proposed regime of GST is demonstrated in Figure 7.1.

Like the petroleum sector, subsidy-cum-tax system is also prevailing in the electricity sector. State electricity boards (SEBs) are obliged to pay electricity duty

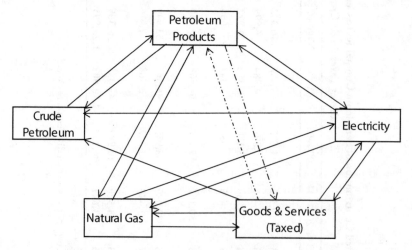

Figure 7.1   Input Tax Credit Pass-through Mechanism (6 Sector Model)
Note: Directions of arrows show the flow of uncredited input taxes. Partial input tax credit is available for petroleum products sector for purchase of inputs from Goods and Services (Taxed) Sector and vice versa.

---

[13] In the present study we have considered agriculture and allied activities (including fishing), forestry and logging, water supply, education and R&D, public administration, social security and health and social work as exempt goods and services.
[14] In the present regime, there is some input tax credit available to refineries within the State regimes. These are State specific rules and vary across States.

to State Governments and the State Governments provide subsidy to electricity utilities. The tax rate on electricity has varied over the years and for 2010–11, it is 9.38 per cent (Ministry of Finance 2013; PFCL 2013). However, since electricity duty is a separate levy not integrated with VAT/GST, taxes on goods and services being used as inputs for generation and distribution of electricity would remain embedded and further, electricity duty on supplies to GST dealers too would remain embedded.[15] Both these contribute to some more cascading in the economy.

Figure 7.1 shows that there are quite a few sources of embedded taxes, which could dilute the potential gains from moving to a GST regime.

Methodology and Data Sources

To capture the economy-wide cascading impact of any change in taxes of petroleum products, we have estimated the direct and total tax incidences for each of the sectors under alternative policy scenarios. We have adopted the Input–Output (I–O) Analysis Framework to capture the impact of limited pass through under the VAT system. The analysis is based on the Input–Output Transaction Table (Commodity by Commodity) for 2007–08 released by the CSO (2012a).[16]

Methodology for Estimation of Direct and Total Tax Incidences

The methodology adopted for the current exercise is presented using a six sector model. The sectors considered are natural gas, crude petroleum, petroleum products, electricity, exempted goods and services, and other goods and services which are taxed, since these are distinct segments in terms of the tax treatment accorded to them. The same methodology is adopted to the 48 sector model to get the results for the study.

The chief characteristics of the proposed GST regime are incorporated as follows:

I. There is no tax associated with intra-sector transactions.[17]
II. Except diesel, petrol and ATF, other petroleum products are under the present VAT system and for them full input tax credit is admissible.

---

[15] Unless inputs or capital goods used in electricity generation are especially exempted from State taxes.

[16] The Central Statistical Organisation (CSO) has released the Input-Output Transaction Table (Commodity x Commodity) at Factor Cost (Rs Lakh) for 2007–08 and it covers 130 items (CSO 2012a). For the purpose of this study, these 130 items are clubbed into 48 sectors. The Input–Output Coefficient Matrix (Commodity x Commodity) is derived from the Input-Output Transaction Table (see detailed methodology provided in Appendix 7A.1). Each cell in Input–Output Coefficient Matrix (Commodity x Commodity), say a_{ij}, shows the amount (in Rs) of ith good required to produce Re. 1 value of jth good.

[17] Though intra-sector inter-companies transactions are subject to Central and State taxes, for simplicity, we exempted such transactions from taxation.

III. I–O table, however, does not differentiate between different outputs produced by refineries. Given the available disaggregation, it is not possible to separate the refinery products into two baskets (VAT and non-VAT items). In order to capture the impact of partial credit available to their users, in this chapter, it is assumed that all petroleum products are homogenous. The impact of differential treatment of the products is captured in the form of partial tax credit – $(1 - \mu)$ is the extent of partial credit available to refineries and $(1 - \sigma)$ is the partial credit available to users of petroleum products.

The system of price equations for the sectors can be written as:

$$P_g = P_g a_{11} + P_c(1 + \beta)\, a_{21} + P_p(1 + s\gamma)\, a_{31} + P_e(1 + \delta)\, a_{41} + P_{oe}\, a_{51} + P_{ot}(1 + \tau)\, a_{61} + V_g$$

$$P_c = P_g(1 + \alpha)\, a_{12} + P_c\, a_{22} + P_p(1 + s\gamma)\, a_{32} + P_e(1+ \delta)\, a_{42} + P_{oe}\, a_{52} + P_{ot}(1 + \tau)\, a_{62} + V_c$$

$$P_p = P_g(1 + \alpha)\, a_{13} + P_c(1 + \beta)\, a_{23} + P_p\, a_{33} + P_e(1 + \delta)\, a_{43} + P_{oe}\, a_{53} + P_{ot}(1 + \mu\tau)\, a_{63} + V_p$$

$$P_e = P_g(1 + \alpha)\, a_{14} + P_c(1 + \beta)\, a_{24} + P_p(1 + s\gamma)\, a_{34} + P_e\, a_{44} + P_{oe}\, a_{54} + P_{ot}(1 + \tau)\, a_{64} + V_e$$

$$P_{oe} = P_g(1 + \alpha)\, a_{15} + P_c(1 + \beta)\, a_{25} + P_p(1 + s\gamma)\, a_{35} + P_e(1 + \delta)\, a_{45} + P_{oe}\, a_{55} + P_{ot}(1 + \tau)\, a_{65} + V_{oe}$$

$$P_{ot} = P_g(1 + \alpha)\, a_{16} + P_c(1 + \beta)\, a_{26} + P_p(1 + s\sigma\gamma)\, a_{36} + P_e(1 + \delta)\, a_{46} + P_{oe}\, a_{56} + P_{ot}\, a_{66} + V_{ot}$$

where

P_i: the price of the ith sector ($i = g$ represents natural gas, $i = c$ represents crude petroleum, $i = p$ represents petroleum products, $i = e$ represents electricity, $i = oe$ represents other goods and service which are exempted, and $i = ot$ represents other goods and services which are taxed)

a_{ij}: to produce Re 1 value of output in the jth sector, input requirement from the ith sector

α: tax on natural gas (e.g., State sales tax, etc.)

β: tax on crude petroleum (e.g., State sales tax, etc.)

γ: tax on petroleum products (e.g., Central excise duty and State sales tax, etc.)

δ: tax on electricity (e.g., State electricity duty)

τ: tax on goods and services (other than on natural gas, crude petroleum, petroleum products and electricity) (e.g., Central excise duty and State sales tax/VAT, etc.)

μ: the percentage of tax (τ) which is not set off as input tax credit for petroleum sector. For example, if 60 per cent of input tax credit (ITC) is availed, $\mu = 0.40$.

σ: is the portion of petroleum tax (γ) which is not set off as input tax credit for using petroleum products in sectors which are under the VAT system. For 2010–11, VAT sales of oil companies is Rs 1,06,453.03 crore (sales of petroleum products other than petrol, diesel and ATF), whereas total sales of all petroleum products (including sales of petrol, diesel and ATF) is Rs 4,78,905.00 crore (NIPFP 2011). The ratio of VAT sales to total sales is 0.22. Therefore, the value of σ is 0.78 (i.e., 1 – 0.22) and shows the portion of input tax which is not set off. In other words σ implies the proportion of input petroleum products for which ITC is not admissible.

V_i: value added per unit of output

In matrix notation, we could write the above set of price equations as follows:

$$
\begin{pmatrix} P_g \\ P_c \\ P_p \\ P_e \\ P_{oe} \\ P_{ot} \end{pmatrix}^T = \begin{pmatrix} P_g \\ P_c \\ P_p \\ P_e \\ P_{oe} \\ P_{ot} \end{pmatrix}^T
$$

$$
*diag \left[\begin{pmatrix} 1 & 1+\beta & 1+s\gamma & 1+\delta & 1 & 1+\tau \\ 1+a & 1 & 1+s\gamma & 1+\delta & 1 & 1+\tau \\ 1+a & 1+\beta & 1 & 1+\delta & 1 & 1+\mu\tau \\ 1+a & 1+\beta & 1+s\gamma & 1 & 1 & 1+\tau \\ 1+a & 1+\beta & 1+s\gamma & 1+\delta & 1 & 1+\tau \\ 1+a & 1+\beta & 1+s\sigma\gamma & 1+\delta & 1 & 1 \end{pmatrix} \begin{pmatrix} a_{11} & a_{12} & a_{13} & a_{14} & a_{15} & a_{16} \\ a_{21} & a_{22} & a_{23} & a_{24} & a_{25} & a_{26} \\ a_{31} & a_{32} & a_{33} & a_{34} & a_{35} & a_{36} \\ a_{41} & a_{42} & a_{43} & a_{44} & a_{45} & a_{46} \\ a_{51} & a_{52} & a_{53} & a_{54} & a_{55} & a_{56} \\ a_{61} & a_{62} & a_{63} & a_{64} & a_{65} & a_{66} \end{pmatrix} \right]
$$

$$
+ \begin{pmatrix} V_g \\ V_c \\ V_p \\ V_e \\ V_{oe} \\ V_{ot} \end{pmatrix}^T
$$

$$
P^T = [I - diag[\hat{T}A]]^{-1} * V^T \tag{1}
$$

where P is the price vector, A is the input coefficient matrix, V is the value added vector and $\hat{T}$ is the tax matrix and represents the input tax pass forward mechanism of the economy. In a perfect VAT or GST system (full input tax credits, without exempted goods and services), all elements of the $\hat{T}$ matrix will be one and the tax will be on final consumption alone. Cascading in the tax regime is therefore captured by the elements of the $\hat{T}$ matrix which are higher than one.

To estimate the direct tax incidence of a sector, we need to multiply the tax vector with the final demand vector (FD).[18]

$$\text{Direct Tax Incidence (DTI)} = T * FD$$

where T is the tax rate vector on final use and FD is the Final Demand vector [FD = C + I + G + (X − M)]

With reference to the price equation presented above,

$$T = \begin{pmatrix} \alpha \\ \beta \\ s\gamma \\ \delta \\ 0 \\ \tau \end{pmatrix}, \text{ where '}s\text{' is the extent of under-recovery in petrol and diesel}^{19}$$

To take into account the extent of subsidy provided (either directly and/or indirectly) to oil companies on account of sales of diesel and petrol below the desired market price, we have estimated the value of 's' as follows:

$$S = \begin{cases} 1, \textit{if there is no under-recovery of OMCs} \\ \left(1 - \dfrac{UR_{2010-11}}{VOP_{2010-11}}\right), \textit{if the government provides the subsidy to compensate the under-} \\ \textit{recoveries of OMCs on account of sales of diesel and petrol below the desired market price.} \end{cases}$$

---

[18] It is to be mentioned here that Input Flow Matrix provides information for 130 items on Private Final Consumption Expenditure (C), Government Final Consumption Expenditure (G), Gross Capital Formation [I, comprises of gross fixed capital formation (GFCF) and change in stock (CIS)], Export (X) and Import (M). According to national accounting framework, the output (Y, final demand) or Total Final Use is determined by Y (or FD) = C + I + G + (X − M). We adopted the same framework and found that for a few sectors either import (M) is substantially higher than C + I + G + X and/or Change In Stock is negative (implies depletion of stock) and therefore FD is negative. For those sectors, we have taken FD as zero. To get final demand for 48 sectors from 130 sectors we have followed the same methodology as discussed in Appendix 7A.1.

[19] The present study only explores the policy option of withdrawing petroleum subsidy on account of sales of diesel and petrol below the desired market price and assumes that petroleum subsidy on account of sales of PDS kerosene and domestic LPG will continue under the GST regime as well. Though petrol price has been decontrolled since June 2010, OMCs cannot change the price automatically. For our empirical analysis, we have considered the year 2010–11, when petrol price was not decontrolled.

where,

$UR_{2010-11}$ is the Under-recovery on account of Sales of Diesel and Petrol in 2010–11 = Rs 36,933.16 crore (Table 7.1)

$VOP_{2010-11}$ is the Value of Output of Petroleum Products (registered and unregistered) in 2010–11 = Rs 7,14,044.04 crore[20]

Therefore, $\dfrac{UR_{2010-11}}{VOP_{2010-11}} = 0.05$ and $s = \left(1 - \dfrac{UR_{2010-11}}{VOP_{2010-11}}\right) = 0.95$

The provision of subsidy reduces prices of petroleum products and at lower prices a higher tax rate is required to meet a certain revenue target. Subsidy-adjusted tax rate on petroleum products is expected to be lower than the nominal tax rate and the present study takes into account this divergence by suitably adjusting the tax rate. The withdrawal of subsidy is expected to increase the prices of petroleum products.

Total tax incidence (TTI) is estimated as follows:

Total tax incidence (TTI) = Direct tax incidence (DTI) + Tax cascading (TC)

Tax cascading = Tax on total (direct and indirect) input use + Final tax on total input use

Tax cascading = $(1 + T) * diag[Z] * FD$

where, Z is defined as follows:

$$Z = (\hat{T} - U)^{T}[(I - A)^{-1} - I]$$

In the equation above, U is a matrix consisting of all 1s and having same order as $\hat{T}$.

We can define a matrix K, where $K = (I - A)^{-1}$. The vector $K_{.j} = \sum_{i=1|j}^{m} K_{ij}$ captures the levels of output across all the sectors that are required to sustain a unit increase in final demand in the jth sector (m is the number of sectors considered). Similarly, $K_{i.} = \sum_{j=1|i}^{m} K_{ij}$ captures the increase in gross output levels of the ith sector required to sustain a unit increase in the final demand for each of the sectors considered.

For comparing the alternative scenarios, it is assumed government gets the same TTI as in the baseline scenario. The tax rate on one or more commodities is adjusted to ensure revenue neutrality. Here it should be noted that revenues under all alternative scenarios are derived under the assumptions that all economic activity in a taxed

---

[20] National Account Statistics provides value of output (at current prices) for 'rubber and petroleum products' (CSO 2012b). To estimate the value of output for petroleum products from combined value of output of rubber and petroleum products, we have used the same percentage share petroleum products in sum total value of output of rubber and petroleum products, as separately available in Input–Output Table 2007–08 (CSO 2012a).

sector will be subject to tax, that is, there are no turnover-based exemptions and there is full compliance. While these are strong assumptions, the Input–Output (I–O) framework adopted for the study does not allow for further calibration to incorporate these structural features of the tax system. Further, this framework does not permit calculation of revenues for the Central and State Governments separately.[21]

For the present exercise, the proposed GST design is considered as the baseline. Since the revenue streams from the proposed GST regime are not yet known, in the present analysis, we work with total revenues that could be derived from the economy provided all economic activity is subject to tax. The revenue neutral rates (RNRs) for the alternative scenarios therefore are the rates which yield the same computed revenues as the baseline scenario for the study, that is, the revenue subsequent to introduction of proposed GST. It should be noted that these would correspond to the total revenues for the Centre and the States put together, but would not incorporate the effects of specific features such as exemptions, thresholds, differential tax rates and less than full compliance, and so on.

Baseline and Alternative Scenarios

Baseline Scenario

Natural gas, crude petroleum, petroleum products and electricity are out of GST. Goods as well as services sectors attract a harmonised tax rate of 20 per cent and there are some exempted goods and services. The government compensates under-recoveries of OMCs on account of sales in diesel and petrol. Partial ITC is available for the petroleum product sector and for other sectors which use petroleum products and are under the GST regime.

Following equation 1, Baseline Price (P_b) can be estimated. The taxes for this scenario can be represented by T_b and $\widehat{T}_b$ and they are as follows:

$$
T_b = \begin{pmatrix} \alpha \\ \beta \\ s\gamma \\ \delta \\ 0 \\ \tau \end{pmatrix} \quad \text{and} \quad \widehat{T}_b = \begin{pmatrix} 1 & 1+\beta & 1+s\gamma & 1+\delta & 1 & 1+\tau \\ 1+\alpha & 1 & 1+s\gamma & 1+\delta & 1 & 1+\tau \\ 1+\alpha & 1+\beta & 1 & 1+\delta & 1 & 1+\mu\tau \\ 1+\alpha & 1+\beta & 1+s\gamma & 1 & 1 & 1+\tau \\ 1+\alpha & 1+\beta & 1+s\gamma & 1+\delta & 1 & 1+\tau \\ 1+\alpha & 1+\beta & 1+s\sigma\gamma & 1+\delta & 1 & 1 \end{pmatrix}
$$

---

[21] The Input–Output system for the entire country would not be representative for I–O system for individual States. The structure of production, any specialisation, and so on, could alter the I–O for the individual States. Assuming these differences away would not be correct. Further, the Final Demand (FD) vector for individual States is unknown.

The regime in the baseline scenario corresponds to the GST regime as proposed by the Empowered Committee of State Finance Ministers (2009). Further, it is assumed that there is no change in the price regime of petroleum products. Under-recoveries in the petroleum sector persist at the present levels.

Scenario 1: Proposed design of GST with no under-recoveries in petroleum sector

The tax structure remains same as the baseline. However, it is assumed that OMCs charge the desired market price and there are no under-recoveries on account of sales in diesel and petrol.

Following equation 1, price in scenario 1 (P_1) can be estimated, and T_1 and $\hat{T}_1$ can be presented as follows:

$$
T_1 = \begin{pmatrix} a \\ \beta \\ \gamma_1 \\ \delta \\ 0 \\ \tau \end{pmatrix}, \quad \text{and} \quad \hat{T}_1 = \begin{pmatrix}
1 & 1+\beta & 1+\gamma_1 & 1+\delta & 1 & 1+\tau \\
1+a & 1 & 1+\gamma_1 & 1+\delta & 1 & 1+\tau \\
1+a & 1+\beta & 1 & 1+\delta & 1 & 1+\mu\tau \\
1+a & 1+\beta & 1+\gamma_1 & 1 & 1 & 1+\tau \\
1+a & 1+\beta & 1+\gamma_1 & 1+\delta & 1 & 1+\tau \\
1+a & 1+\beta & 1+\sigma\gamma_1 & 1+\delta & 1 & 1
\end{pmatrix}
$$

In order to ensure that the revenue needs of governments are not compromised, the tax rate for petroleum products in this scenario is calibrated to yield the same amount of net revenue as in the baseline scenario, that is, γ_1 is altered both in the T_1 vector and $\hat{T}_1$ matrix. Since the under-recoveries are borne by the public sector enterprises alone, it is assumed that increase in prices (due to withdrawal of subsidy) would result in higher revenues for these companies which in turn would translate into higher revenue for the government as dividends. The revenue that is sought from the tax regime in this scenario would therefore be lower to this extent. We estimate the γ_1 such that the total tax incidence for scenario 1 (TTI_1) exactly matches the total tax incidence for the baseline scenario net of under-recoveries of OMCs (i.e., $TTI_b - TTI_1 - UR = 0$, where UR is the under-recovery on account of sales in diesel and petrol).

Scenario 2: GST covering petroleum refineries with subsidy in place

In this scenario, natural gas, crude petroleum, petroleum products and electricity are brought under the GST system. This would mean that for both natural gas and crude petroleum, the taxes on inputs would be set off and similarly other sectors will get full ITC for the purchase of natural gas and crude petroleum as inputs. Further, for refineries, there will be full ITC available. For the electricity sector, while it gets partial ITC for refined petroleum products used as inputs, for all sectors using electricity as an input, full ITC would be available. Full ITC for the purchase of petroleum products as inputs by other activities, however, is not allowed. Goods as well as services sectors attract a harmonised standard GST rate of 20 per cent (including natural gas and crude petroleum) and there are some exempted goods and services. The tax on electricity is increased to 10 per cent and the petroleum products sector attracts a differential tax (higher than the standard GST rate). Compensation on account of under-recoveries of OMCs is provided by the government.

Following equation 1, price in scenario 2 (P_2) can be estimated, and T_2 and $\hat{T}_2$ can be presented as follows:

$$
T_2 = \begin{pmatrix} \tau \\ \tau \\ s\gamma_2 \\ \bar{\delta} \\ 0 \\ \tau \end{pmatrix}
\quad \text{and} \quad
\hat{T}_2 = \begin{pmatrix}
1 & 1 & 1+s\sigma\gamma_2 & 1 & 1 & 1 \\
1 & 1 & 1+s\sigma\gamma_2 & 1 & 1 & 1 \\
1 & 1 & 1 & 1 & 1 & 1 \\
1 & 1 & 1+s\sigma\gamma_2 & 1 & 1 & 1 \\
1+\tau & 1+\tau & 1+s\gamma_2 & 1+\bar{\delta} & 1 & 1+\tau \\
1 & 1 & 1+s\sigma\gamma_2 & 1 & 1 & 1
\end{pmatrix}
$$

To estimate the revenue neutral condition for a shift from the baseline to Scenario 2, we estimate the γ_2 such that the total tax incidence of Scenario 2 becomes equal to that of the baseline scenario (i.e., $TTI_b - TTI_2 = 0$). The tax rate on petroleum products is likely to be higher than the baseline scenario and it would be a cascading type of tax.

Scenario 3: GST for petroleum refineries without petroleum subsidy[22]

The conditions of this scenario remain the same as Scenario 2, except that there is no under-recovery of OMCs on account of sales in diesel and petrol (i.e., $s = 1$).

Following equation 1, price in Scenario 3 (P_3) can be estimated, and T_3 and $\hat{T}_3$ can be presented as follows:

$$
T_3 = \begin{pmatrix} \tau \\ \tau \\ \gamma_3 \\ \bar{\delta} \\ 0 \\ \tau \end{pmatrix}
\quad \text{and} \quad
\hat{T}_3 = \begin{pmatrix}
1 & 1 & 1+\sigma\gamma_3 & 1 & 1 & 1 \\
1 & 1 & 1+\sigma\gamma_3 & 1 & 1 & 1 \\
1 & 1 & 1 & 1 & 1 & 1 \\
1 & 1 & 1+\sigma\gamma_3 & 1 & 1 & 1 \\
1+\tau & 1+\tau & 1+\gamma_3 & 1+\bar{\delta} & 1 & 1+\tau \\
1 & 1 & 1+\sigma\gamma_3 & 1 & 1 & 1
\end{pmatrix}
$$

To estimate the revenue neutral condition for a shift from the baseline to Scenario 3, we estimate the γ_3 such that the total tax incidence under Scenario 3 becomes equal

---

[22] Subsidy (or compensation) on account of under-recovery of OMCs for sales of petrol and diesel are not allowed in this scenario.

to the total tax incidence of Scenario 1, which is the baseline scenario net of under-recovery of OMCs (i.e., $TTI_b - TTI_3 - UR = 0$).

Scenario 4: GST for petroleum refineries with additional regulatory levy on petroleum products without petroleum subsidy

This is an extension of Scenario 3, except that full ITC is allowed up to the standard GST rate for the purchase of petroleum products as inputs. In other words, the tax on petroleum products is assumed to have two components, a GST and a non-rebatable levy. In this scenario, the non-rebatable levy is calibrated to satisfy revenue neutrality.

Following equation 1, price in Scenario 4 (P_4) can be estimated, and T_4 and $\widehat{T}_4$ can be presented as follows:

$$
T_4 = \begin{pmatrix} \tau \\ \tau \\ \gamma_3 \\ \delta \\ 0 \\ \tau \end{pmatrix} \quad \text{and} \quad \widehat{T}_4 = \begin{pmatrix} 1 & 1 & 1+\sigma(\gamma_4-\tau) & 1 & 1 & 1 \\ 1 & 1 & 1+\sigma(\gamma_4-\tau) & 1 & 1 & 1 \\ 1 & 1 & 1 & 1 & 1 & 1 \\ 1 & 1 & 1+\sigma(\gamma_4-\tau) & 1 & 1 & 1 \\ 1+\tau & 1+\tau & 1+\gamma_4 & 1+\delta & 1 & 1+\tau \\ 1 & 1 & 1+\sigma(\gamma_4-\tau) & 1 & 1 & 1 \end{pmatrix}
$$

To estimate the revenue neutral condition for a shift from the baseline to Scenario 4, we estimate the γ_4 such that the total tax incidence under Scenario 4 becomes equal to the total tax incidence of the baseline scenario net of under-recovery of OMCs (i.e., $TTI_b - TTI_4 - UR = 0$).

Scenario 5: Comprehensive GST with uniform rates of tax and with no petroleum subsidy

The conditions of this scenario are similar to Scenario 3, except that full ITC is allowed for the purchase of petroleum products as inputs for sectors subject to GST. In this scenario, instead of a special tax on petroleum products we estimate a standard GST rate that will maintain revenue neutrality of the governments.

Following equation 1, price in Scenario 5 (P_5) can be estimated, and T_5 and $\widehat{T}_5$ can be presented as follows:

$$
T_5 = \begin{pmatrix} \bar{\tau} \\ \bar{\tau} \\ \bar{\tau} \\ \delta \\ 0 \\ \bar{\tau} \end{pmatrix} \quad \text{and} \quad \widehat{T}_5 = \begin{pmatrix} 1 & 1 & 1 & 1 & 1 & 1 \\ 1 & 1 & 1 & 1 & 1 & 1 \\ 1 & 1 & 1 & 1 & 1 & 1 \\ 1 & 1 & 1 & 1 & 1 & 1 \\ 1+\bar{\tau} & 1+\bar{\tau} & 1+\bar{\tau} & 1+\delta & 1 & 1+\bar{\tau} \\ 1 & 1 & 1 & 1 & 1 & 1 \end{pmatrix}
$$

To estimate the revenue neutrality condition for a shift from baseline to Scenario 5, we estimate the $\bar{\tau}$ such that total tax incidence for Scenario 5 becomes equal to total tax incidence of baseline net of under-recovery of OMCs (i.e., $TTI_b - TTI_5 - UR$). It should be mentioned here that even in this scenario, the tax on electricity is held fixed at 10 per cent, since it is expected that such a reform would face lot of resistance, because of increase in prices for electricity.

Assumptions on Tax Rates

To derive the tax rates on petroleum products for the baseline scenario, we used the effective tax rates for these products in the present regime, for taxes that are expected to be subsumed into GST – Central excise, sales tax and entry tax. The tax rates (ETRs) for six policy sectors are presented in Table 7.3.

Estimation of Input Tax Credit Claimed by Petroleum Refineries against Central Taxes and State Sales Tax/VAT

Petroleum companies (refineries) are allowed to avail ITC against Central Taxes (Central excise duty and Service tax). Table 7.4 shows the percentage of ITC claimed

Table 7.3 Effective Tax Rates as on 2010–11 and Assumptions*

Sl. No.	Description	Central Excise Duty (%)[a]	State Sales Tax (%)[b]	Central Sales Tax (%)	Entry Tax (%)[c]	Total ETR (%)
1	Natural Gas	Nil	12.15	1.75	2.78	16.68 Approximately 17.00
2	Crude Petroleum	Nil	0.94	0.05	0.17	1.17 Approximately 2.00
3	Petroleum Products	17.72	16.71	1.78	3.29	39.5 Approximately 40.00
4	Electricity[d]	Nil	9.38	—	—	9.38 Approximately 10.00
5	Goods and Services	10.00	10.00	—	—	20.00[e]

Source: NIPFP (2011).

Notes: *The taxes are on output. However, when the output of a sector is going as inputs for other sectors the same tax rate will apply.

[a]Includes basic excise duty, additional excise duty and special additional excise duty.

[b]Includes State sales tax and State cesses on all petroleum products.

[c]In estimation of ETR we did not take into consideration the Entry Tax paid to Bombay Municipal Corporation and the Government of Maharashtra, as it will continue under the GST regime.

[d]Statutory tax rate on electricity (as electricity duty) across the States is 5.00 per cent. Effective tax rate on electricity is estimated for 2010–11 as 9.38 per cent or approximately 10.00 per cent.

[e]The effective tax rate on goods and services is taken as 20.00 per cent with equal share of Central excise duty and State sales tax.

Table 7.4   Input Tax Credit Claimed against Central and State Taxes (Rs Crore): 2010–11#

Central Taxes		State Taxes		Total
Value of Purchase of Goods and Services (Rs Crore) (A)	61,719	Value of Purchase of Goods (Rs Crore) (A)	10,004	71,723
Percentage Share in Total Value of Purchase (%) (B)	86.05	Percentage Share in Total Value of Purchase (%) (B)	13.95	
Excise Duty (ED)/Service Tax (ST) Charged	5,769	VAT & CST Paid	565.1	6334.1
CENVAT setoff of Excise Duty/Service Tax	3,342	Input tax credit (ITC) Claimed	285.2	3627.2
Weighted ED/ST Set off (%) (C)*	61.4	Weighted VAT Set off (%) (C)*	47.6	
Final Weighted Effective Tax Rate (%)@ (D) [(B)*(C)/100]	52.84	Final Weighted Effective Tax Rate (%)@ (D) [(B)*(C)/100]	6.64	59.48

Source: NIPFP (2011).

Notes: # this is based on company-wise information provided in NIPFP (2011).
*Weights are based on company-wise share in Total Value of Purchase.
@Weights are based on share in Total Value of Purchase.

against Central Taxes during 2010–11. Since crude oil and natural gas are exempted from Central excise duty, there are no provision for Exploration and Production companies to avail ITC against Central Taxes paid on input goods and services. Table 7.4 shows that 61.4 per cent of the ITC is claimed against Central Taxes.

Andhra Pradesh, Bihar, Gujarat, Haryana, Jharkhand, Karnataka, Kerala, Madhya Pradesh, Maharashtra, Orissa, Tamil Nadu, Delhi, Uttar Pradesh and West Bengal allow petroleum companies to avail the ITC against their State purchases of inputs (goods). The details of value of purchase and VAT and CST paid to State Governments are presented in Table 7.4. The percentage of setoff availed by the companies vary depending on the States where the companies are operating and their input and output baskets. In aggregate, available data suggests that 47.6 per cent of the State taxes that the companies paid are availed off as ITC.

From Table 7.4, we could conclude that petroleum companies on an average claim 59.48 or approximately 60 per cent of the taxes paid to Central and State Governments as ITC, the rest is their stranded costs. This ratio is assumed to remain constant in the baseline as well as in any other scenarios and is captured in the parameter μ (1 – 0.60).

Results and Analysis

Revenue Neutral Rates Corresponding to Alternative Scenarios

In the baseline scenario, government provides compensation to OMCs on account of under-recoveries due to sales of diesel and petrol below the desired market price.

In Scenario 1, as an alternative to baseline, there is no under-recovery of OMCs. In this case, there will be upward pressure on prices of petroleum products but at the same time the revenue required to meet the revenue neutrality condition will be lower by the amount of under-recovery of OMCs as prevailing in baseline. These joint effects put a downward pressure on tax rate of petroleum products. The estimated tax rate on petroleum products in Scenario 1 is 29 per cent which is considerably lower than 40 per cent of baseline (Table 7.5).

To move from baseline to Scenario 2, tax rate on petroleum products would be 48 per cent (Table 7.5). In Scenario 2, petroleum products sector will get full ITC against the purchase of goods and services (including crude oil, natural gas and electricity) as inputs whereas partial ITC against the purchase of petroleum products is allowed for sectors which are under the VAT or GST system. To move from the baseline to Scenario 3, the tax rate on petroleum products would be 36 per cent to protect the revenues of the government.

Scenario 4 is an improvement over Scenario 3. To move from the baseline to Scenario 4, the tax rate on petroleum products would be 47 per cent (Table 7.5). In this scenario, full ITC for the purchase of input petroleum products is allowed up to the

Table 7.5   Alternative Scenarios and Revenue Neutral Rates

Subsidy	Scenario	Natural Gas (%)	Crude Petroleum (%)	Petroleum Products* (%)	Electricity (%)	Tax Exempted Goods & Services (%)	Other Goods and Services (%)
With Subsidy	**Baseline Scenario**	17.00	2.00	40.00	5.00	0.00	20.00
	Scenario 2	20.00	20.00	48.00 (RNR)	10.00	0.00	20.00
Without Subsidy	**Scenario 1**	17.00	2.00	29.00 (RNR)	5.00	0.00	20.00
	Scenario 3	20.00	20.00	36.00 (RNR)	10.00	0.00	20.00
	Scenario 4	20.00	20.00	47.00 (RNR)	10.00	0.00	20.00
	Scenario 5	23.00 (RNR)	23.00 (RNR)	23.00 (RNR)	10.00	0.00	23.00 (RNR)

Source: Computed by authors.
Notes: *Petroleum Products includes Motor Spirit (also known as Gasoline/Petrol), High Speed Diesel and Aviation Turbine Fuel and all other Petroleum Products. Separate Revenue Neutral Tax Rates are not calculated for the following two baskets – (a) MS, HSD & ATF and (b) other petroleum products. Input tax credit availed by refineries are taken into consideration in this analysis.

standard GST rate of 20 per cent. However, to meet the revenue neutrality condition, there will be an additional 27 per cent regulatory levy (cascading type) on petroleum products. This scenario is in line with the international experience of taxation of petroleum products where an additional regulatory levy on petroleum products is proposed (Daniel et al. 2010). This scenario also has significant implications for the operationalisation of environmental fiscal reforms (UNEP 2010).

In Scenario 5, we explore the possibilities for the introduction of a full-fledged GST including petroleum products. To move from the baseline scenario to the full-fledged GST, government has the option to either put special cascading tax on petroleum products or evise the standard GST rate and apply the same across all sectors (including petroleum products).[23] If the government chooses the first option, the tax rate on petroleum products will be 78 per cent (not shown in Table 7.5). Alternatively, the standard GST rate needs to be revised to 23 per cent (Table 7.5). Increasing the standard GST by 3 per cent is adequate to compensate the revenue loss in terms of full ITC payment for all goods and services (including petroleum products).

Phasing out of petroleum subsidy will initially result in a rise in prices of petroleum products. However, the higher prices mean that the same desired revenue can be raised with lower tax rates. Further, since higher prices provide a payback to the government in terms of dividends, the revenue needs of the government would be lower, further decreasing the RNR. This is reflected in the results in Table 7.5. A shift from the baseline to Scenario 2 would require an 8 per cent increase in the tax rate on petroleum products whereas a shift from the baseline to Scenario 3 could be achieved by reducing the tax rate on petroleum products by 4 percentage points.

Cascading of Taxes

One of the reasons for seeking a reform of trade taxes is to reduce the extent of cascading in the system. It is therefore important to check what the impact on cascading is in the alternative scenarios considered. Cascading of taxes varies across the scenarios and it can be captured by the difference between total and direct tax incidence. The extent of cascading for a sector depends not only on the tax treatment of the sector but also on the overall indirect tax structure of the economy. We have adopted the following ratio as a measure of the extent of cascading of taxes:

Degree of Cascading of Taxes under the ith Scenario = $(TTI_i - DTI_i)/FD_i * 100$

where, TTI_i and DTI_i are Total and Direct Tax Incidences for the ith sector respectively and FD_i is the final demand for the ith sector.

The ratio shows the cascading of taxes as a percentage of final demand – the higher the ratio the higher the extent of cascading of taxes. The level of cascading of taxes (as percentage of Total Tax Incidence) goes down as we move away from the

---

[23] Standard GST rate is the rate at which most of the goods and services are taxed.

baseline scenario. The direct incidence of taxes goes up which shows that the tax system becomes cleaner.

The degree of cascading of taxes can be measured for individual sectors as well (for a detailed table of cascading across different scenarios, see Appendix 7A.2). For some of the sectors, like textiles (including apparels), petroleum products, chemicals, ferrous and non-ferrous basic metals, metal products (excluding machinery), machinery and machine tools (including tractors and agricultural implements), electronic and communication equipment and all transport equipment (excluding motor vehicles other than two-wheelers), cascading as a percentage of final demand (FD) is more than 2 per cent (baseline scenario). These are sectors which have substantial share in India's total export (Table 7.6). Therefore, any change in prices (through elimination of cascading of taxes) of these products could increase their competitiveness in the international market.

A substantial reduction in cascading of taxes is observed for a shift from the baseline to alternative scenarios.

Impacts on Prices of Policy Sectors

One of the primary reasons for sector-specific policies for the petroleum sector is an apprehension that reforms would raise prices, the latter being politically unacceptable. In proposing alternatives, therefore it is important to assess the likely impact on prices as well. Table 7.7 shows that prices across all scenarios fall for natural gas, crude petroleum, petroleum products and electricity (as compared to the baseline scenario). For petroleum products, as compared to the baseline scenario, price remains unchanged in Scenario 1 (due to the withdrawal of petroleum subsidy), but starts falling from Scenario 2 onwards (due to the combined effects of withdrawal of subsidy and introduction of GST). Table 7.7 shows that dismantling the administered pricing mechanism for petrol and diesel along with introduction of comprehensive GST for petroleum products benefits both the upstream (crude oil and natural gas) and downstream (electricity) sectors. The prices in Scenario 4 lie in between Scenarios 3 and 5 and it shows that the government could introduce an additional regulatory levy on petroleum products and allow full ITC for petroleum products up to the standard GST rate.

Conclusions

This study shows that keeping crude petroleum, natural gas, petroleum products and electricity out of the GST system will result in cascading across the sectors. The degree of cascading will vary across the sectors depending on their direct as well as indirect (inputs embedded in outputs of other sectors) input use. The present study documents that the extent of cascading is non-negligible and identifies alternative designs for the tax without compromising revenue considerations of the government. Non-availability or partial availability of ITC will result in stranded costs for some

Table 7.6 Share of Selected Sectors in India's Export of Principal Commodities and Degree of Cascading of Taxes

Industry Code	Commodity Description	Export as % of GVA: 2007–08[a]	% Share in Export of Principal Commodities: 2010–11[b]	Cascading – Baseline[c]	Cascading – Scenario 3[c]	Cascading – Scenario 4[c]
6	Metallic minerals	59.6	1.9	1.4	1.1	0.8
10	Textiles (including apparels)	80.9	9.7	2.9	2.2	1.6
16	Rubber and plastic products	36.4	3.3	3.2	2.3	1.7
17	Petroleum products	118.1	16.5	8.7	0.0	0.0
18	Chemicals	73.7	8.2	4.9	3.5	2.6
20	Ferrous and non-ferrous basic metals	57.9	2.0	3.6	2.4	1.8
21	Metal products (excluding machinery)	24.8	3.4	3.0	2.1	1.5
22	Machinery and machine tools (including tractors and agri. implements)	45.8	8.1	2.6	1.8	1.3
24	Electronic and communication equipment	53.3	6.4	2.4	1.7	1.2
25	All transport equipment (excluding motor vehicles other than 2 wheelers)	85.0	3.3	2.7	1.9	1.4

Sources: [a] Estimated from Input–Output Table 2007–08 (CSO 2012a).
[b] Estimated from Reserve Bank of India (RBI)'s Handbook of Statistics of Indian Economy (Table 130: Exports of Principal Commodities – Rupees, available at http://www.rbi.org.in/scripts/PublicationsView.aspx?id=15251 (last accessed on 3 March 2014).
[c] See Appendix 7A.2 for detailed Table.

Table 7.7　Percentage Change in Prices across Scenarios as Compared to Baseline Scenario*

Sector Description	Scenario 1	Scenario 2	Scenario 3	Scenario 4	Scenario 5
Natural gas	−0.11	−3.62	−3.69	−3.77	−4.00
Crude petroleum	−0.30	−7.02	−7.23	−7.44	−8.05
Petroleum products	0.00	−12.96	−12.96	−12.96	−12.96
Electricity	−2.08	−16.77	−18.64	−20.97	−23.96

Source: Computed by authors.
Note: *Estimated by [(Price in Alternative Scenario − Price in Baseline Scenario)/ Price in Baseline Scenario *100].

sectors (where the direct use of out-of-GST items are high) but the costs will be spread across all sectors of the economy, through sectoral inter-linkages. Moreover, some sectors with considerable export presence are shown to be facing significant incidence of tax cascading, which could be detrimental for competitiveness in the international market. The study explores various policy options and suggests alternative designs for GST. In none of the policy options the estimated RNR is beyond the level that could make the design of the GST unacceptable. The results also show that in all improved designs of GST (as compared to the proposed design of GST), the prices across the sectors either remain unchanged or decline (except for tax exempted sectors). These results suggest that there is little ground for separating out petroleum products for special treatment by keeping them out of the base for GST. GST reforms implemented alongside price correction could provide an interesting opportunity to reform without worries about price rise.

Appendix 7A.1　Methodology for Construction of Input–Output Coefficient Matrix (Commodity x Commodity) for 48 Sectors from 130 Items

The methodology used to construct the Input–Output (I–O) Coefficient Matrix from I–O Transaction Table (Commodity by Commodity) is as follows:

$$\sum_{i=1\forall j}^{130} X_{ij} + NIT_j + GVA_j = TO_j \forall j$$

where, X_{ij} is the input flow from ith commodity to jth commodity in Rs Lakh

$\sum_{i=1\forall j}^{130} X_{ij}$ is the total input/commodity used by the jth commodity (in Rs Lakh)

NIT_j is the Net Indirect Taxes of the jth commodity (in Rs Lakh)

GVA_j is the Gross Value Added by the jth commodity (in Rs Lakh)

TO_j is the Total Output of the jth commodity (in Rs Lakh)

V_j is the value added vector for the jth commodity, where $V_j = GVA_j/TO_j$

First, we sum up X_{ij} across j at given i to combine 130 items under 48 sectors and get X_{ij^*}. Then, we sum up X_{ij^*} across i at given j^* to get the input flow matrix for 48 sectors, that is, $X_{i^*j^*}$. Similarly, we also get the GVA_{j^*} and TO_{j^*} for 48 sectors. We estimate the I–O Coefficient Matrix for the 48 sectors by dividing $X_{i^*j^*}$ for given j^* by TO_{j^*} and get $a_{i^*j^*}$.

Therefore, $a_{i^*j^*} = X_{i^*j^*|j^*} /TO_{j^*}$.

Appendix 7A.2   Cascading of Taxes under Different Scenarios

Industry Code	Commodity Description	Baseline	Scenario 1	Scenario 2	Scenario 3	Scenario 4	Scenario 5
1	Crops and livestock products (including fishing)	7.7	7.5	8.4	8.1	8.4	8.7
2	Forestry and logging	6	5.8	6.6	6.4	6.7	6.7
6	Metallic minerals	1.4	1.1	1.4	1.1	0.8	0
8	Food products and beverages (including edible vegetable oils)	2.1	1.7	2	1.6	1.2	0
9	Tobacco products	1.1	0.9	1.1	0.9	0.7	0
10	Textiles (including apparels)	2.9	2.4	2.7	2.2	1.6	0
11	Furniture and fixtures—wooden	1.7	1.4	1.7	1.3	1	0
12	Wood and wood products (excluding furniture)	1.6	1.3	1.6	1.3	1	0
13	Paper, paper products. and newsprint	3.4	2.7	3.2	2.6	1.9	0
14	Printing and publishing	2.9	2.4	2.8	2.3	1.7	0
15	Leather products (including footwear)	1.9	1.5	1.8	1.5	1.1	0
16	Rubber and plastic products	3.2	2.7	2.9	2.3	1.7	0
17	**Petroleum products**	**8.7**	**8.1**	**0**	**0**	**0**	**0**
18	Chemicals	4.9	4.1	4.3	3.5	2.6	0

Contd.

Industry Code	Commodity Description	Baseline	Scenario 1	Scenario 2	Scenario 3	Scenario 4	Scenario 5
19	**Non-metallic mineral products (including cement)**	**5.8**	**4.7**	**5.5**	**4.4**	**3.3**	**0**
20	Ferrous and non-ferrous basic metals	3.6	3.1	3	2.4	1.8	0
21	Metal products (excluding machinery)	3	2.5	2.6	2.1	1.5	0
22	Machinery and machine tools (including tractors and agri. implements)	2.6	2.1	2.2	1.8	1.3	0
23	Electrical machinery and appliances	3	2.5	2.7	2.1	1.6	0
24	Electronic and communication equipment	2.4	2	2.1	1.7	1.2	0
25	All transport equipment (excluding motor vehicles other than 2 wheelers)	2.7	2.2	2.4	1.9	1.4	0
26	Motor vehicles	2.7	2.2	2.3	1.8	1.4	0
27	Medical, precision and optical instruments (including watches and clocks)	2.8	2.3	2.6	2	1.5	0
28	Gems and jewellery, misc. manufacturing	2.5	2	2.4	1.9	1.4	0
29	Construction	2.6	2.1	2.4	1.9	1.4	0
30	**Electricity**	21.2	20.1	6.2	4.7	2.7	0
31	Water supply	15.6	15.1	16.8	16.3	16.9	17.6
32	Railway transport services	2.4	2	1.8	1.5	1.1	0
33	**Land transport (including via pipeline)**	**9.6**	**7.5**	**10.5**	**8.4**	**6.3**	**0**
34	Water transport	2.2	1.8	2.2	1.8	1.3	0
35	Air transport	4.9	3.9	5.2	4.1	3.1	0
36	Supporting and aux. transport activities (including storage and warehousing)	2.5	2	2.3	1.9	1.4	0

Contd.

Industry Code	Commodity Description	Baseline	Scenario 1	Scenario 2	Scenario 3	Scenario 4	Scenario 5
37	Communication	1.2	1	1.1	0.9	0.7	0
38	Trade	1.2	1	1.2	1	0.7	0
39	Hotels and restaurants	1.7	1.3	1.6	1.3	0.9	0
40	Banking and insurance	0.7	0.6	0.6	0.5	0.4	0
41	Ownership of dwellings	1.9	1.9	2	2	2	2.2
42	Education and research, medical and health, public administration	4.9	4.8	5.1	5	5.2	5.5
43	Business services	0.9	0.8	0.7	0.6	0.4	0
44	Computer and related activities	0.6	0.5	0.4	0.3	0.2	0
45	Legal services	0.8	0.7	0.5	0.4	0.3	0
46	Real estate activities	0.2	0.2	0.2	0.1	0.1	0
47	Renting of machinery and equipment	0.9	0.8	0.6	0.5	0.4	0
48	Other commercial, social and personal services, other services	0.5	0.4	0.5	0.4	0.3	0

Source: Computed by authors.
Note: Sectors shaded are exempted sectors.

References

Agrawal, Pradeep (2012). 'India's Petroleum Demand: Empirical Estimations and Projections for the Future', IEG Working Paper No. 319, Institute of Economic Growth, New Delhi.

Central Statistics Office (CSO) (2012a). 'Input–Output Transactions Table 2007–08', *CSO, Ministry of Statistics and Programme Implementation*, Government of India, New Delhi.

———— (2012b). 'National Account Statistics 2012', *Ministry of Statistics and Programme Implementation*, Government of India, New Delhi.

Daniel, P., M. Keen and C. McPherson (2010). *The Taxation of Petroleum and Minerals: Principles, Problems and Practice*, Routledge, New York.

Greening, Lorna A., David L. Greene and Carmen Difiglio (2000). 'Energy Efficiency and Consumption – the Rebound Effect – a Survey', *Energy Policy* 28(6–7): 389–401.

Ministry of Finance (2013). 'Indian Public Finance Statistics 2012–13', Economic Division, Department of Economic Affairs, Ministry of Finance, Government of India, New Delhi.

——— (2012). 'Indian Public Finance Statistics 2011–12', Economic Division, Department of Economic Affairs, Ministry of Finance, Government of India, New Delhi.

——— (2011). 'Indian Public Finance Statistics 2010–11', Economic Division, Department of Economic Affairs, Ministry of Finance, Government of India, New Delhi.

National Institute of Public Finance and Policy (NIPFP) (2011). 'Study on GST in the Context of Petroleum and Natural Gas', Project Report Submitted to the Petroleum Federation of India, New Delhi.

Petroleum Policy Analysis Cell (PPAC) (2012). 'PPAC Ready Reckoner 2012', Petroleum Policy Analysis Cell, Ministry of Petroleum and Natural Gas, Government of India, New Delhi.

——— (2010). 'PPAC Ready Reckoner 2010', Petroleum Policy Analysis Cell, Ministry of Petroleum and Natural Gas, Government of India, New Delhi.

——— (2009). 'PPAC Ready Reckoner 2010', Petroleum Policy Analysis Cell, Ministry of Petroleum and Natural Gas, Government of India, New Delhi.

——— (2008). 'PPAC Ready Reckoner 2010', Petroleum Policy Analysis Cell, Ministry of Petroleum and Natural Gas, Government of India, New Delhi.

Power Finance Corporation Ltd. (PFCL) (2013). 'Report on the Performance of State Power Utilities for the Years 2009–10 to 2011–12', New Delhi.

Srivastava, D. K., C. Bhujanga Rao, Pinaki Chakraborty and T. S. Rangamannar (2003). *Budgetary Subsidies in India: Subsidising Social and Economic Services*, National Institute of Public Finance and Policy, New Delhi.

The Empowered Committee of State Finance Ministers (2009). 'First Discussion Paper on Goods and Service Tax in India', Government of India, New Delhi, 10 November 2009.

United Nations Environment Programme (UNEP) (2010). 'Driving a Green Economy through Public Finance and Fiscal Policy Reform'. Available online at http://www.unep.org/greeneconomy/Portals/88/documents/ger/GER_Working_Paper_Public_Finance.pdf (last accessed on 22 April 2014).

III

GST Administration and Possible Impacts of GST on Indian Economy

III

8

Administration of GST

Can We Continue with Present Structures?

R. Kavita Rao *and* Sacchidananda Mukherjee

Introduction

With some progress in the design of the Goods and Services Tax (GST), there is an emerging need to explore the options for administering the new tax regime. From the discussions and decisions taken so far, one of the important parameters of the new regime is the applicability of two taxes (Central GST, CGST, and State GST, SGST) on each and every transaction of supply of good and/or service in the country. The central tax would accrue to the central government and the state tax would accrue to the state governments. Inter-state sales and imports will attract Integrated GST (IGST) and it is likely to be administered by the central government. IGST will comprise of the prevailing SGST and CGST rates for the concerned good and it will work as a mechanism (or clearing house) to transfer input tax credits from the origin state to the destination state. Compared to the existing regime, the proposed tax represents a significant change in the tax administration. The central tax administration would need to deal with wholesale and retail traders in addition to the existing taxpayers (e.g., manufacturers, service providers). Similarly, the state tax departments would need to deal with service providers. The workload per employee as well as the skill set associated with tax administration would have to undergo a sharp change if the taxes are to be administered by maintaining a status quo on the forms of administration. In other words, grafting the new tax on to existing tax administrations would impose a significant cost of transition in addition to the higher costs of collection. On the other hand, there would be quite a sharp change in the tax environment faced by a segment of the taxpayers – all taxpayers other than the manufacturers who had faced one tax and one tax department (e.g., service providers, wholesale and retail traders). Under the new regime potentially they will face two tax departments, and potentially an increase in the compliance cost associated with the new regime, thereby raising the opportunity cost of being in the tax system. The result could either be higher evasion or higher resistance to the new tax regime. Some segments of the taxpayers are already articulating a demand for addressing the sharp increase in the compliance requirements of the new regime. In this context, it is tempting to ask whether the only way to administer the tax regime is through a business-as-usual model or whether there exist alternatives to the same. This chapter attempts to discuss the options available and presents a brief summary of the international experience in the context.

The above suggests that the new regime grafted onto the existing tax administration set-up would imply higher costs of administration as well as compliance. In any discussion on exploring the alternative forms, the key factors which will potentially drive or condition the choice within the options available are: first, two levels of tax administrations would be collecting taxes on the same base and if, as the discussion paper suggests (Government of India 2009), there would be a significant degree of harmonisation in the forms and procedures across the different levels of administration and uniformity in the rates of tax, separate central and state administrations would mean significant duplication of effort. Second, any discussion on change in forms of administration, however, has to contend with potential resistance or discomfort from the respective governments: since these taxes represent a significant share of the total tax base for the central government as well as the state governments, both these levels of governments may not be comfortable to delegate the collection of the tax to the other level.

Keeping these factors in perspective, this chapter tries to build an argument in favour of a new system of tax administration which could potentially reduce the transaction costs, could be transparent and also enable joint tax administration with an objective to safeguard the interests of both the central and state governments. Drawing experience from both developed and developing countries, this note discusses the merits and demerits of the alternatives available and provides a choice for policy makers to think about the alternative systems.

International experience on alternative forms of organisation has thrown up varied experiments – the first and most radical form is called the Autonomous or Semi-Autonomous Revenue Agency (ARA or SARA). This form moves the actual administration of the tax from directorates within the Ministry of Finance in any government into a separate and partly autonomous agency. The lessons we can learn from these experiments are summarised in the section titled 'Semi-Autonomous Revenue Agencies'. Another set of experiments deal with various mechanisms to bring in cooperation between tax departments so as to improve the efficiency of tax collection. Some of the lessons from these experiments are summarised in the section titled 'Coordinated Tax Administration'. This is followed by a discussion of the possible options for India. This discussion draws on the earlier sections and attempts to identify a middle path between the two broad extremes discussed in the earlier sections.

Semi-Autonomous Revenue Agencies

Starting from the early 1980s, there is a growing tendency among developed countries under OECD and developing countries in Africa and Latin America to separate out tax administration from the Ministry of Finance through the establishment of Semi-Autonomous Revenue Agencies (SARAs) (see OECD 2009; Mann 2004; von Haldenwang et al. 2014). Although there are several variations among SARAs, the basic characteristics of SARA include a personnel system outside civil service purview, a self-financing mechanism and a board of directors with members from among Ministers of Finance, other ministers from key ministries and private sector representatives. Table 8.1 summarises the functions undertaken by these institutions in the different countries.

Apart from broad political and economic conditions, factors which induced developing countries to go for SARA are summarised as follows (Mann 2004):

- level of inefficiency of revenue collections in the face of fiscal deficits and expanding public expenditure needs
- tax evasion and generalised corruption
- high compliance costs
- high level of political interference

Assessment of the experiments with SARA suggests a mixed bag of results. Studies suggest that the improvements in tax administration are not necessarily consistent (Mann 2004). The establishment of these institutions, it is argued, can be considered a first step in the process of reforms in tax administration. Autonomy in functioning does not necessarily follow the establishment of such an organisation. Some of the arguments in favour of establishing a SARA are as follows (Mann 2004):

- Public revenue enhancement reflected in higher tax ratios and real revenue growth
- Greater efficiency in public resource utilisation via financial and administrative independence/autonomy
- Employment of a competent, disciplined and more qualified staff via the freedom to offer higher compensation than the civil service and the freedom to recruit and fire on own terms
- De-politicisation of tax administration
- Reduced corruption, thereby improving the credibility of taxation in particular and government in general
- Better work ethic and modification of administrative culture from reactive, bureaucratic, and hostile to proactive and professional

Table 8.1 Delegated Authority That Can Be Exercised by the Unified Semi-Autonomous Body

Country	Make Tax Law Rulings	Remit Administrative Penalties and/or Interest	Establish Internal Design/ Structure	Allocate Budget	Fix Levels and Mix of Staff	Set Service Performance Levels	Influence Staff Recruitment Criteria	Hire And Dismiss Staff	Negotiate Staff Pay Levels
1) OECD countries									
Australia	Yes	Yes*	Yes	Yes	Yes	Yes	Yes	Yes	Yes
Canada	Yes	Yes	Yes	Yes	Yes	Yes	Yes	Yes	Yes
Finland	Yes	Yes	Yes	Yes	Yes	Yes	Yes	Yes	Yes
Hungary	Yes	Yes	×	Yes	Yes	Yes	Yes	Yes	Yes
Iceland	Yes	Yes	Yes*	Yes*	Yes	Yes	Yes	Yes*	Yes*
Ireland	Yes	Yes	Yes	Yes	Yes	Yes	Yes	Yes	×
Japan	Yes	Yes	×	×	×	Yes	Yes	Yes	×
Korea	Yes	Yes	Yes	Yes	×	Yes	Yes	Yes	Yes
Mexico	Yes	Yes	Yes	Yes	Yes	Yes	Yes	Yes	Yes
New Zealand	Yes	Yes	Yes	Yes	Yes	Yes	Yes	Yes	Yes
Norway	Yes	Yes	×	Yes	Yes	Yes	Yes	Yes	Yes
Slovak Rep.	Yes	Yes	Yes	Yes	Yes	Yes	Yes	Yes	Yes
Spain	Yes	Yes	Yes	Yes	Yes	Yes	Yes	Yes	Yes
Sweden	Yes	Yes	Yes	Yes	Yes	Yes	Yes	Yes	Yes
Turkey	Yes	Yes	Yes	×	×	Yes	Yes	×	×
UK	Yes	Yes	Yes	Yes	Yes (limited)	Yes*	Yes	Yes	Yes
USA	Yes	Yes	Yes	Yes	Yes	Yes	Yes	Yes	Yes
2) Selected non-OECD countries									
Argentina	Yes	Yes	Yes	Yes	Yes	Yes	Yes	Yes	Yes
Bulgaria	Yes	×	Yes	Yes	Yes	Yes	Yes	Yes	Yes
Latvia	Yes	Yes	Yes	Yes	Yes	Yes	Yes	Yes	–
Romania	Yes	Yes	Yes	Yes	Yes	Yes	Yes	Yes	×
Singapore	Yes	Yes	Yes	Yes	Yes	Yes	Yes	Yes	Yes
Slovenia	Yes	Yes	Yes	Yes	Yes	Yes	Yes	Yes	Yes
South Africa	Yes	Yes	Yes	Yes	Yes	Yes	Yes	Yes	Yes

Source: Compiled from Table 1 and Table 2 from OECD (2009).

Note: *-Australia – not for penalties imposed by a court; Iceland – not including the regional tax offices; UK – Public Service Agreement targets have to be agreed with Ministers

- Improved taxpayer services and reduced taxpayer compliance costs
- Comprehensive accounting for all tax revenues
- Integration of tax and taxpayer-related databases

For the Indian context, while all of the above arguments might not be immediately on the policy makers' agenda, it would appear that the last three would be important to keep in focus. While the immediate impetus in considering this model would not be directly related to the issue of establishing autonomy of the tax departments from political interference, there are two key lessons from the experiments with SARA – one, this mode of functioning addresses both the issues raised in the discussion – the need for change in the forms of administration. This form of organisation can potentially reduce the compliance cost for the taxpayer and the costs of administration for the tax administrator. Further, given the potential reluctance in both levels of government in allowing the entire function of tax collection to rest with the other, this mode of functioning can allow the revenue agency to report to the respective finance ministries. This agency potentially could draw on the employees of all the existing tax departments. Two examples of an independent public agency which undertakes the task of tax collection for a number of governments are discussed below. In both these examples, the tax administrator is an independent public sector organisation that has been assigned or has taken on the task of tax administration on behalf of more than one tax authority. In the first example, the agency provides revenue administration services to 140 town councils from provinces. The number of functions assigned to this agency varies across the town councils and could change over time. The second example is that of the Canadian Revenue Agency (CRA). This example too captures an evolving relationship. The CRA, set up initially to administer taxes for the central government in Canada, has also been given the authority to sign agreements with the provinces to collect and remit the taxes for them. In signing such agreements, the CRA does not mandate a uniform rate of tax across the participating provinces nor does it require complete homogenisation of the exemptions.

Box 8.1   Suma experience in Alicante, Spain

Suma (meaning addition) is a public organisation that provides tax administration services to 140 town councils in the province of Alicante, Spain. The Suma performs an integrated tax management service and is responsible for the processing of local taxes from the first instance of a taxable activity or property to the receipt of tax payment by the municipal authorities. This involves payment, management, inspection and collection. Suma has implemented an efficient system which has enabled the municipalities to (1) improve ratios in tax collection; (2) increase the accessibility of information to citizens in its office or mobile offices and Internet Virtual Offices; (3) improve the quality of work for employees by providing tools for the autonomous and complete solution of taxpayers' problems. This model, mainly based on technology but also with organisational components, has proved to be an excellent solution for other local authorities in Spain.

In this context the role of a supra-municipal authority is crucial, as not all councils have resources enough to do the job: updating of censuses for local tax purposes (property tax, the economic activities tax, the motor vehicle tax, capital gains on land, the tax on constructions installations and works, as well as other local taxes specific to each municipal authority [rubbish collection, drains, private entrances, etc.]). The existence of a supra-municipal authority dealing with these issues is perhaps the best and most cost-effective way for the councils as it uses 'economies of scale + dimension' management principle. For the small towns it is probably the only solution, as they cannot usually afford to have or maintain tax-dedicated information systems, nor tax specialists, nor do the billing and collection efficiently. It is also simpler for the customers as they only have to go to one place to fulfil their local tax obligations.

The governing body (the Board) of Suma consists of a President, who is the President of the Provincial Council, and seven Provincial Representatives and the Director of Suma himself. The Director is appointed by the President. The Board has also a legal advisor, the Secretary of Suma, and an economic auditor, the Head of Finance. Their duties are regulated by Suma statutes. There is, in addition, a consultative body, called the Council of Mayors, which guarantees the participation of the delegating Town Councils in the strategies adopted by Suma.

To fully understand the complexity of this activity we must keep in mind that the powers are not uniformly delegated to this authority by the local governments – not all local governments collect all the potential taxes. In other words, variation in the demands to be raised across local bodies is incorporated into the system. Further, given the large number of levies administered by them, they must establish close relationships with a number of organisations: State Tax Agency, Central Vehicle Registry, Central Cadastre, notaries, among others. It should also be mentioned that the relation established between SUMA and the local authorities is not fixed and given. Local authorities can propose new services at the annual meeting between Suma and the technical and political representatives of each of the 140 town councils associated to Suma. The Suma officers gather suggestions and requests from the Council that will later form part of the development plans for the coming year. Services provided therefore can evolve over time.

Source: http://www.epractice.eu/en/cases/sumaalicanteawards, posted on 2 February 2010; Suma website: http://www.suma.es/.

The Canadian CRA Experience

In Canada, there are three types of tax regimes on goods and services that are operational across provinces.

- Provinces with a central goods and services tax (GST), and a provincial retail sales tax (PST) are levied and collected. The former would be collected by the CRA and the latter by the provincial tax administration. Examples are Prince Edward Island, Manitoba and Saskathchewan.
- Provinces which choose to collect no taxes from their residents. Here only the central GST applies and is collected by the CRA. Examples are Alberta, Northwest Territories and Yukon Territory.
- Provinces where these two levies are replaced by a harmonised sales tax (HST). This levy has a central component equivalent to the GST above and a state component in the form of a VAT. This tax is administered by the CRA and the revenue accruing to the states are passed on the states. Examples of this regime are found in Newfoundland, Nova Scotia and New Brunswick. A variant of this regime is that of Quebec, where, though the tax is an HST, it is collected by the provincial government and the central share is remitted to it.[1]

A few interesting features of the last regime are useful to note. First, this regime is evolving in terms of participation by states – Ontario and British Columbia are joining the regime from 1 July 2010. Second, while the HST regime began with a uniform rate across provinces, that is not a requirement any longer. The rate for the above provinces is 13 per cent. Ontario proposes to stick to this rate while British Columbia chooses a lower rate of 12 per cent. One of the earlier partners – Nova Scotia – on the other hand seeks to raise its rate to 15 per cent. Third, the Canadian provinces have different lists of exemptions and different thresholds for taxing business entities, even with a change over to HST – some of these exemptions and thresholds would be retained. Fourth, with the introduction of the new regime for Ontario and British Columbia, the CRA has signed a Human Resource Agreement whereby a number of provincial employees currently administering sales taxes in these states would transition to the CRA. Through this step, the transition to

---

[1] The Comprehensive Integrated Tax Coordination Agreement (CITCA) could be signed between the Federal Government of Canada and participating provincial government. Under this agreement, the CITCA provinces agree to pay the Harmonised Sales Tax (HST) in respect of supplies acquired by their governments, agents and entities. The HST replaces the federal Goods and Service Tax (GST) and the Provincial General Sales Tax (PST) that would otherwise be charged (TBCS undated). The objectives of this agreement are to reduce tax administration burden by entrusting a single agency to administer both federal GST and provincial sales taxes; to build upon the existing sales tax harmonisation framework; to simplify compliance and promote federal-provincial fiscal co-operation and harmonisation.

an HST regime by the provincial government is supported, since the provincial government, while retaining the right to formulate policy need not worry about relocating employees that were formerly in tax administration.

The Canadian experience of integrated tax administration underlines the fact that the uniform rates and exemptions/thresholds are not essential for introducing and implementing a regime such as the HST which is administered by an independent revenue agency. Box 8.2 provides the details about CRA.

Box 8.2   Canadian Revenue Agency

Canadian Revenue Agency (formerly known as Canada Customs and Revenue Agency) was established by an Act in the Parliament, viz., Canada Customs and Revenue Agency Act, 1999. The CRA is responsible for the administration of tax programmes, as well as the delivery of economic and social benefits. It also administers certain provincial and territorial tax programmes. In addition, the CRA has the authority to enter into new partnerships with the provinces, territories, and other government bodies to administer non-harmonised taxes and other services, at their request and on a cost-recovery basis. The CRA promotes compliance with Canada's tax legislation and regulations.

The Canadian Minister of National Revenue (hereafter Minister) is accountable to the Parliament for all the CRA's activities, including the administration and enforcement of the Income Tax Act and the Excise Tax Act. The Minister ensures that the CRA operates within the overall government framework and consistently treats its clients with fairness and integrity. The CRA has a Board of Management which consists of 15 members appointed by the Governor in Council. Eleven of these members have been nominated by the provinces and territories. The Board is responsible for overseeing the organisation and management of the CRA, including the development of the Corporate Business Plan, and the management of policies related to resources, services, property and personnel. The CRA's Board of Management is not involved in all the CRA's business activities. It does not have the authority to administer and enforce legislation or to access confidential client information.

As the CRA's chief executive officer, the Commissioner is responsible for the day-to-day administration and enforcement of programme legislation that falls under the Minister's delegated authority. The Commissioner is accountable to the Board of Management for the daily management of the CRA, supervision of employees, and implementation of policies and budgets.

The CRA Annual Report to Parliament is tabled by the Minister of National Revenue, pursuant to the statutory requirements of the Canada

Revenue Agency Act. The document is a comprehensive report on the performance of the CRA for the previous fiscal year, and a rating of the CRA's achievements against the key targets and indicators set out in CRA's Corporate Business Plan. The Annual Report and the Performance Report also contain an assessment of the fairness and reliability of the information contained in the report, and an audit of the agency and administered financial statements, by the Auditor General of Canada.

Source: http://www.cra-arc.gc.ca/menu-eng.html (accessed on 3 May 2010).

In considering a similar regime for India, it is possible to imagine a unified tax administration for GST, where the revenue accruing to different governments can be transferred to it. The agency could be made answerable to the Ministry of Finance, Government of India, and the Empowered Committee of State Finance Ministers, or its equivalent. Its autonomy would be critical for its success. The Canadian experiment suggests that such a model can even be adopted partially, that is, for some states, but would likely complicate the administration, at least initially. Further, attempting such a major change in the form of administration would not seem acceptable to the various tax departments and possibly delay the implementation of the new regime. Considering these factors, it is important to explore some of the other alternatives.

Coordinated Tax Administration

Administrative cooperation in VAT administration is another area which is highlighted by Cnossen (2008). 'Cnossen (2008) argues that carousel fraud is not facilitated or caused by the break in the VAT collection chain on which all other proposals focus, but by a break in the VAT audit chain. The answer to VAT fraud, he argues, is not to change the VAT system but to increase VAT audit, investigation, and prosecution capacity...' (Ahmad and Al Faris 2010).

Turning to the other extreme position, we look at experiments on how tax administrations have worked out mechanisms for coordinated effort. It is common knowledge that a variety of agencies seek to share information with each other in order to optimise on their functions. This is true more so in the case of tax agencies. Denison and Facer II (2005) argue that as regional economies have become more interconnected, the administration of tax revenue systems has become increasingly complex, motivating states to consider tax coordination efforts through a variety of arrangements to improve tax administration and enforcement. A tax coordination agreement permits the participating states to engage in specified collection or enforcement activities associated with a tax on behalf of another jurisdiction.

A very prominent experiment in this field is the design and administration of value added tax and corporate taxes in Europe. The sixth Directive of the European Union spells out a number of parameters on which the tax systems of different countries have to agree. The treatment of any transaction which involves agents from more than one country, member or otherwise is debated and once some decisions are arrived at, they are specified by the Union and adopted by the member states. Further, evolving over time, there are agreed upon formats for sharing information between the member states. Given that the member states in the Union are keen to maintain their autonomy and yet seek to find mechanisms to protect their tax base from erosion through evasion and avoidance, some standardised formats have been worked out to share information among the member states.

Administrative Cooperation in VAT Administration across EU Member States

The EU requires the member states to collect from VAT registered suppliers of goods a European Community Sales List (ESL), also known as recapitulative statement, concerning all their supplies to VAT registered acquirers/consignees of other EU member states.[2] The submission of ESL is mandatory under 6th VAT Directive (77/388/EEC) and it is submitted on calendar quarterly basis or monthly basis as specified.[3] The ESL captures identification information on the intra-community suppliers/acquirers and consignees of goods and services (VAT registration number, address details and country code of the suppliers and their acquirers/consignees) and their total value of transactions (total value of goods and services supplied to each VAT registered acquirers).[4]

After compiling the data from the ESL, the member state concerned, say state B, communicates the following information to all other member states on an automatic basis (EC Regulation No. 1798/2003 of 7 October 2003):[5]

---

[2] From 1 January 2010, ESL reporting becomes mandatory for intra-community service providers also.

[3] In an effort to curb evasion, the periodicity for these lists is being consistently reduced to one month (EU Directive 2006/112/EC of 16 December 2008; Amendment of Regulation 1798/2003 of 16 December 2008).

[4] It may be mentioned that while the EU regulations require this minimum information to be collected, any individual member state may ask for additional information through ESL (77/388/EEC).

[5] The competent authority of a member state is obliged to grant access to information and it shall do so as soon as possible and within one month at the latest of the end of the calendar quarter to which the information relates. Member states store information in electronic databases and exchange such information by electronic means (EC Regulation No. 1798/2003 of 7 October 2003; Council Regulation (EC) No. 37/2009 of 16 December 2008 amending Regulation (EC) No. 1798/2003).

a. VAT identification numbers of the acquirers / consignee of state A who are receiving the goods and services from state B.[6]
b. Total value of all goods and services that a person (identified by VAT registration number) receives from all suppliers of state B in the reporting period.[7]

In addition to the above information, the importing state could also (if it considers necessary) obtain direct and immediate access to the following information:

c. VAT identification numbers of the suppliers who effected supplies referred to in point (b) above; and
d. Total value of such supplies from each person to each person holding a VAT identification number referred to in point (a) above.

At present, information collected through ESL are processed and maintained in an electronic database (for at least five years from the end of the calendar year for which the information is collected) by each member state, instead of at the EC level. Each member state exchanges information with other member states on automatic as well as on request basis.

The institutional agreements within the EU allow for requests on specific cases as well, in order to help in arriving at a correct assessment of VAT on intra-community transactions. On request, the requested authority is expected to conduct the required administrative enquiries necessary to obtain such information and communicate any pertinent information available in its records or obtained through enquiries. There are prescribed time limits for responding to such queries to support timely action.

The EU model, thus, works on the basis of a minimum prescribed format for information collection and sharing, to address the issues of potential revenue evasion. All member states agree on the minimum prescribed formats. In addition, pairs of member states could also enter into agreements for close cooperation (e.g., Belgium and the Netherlands,[8] France and Germany[9]).

---

[6] To ensure that the exporters can obtain confirmation of the tax status of the buyer/consignee, all tax administrations in the member states provide for a computerised system for checking validity of the same. This information is maintained by the individual member states and made accessible to all concerned.

[7] The value is expressed in the currency of the member state providing the information and it is related to calendar quarter.

[8] On 11 March 2008, Belgium and the Netherlands signed an agreement regarding the presence of tax officials of one country in the territory of the other country to collect information that may be relevant for the correct levy of taxes on income and capital, as well as of VAT and excise duties (IBFD Online database on Tax Treaties – accessed on 10 May 2010).

[9] The competent authorities of France and Germany signed an exchange of information agreement on 18 October 2001.The agreement provides for the spontaneous and automatic exchange of information between the tax administrations of the states with regard to VAT refunds under the EC 8th VAT Directive (Directive 79/1072/EEC of 6 December 1979) (IBFD Online database on Tax Treaties – accessed on 10 May 2010).

With specific to Sweden's exchange of tax information for VAT purposes with 14 EU member states, Ligthart (2007) argues that the size of the country (as measured by population size and net trade with Sweden) significantly influences the bilateral exchange of information on request. The countries which are net exporters of goods to Sweden are also net importers of information from Sweden, which helps to curtail their export-related VAT fraud. Unless tax information is shared on spontaneous basis, it becomes difficult for small countries (in terms of population size and trade) to get information from their comparatively large trade partners.

Other Examples of Coordinated Tax Administrations

In the United States of America, for instance, to increase tax revenues and taxpayer compliance, and to reduce duplicate resource expenditures, an *Agreement on Coordination of Tax Administration (ACTA)* is in place for the exchange of Federal Tax Information with State Tax Agencies, US Territories, and Municipalities with populations in excess of 2.50 lakh that impose taxes on income or wages. The Internal Revenue Service has written agreements with 126 State agencies representing 50 States, the District of Columbia, American Samoa, Guam, Puerto Rico, the Virgin Islands, New York City, Louisville, St. Louis, Cincinnati, Cleveland, Toledo, Philadelphia, Pittsburgh, Kansas City and Columbus. The State Tax Agencies are required to maintain a system of standardised records of requests for inspection or disclosure (CFDA undated).

Agreements on Exchange of Tax Information

Luxembourg Parliament passed a bill on *Cooperation among Authorities and Measures to Combat Tax Fraud and Tax Evasion* (a bill no. 5757, enacted into law on 17 December 2008). The main purpose of the new act is to (PriceWaterhouseCoopers 2008):

- Combat tax fraud and tax evasion,
- Clarify and strengthen the legal framework governing cooperation and exchange of information among tax authorities and other government bodies, and
- Lighten the administrative burden for taxpayers.

The law clarifies and strengthens the legal framework governing cooperation and exchange of information among the tax authorities, as well as between tax authorities and other government bodies (e.g., social security authorities) or judicial authorities.

Another example of such efforts is the *Joint Tax Shelter Information Centre (JITSIC)* – a joint effort between the tax bodies of Australia, Canada, China (included recently), the United Kingdom and the United States to combat abusive tax avoidance transactions and broaden activities against cross-border transactions involving tax compliance risk in light of the financial crisis. The JITSIC participants commit to share best practices, identify emerging trends and patterns, identify and curb tax avoidance and shelters and those who promote and invest in them and enhance compliance through 'coordinated and "real time" exchange of tax information'. JITSIC's stated purposes are to (Ernst & Young undated):

a. identify and understand abusive tax schemes;
b. share expertise, best practices, and experience in combating these schemes;
c. exchange information on abusive tax schemes, promoters, and investors; and
d. enable participants to better address these schemes 'without regard to national borders'.

The *Seven Country Working Group on Tax Havens* (Australia, Canada, France, Germany, Japan, the United Kingdom and the United States) is another example of multiple jurisdictions working together to improve each country's capacity to deal with the risks that tax havens pose to their tax systems and to share information on perceived tax abuses – specifically, those arising from the use of tax havens (Ernst & Young undated).

The members bilaterally exchange information at a case and promoter level, share research and information on transactions encounter and strategies adopted, and conduct joint training sessions. One of the group's major initiatives is the issuance of international alerts to its member tax administrations on tax-motivated transactions involving domestic and tax havens.

OECD's Forum on Harmful Tax Practices aims to eliminate harmful tax practices from both OECD member countries and non-member countries (such as tax havens). Members of the forum have agreed to work together, particularly to explore new tools to help detect international non-compliance. Since 2002, the OECD has sponsored the Forum on Tax Administration (FTA), a group consisting of the tax administrators from its 30 member nations plus several other non-member countries. The FTA has promoted dialogue between the tax authorities to identify good tax administration practices and to promote tax enforcement. The FTA's areas of focus include the following (Sullivan & Cromwell LLP, 2009):

- Developing a directory of aggressive tax planning schemes in order to identify trends and countermeasures;
- Examining the roles of tax intermediaries, such as lawyers and accountants, in enabling tax evasion;
- Expanding the 2004 Corporate Governance Guidelines to encourage companies to issue a set of tax principles to guide their tax activities; and
- Improving the training of tax officials, especially on international tax matters.

Recently, developing countries such as India, China and South Korea have also participated for the first time in a formal, multilateral tax information exchange discussion forum, viz., *Leeds Caste Group*. Under this new arrangement, the commissioners of the revenue bodies of Australia, Canada, China, France, Germany, India, Japan, South Korea, the United Kingdom and the United States agreed to meet regularly to consider and discuss issues of global and national tax administration in their respective countries, particularly mutual compliance challenges (Ernst & Young undated).

These coordinated efforts have already resulted in early successes in identifying certain cross-border tax transactions deemed to be of interest by the participating governments. However, exchange of information is not automatic and it is provided upon request (i.e., when the information requested relates to a particular examination, inquiry or investigation). Therefore, it becomes difficult for developing countries to get benefit from information exchange and avoid tax evasion and double taxation. Recently, the UN Committee of Experts on International Cooperation in Tax Matter has proposed a treaty, viz., a treaty process for developing countries, to ensure automatic or spontaneous exchange of information through a multilateral tax treaty (Thuronyi 2009). The information could be provided automatically by financial institutions (on the basis of European Savings Tax Directive).[10] The proposal suggests that the treaty should 'provide a framework for developing countries receiving assistance from developed countries by facilitating exchange of information and by enforcing tax claims'. The proposed multilateral treaty would address the following issues:

- exchange of information;
- administrative cooperation in tax collection;
- non-discrimination;
- residence tie-breaker rule (exclude dual residence for tax purpose); and
- a mutual agreement procedure.

The above highlight the importance and merits of automatic sharing of information and close coordination between the different inter-linked jurisdictions. In the Indian context of GST, this needs to be emphasised since the base for the taxes is the same.

Conservative Options for India

The Discussion Paper on GST put out by the Empowered Committee of State Finance Ministers (Government of India 2009) as well as the response of the Department of Revenue (Government of India undated) to the same present a case for some integration of tax administration across the central government and state governments. These documents emphasise the need for a unified dispute settlement system. One of them even proposes a single advance ruling system. While these are important functions of the total regime, it would appear that there are some other critical functions that need to be looked at as well. It is useful to begin the discussion from the information system.

---

[10] The European Union's Savings Directive (STD), which has since 2005 put in place a working system for multilateral, automatic information exchange (Meinzer 2009).

The information system for the central tax administration, through the way the proposed tax system would be structured, would capture information on all the taxable transactions in the economy. This would suggest that since the state tax departments too would be collecting taxes from the same set of transactions, the same information system should be adequate to capture and reflect this information, unless the central and state departments choose to ask for and capture different levels of detail for the same given set of taxpayers. In this case, it would be suitable to ask for a comprehensive set of information to be provided to one agency instead of requiring two different levels of information capture. This is an important decision in the setting up of the new regime since a large amount of resources would potentially be expended on setting up 30 different information systems, which when taken together would represent 2 completely duplicated systems. At the very least, therefore, it would appear prudent to have one information system that all the tax administrations will have access to.

If it can be accepted that one information system is adequate, then it also follows that the same information system – depending on which agency is organising and maintaining it – should also take up the function of registration and returns filing in addition to data capture for the information system. In other words, these three functions seem closely related to the function of managing and maintaining the information system and it would appear logical to keep them together at one agency. This would make the generation and maintenance of the information system reliable and timely.

Turning to the functions that the discussion paper and the department of revenue mention, a third level of integration would involve a uniform system of dispute settlement and advance ruling, possibly along with a unified taxpayer services unit. The information system as mentioned above along with the services discussed here effectively represent the public face of the tax administrations. If unified across the various tax administrations involved in GST administration, these would considerably reduce the compliance cost for the taxpayer and reduce the duplication of effort for the tax administrators.

If conservation of the efforts of the tax administrators for more useful functions such as audit, survey, inspection, addressing issues of litigation with taxpayers is considered a worthwhile goal, it would be useful to explore the possibility of achieving some integration of the functions as discussed above.

It should be mentioned here that integration of the information system appears a minimum first step in designing the administrative set-up for the new regime. However, even this might be a difficult goal to aim for immediately for two reasons – there appears to exist a basic urge to maintain status quo, given some perceived uncertainty with any regime, and second, the smaller jurisdictions sometimes perceive that the local administration is better poised to capture information on some transactions which are significant locally but might not be significant at the national level. In such cases, the next best alternative to an integrated information system would be for the establishment of two parallel information systems, one for the centre and the other for states, with mandatory cross-verification on a regular and automated basis. Here the key operational words are regular and automated. The Tax Information Exchange System (TINXSYS) by almost becoming a voluntary system failed in its effort to provide timely and regular information for tracking inter-state transactions across states.

In addition, adoption of functional specialisation based scrutiny assessment of taxpayers could reduce compliance as well as administration costs. For example, the central tax authority is dealing with service providers for a long time and they have better understanding to deal with service tax assessees as compared to any state tax administration. Similarly, all state tax administrations are well conversant in dealing with traders/distributors. Therefore, coordination across tax authorities by assigning superiority of decisions taken by one tax authority over other could be mutually beneficial.

References

Ahmad, Ehtisham and Abdulrazaq Al Faris (2010). *Fiscal Reforms in the Middle East: VAT in the Gulf Cooperation Council.* Cheltenham, UK: Edward Elgar.

Catalogue of Federal Domestic Assistance (CFDA) (undated). 'Exchange of Federal Tax Information With State Tax Agencies', http://www.supremelaw.org/rsrc/acta/cfda.htm, last accessed on 11 May 2010.

Cnossen, S. (2008). 'VAT Coordination Issues in the European Union', Commentary on the Mirrlees Review Paper on VAT and Excises, 19 February 2008.

Denison, D. and R.L. Facer II (2005). 'Interstate Tax Coordination: Lessons from the International Fuel Tax Agreement', *National Tax Journal* 58(3): 591–603.

Ernst & Young (undated). *Tax Administration Goes Global: Corporate Tax Departments Confront Complexity, Risks, and Opportunities*, https://eyo-iis-pd.ey.com/drivinggrowth/unprotected/downloads/TaxAdministration.pdf, last accessed on 11 May 2010.

Government of India (2009). 'First Discussion Paper on Goods and Services Tax in India', The Empowered Committee of State Finance Ministries, Government of India, New Delhi 10 November 2009, http://finmin.nic.in/GST/Empowered%20Committee%20of%20SFM%20%20First%20Discussion%20paper.pdf, last accessed on 11 May 2010.

——— (undated). 'Comments of the Department of Revenue (DoR) on the First Discussion Paper on GST', Department of Revenue, Government of India, New Delhi, http://finmin.nic.in/GST/Comments%20of%20DoR%20on%201st%20Discussion%20Paper%20on%20GST.doc – last accessed on 11 May 2010.

Ligthart, J.E. (2007). 'Information Sharing for Consumption Tax Purposes: An Empirical Analysis', *Information Economics and Policy* 19(1): 24–42.

Mann, A.J. (2004). *Are Semi-Autonomous Revenue Authorities the Answer to Tax Administration problems in Developing Countries? A Practical Guide*, The US Agency for International Development (USAID). August 2004.

Meinzer, Markus (2009). 'Tax Information Exchange Arrangements', Tax Justice Network Briefing Paper, http://www.taxjustice.net/cms/upload/pdf/TJN_0903_Exchange_of_Info_Briefing_draft.pdf, last accessed on 11 May 2010.

Organisation for Economic Cooperation and Development (OECD) (2009). *Tax Administration in OECD and Selected Non-OECD Countries: Comparative Information Series (2008)*. Forum on Tax Administration, Centre for Tax Policy and Administration, OECD.

PriceWaterhouseCoopers (2008). *Cooperation among Authorities and Measures to Combat Tax Fraud and Tax Evasion (Bill no. 5757)*. 22 December 2008, http://www.pwc.com/en_LU/lu/tax-consulting/docs/pwc-tax-22122008.pdf – last accessed on 11 May 2010.

Sullivan & Cromwell LLP (2009). *Impact of Multilateral Tax Information Exchange Programs*, 1 July 2009, http://www.sullcrom.com/files/Publication/2be37dd9-0dc6-42c1-a2fc-29b0ea27169a/Presentation/PublicationAttachment/383f8579-5244-43c0-a6e3-2b8481948cf9/SC_Publication_Impact_of_Multilateral_Tax_Information_Exchange_Programs.pdf, last accessed on 11 May 2010.

Thuronyi, V. (2009). 'Tax Treaty Process for Developing Countries', paper presented at the Fifth session of the Committee of Experts on International Cooperation in Tax Matters, Geneva, 19–23 October 2009. United Nations Economic and Social Council, E/C. 18/2009/3, http://www.un.org/ga/search/view_doc.asp?symbol=E/C.18/2009/3&Lang=E, accessed on 25 March 2010.

Treasury Board of Canada Secretariat (TBCS) (undated). 'Policy on the Collection and Remittance of Provincial Sales Taxes (Application of Reciprocal Taxation Agreements and Comprehensive Integrated Tax Coordination Agreements)', http://www.tbs-sct.gc.ca/pol/doc-eng.aspx?id=12198&section=text, last accessed on 11 May 2010.

von Haldenwang, C., A. von Schiller and M. Garcia (2014). 'Tax Collection in Developing Countries – New Evidence on Semi-Autonomous Revenue Agencies (SARAs)', *The Journal of Development Studies* 50(4): 541–555.

9

Goods and Services Tax

Performance and Progress

R. Kavita Rao

After considerable effort by the Goods and Services Tax (GST) council, GST has been ushered into India from 1 July 2017. At the time of writing this chapter, GST has been in operation for over 12 months. The new regime has faced a number of hurdles and has therefore needed some significant changes, spanning changes in rates of tax, changes in the forms and procedures for filing returns and introduction of new compliance-related features like the issue of an e-way bill for the transport of goods from one location to another. This chapter is an attempt to assess the performance of the GST regime in this one year. The economy has been subject to two major shocks in the past two years – the withdrawal of high value currency notes, otherwise referred to demonetisation, and the introduction of GST. Since it is rather early as well as technically difficult to disentangle the effects of these two effects on the economy, in the section titled 'Likely Impact of GST', an attempt is made to identify the kinds of effects change in the indirect tax regime could have on the economy. This is followed by a discussion on the impact of GST on revenues of union and state governments (section titled 'Revenue Performance Under GST'). Finally, with GST bringing with itself a substantially different administration and compliance regime, the final section looks at some of the issues emerging out of the compliance framework for GST. Before exploring these issues, presented below is a brief summary of the key features of the GST regime in place today.

The key features of the GST regime implemented in the country on 1 July 2017 can be summarised as follows:

1. A dual VAT regime covering goods and services: Every transaction of supply of goods and services would be subject to two taxes – a Central GST and a State GST. The tax is designed as a value added tax and it incorporates the feature of input tax credit for taxes paid on purchased goods and services. This represented a big change from the earlier regime where both central and state taxes had access to less than comprehensive tax bases. Centre could not tax sale and purchase of goods while states could not tax services. The new regime therefore meant an expansion in the tax base.

2. Following from the above, while the union government and the state governments have each enacted their own laws and rules, these are following from decisions taken within the GST council. The GST council makes recommendations on the design and structure of the GST regime as well as on the compliance and administration of the regime. In principle, the concerned governments can choose to adopt these recommendations or to adapt them to suit their own needs. This assertion of autonomy, however, might not manifest itself in the near future given the dynamic nature of the tax reform as would be evident in the discussion of the other features of the tax regime.

3. Inter-state transactions in both goods and services as well as imports of goods and services into the country are now subject to IGST (Integrated GST). This meant that on any inter-state transaction, the supplier would charge an IGST (which is equal to the sum of SGST and CGST) and claim input tax credit for IGST, CGST and SGST for purchases towards that supply. The purchasing dealer would charge CGST and SGST on subsequent sales and claim credit for IGST. The IGST is set up as a mechanism to establish a destination-based tax regime without a break in the input tax credit chain. The state tax in this case accrues to the importing state. This is distinct from the earlier regime where the Central Sales Tax (CST) regime established an origin base regime with a cap on the level of tax the state of origin could collect.

4. While the base has been expanded, the coverage is not yet a comprehensive one. Apart from activities and supplies that the Acts could choose to exempt, there are two categories of supplies that are currently beyond the GST regime implemented – one, petrol, diesel, ATF, crude petroleum and natural gas have been kept out of the base for GST. While the constitutional amendment has provided for the inclusion of these goods into the GST regime, the concerned governments have chosen to keep these goods outside the base for GST until the revenues from GST stabilise and productivity is evident. Second, alcoholic beverages for human consumption, electricity and real estate transactions have been kept out of the base for GST – the earlier regimes on these sectors, that is, state excise, electricity duty and stamps and registration duties have not been subsumed into GST.

5. The rates of tax in regime: One of the integral elements of the tax reform process in the last three decades in India has been the gradual rationalisation of the regimes from those containing a large number of tax rates to those with few – two or three – rates. This, it has been argued, reduces the scope for classification disputes and the need for articulating for changes in the rate structure for specific goods and/or for the economy as a whole. In the context of GST, the discussion on number of rates has been fluctuating between three different arguments – few rates to ensure stability in the tax regime, larger number of rates would allow for the policy maker to address the needs of the economy and its population and larger number of rates to ensure acceptability of the regime. Between these arguments, the regime was introduced with five rates, in addition to a few commodity-specific rates. The attempt has been to structure the rates and the classification of the commodities within the rates such that each of the commodities is brought into a rate as close to its rates before the introduction of GST, that is, the rates that would result as a combination of state VATs, CenVAT and service tax. This has meant two things. In the short run, there were some disputes on whether the classification was appropriately done for all supplies and the rates for some supplies had to be changed within the first six months of introduction of the new regime. In the medium term, it is hoped that the number of rate categories would be reduced and the union government reiterates its commitment to such a process. However, it is not yet clear where and when this rationalisation of rates would stabilise.

   a. The rate categories in place at present are: 3 per cent, 5 per cent, 12 per cent, 18 per cent and 28 per cent with additional GST compensation cesses on some selected items.

6. To ease concerns of the states regarding the revenue productivity of the tax regime, the union government has assured the states a minimum rate of growth in revenue of 14 per cent per annum on a base of revenue collections in the year 2015–16. While this structure of determining the needs for compensation is quite different from that in the transition to VAT by the states, the proposal is designed to address the concerns of the states without putting undue pressure on the union government. Given the reduction in the average rate of inflation in the economy, the nominal rates of growth too have reduced. As a result attributing historical growth rates to future years would result in overestimation on the revenue that states need to be compensated for. The new design, however, does have different results for different states. States like Punjab have had low rates of growth and the assurance of 14 per cent would imply augmentation of revenue while states like Bihar and Chhattisgarh might not get the same deal. The cesses have been introduced to raise revenues to compensate the states for any loss of revenue.

While there have been some changes in the GST regime, that is, changes in the rates of tax for some supplies, changes in the regime of tax compliance, gradual introduction of the e-way bill regime, to give a few examples, the basic structure of the regime has not undergone any major change. Two important aspects of the change brought in by the GST regime when compared to the earlier regime are: first, the regime means a comprehensive expansion in the tax base for both the union and the state governments and second, considerable homogenisation of the tax regime across the jurisdictions in the country. This would be an improvement over the earlier regime since it would reduce elements of tax competition among states and provide a relatively stable tax regime in terms of procedures and design of GST.

To discern a measureable impact of the GST regime, it would still be a few years. The data which allow one to draw any unambiguous conclusion on the impact of the change in regime on the economy and its component sectors would become available only in a few years. In the meantime, it is possible to identify some of the channels through which the impact plays itself out and, given the design of the GST regime implemented, to infer about likely impact. The following section explores this aspect in some detail.

Likely Impact of GST

The GST regime is expected to bring in significant changes in the functioning of the economy – these changes, some have argued, would contribute up to 1.5 per cent to GDP. While the quantification of the gains is an interesting intellectual exercise, it is more important to ask where and how these gains are expected to be realised. There are broadly six channels through which the change in the tax regime can bring about increase in economic activity in the economy.

i. A shift to GST from the present regime of indirect taxes is expected to reduce the amount of cascading in the tax regime. Since cascading could result in some price build-up, a reduction in cascading can imply a reduction in the final price. The former could imply some expansion in demand, if demand is sensitive to the changes in prices. This could have implications for exports as well, if exports from India are sensitive to changes in prices.

ii. If the benefits of reduction in cascading are not passed on in the form of lower prices, it should result in an increase in the profits of sectors where these gains are visible. This in turn should attract investments into these sectors.

iii. One major change in the GST regime is the elimination of CST for commodities under GST. Apart from the effect through a lower level of cascading, the removal of CST can have two other kinds of effects. First, it has been argued that the CST regime encourages fragmentation of economic activities in the country – setting up branches in different states allowed companies to send goods on consignment transfer which were not subject to CST. While these transactions did suffer some taxes, since the exporting states denied part of the input tax credit attributable to these transactions, the overall tax liability could be lower. With the elimination of CST, this distortion is eliminated and this could generate incentives for setting fewer and larger factories, thereby allowing companies to benefit from economies of scale. Second, it could allow for the redesign of the supply chain with fewer, larger warehouses instead of having one in each state. These would mean new investments both in production capacities and in redesigning supply chain. With economies of scale, it is argued that the cost of production of goods/services would be lower, which if passed on could further stimulate demand.

iv. The GST regime is also expected to eliminate the incentive regimes associated with the erstwhile indirect tax regimes, whether in the form of area-based exemptions or in the form of incentives to specific sectors. Through these incentives, governments have attempted to influence the choice of investment location and/ or the sector for investment. These initiatives can be viewed in two ways: first, that they bring investment into areas where investment was not forthcoming and hence contributing to better regional distribution of economic activity. The alternative way of looking at these incentives is to recognise the fact that the incentives are not reaching certain locations/sectors is evidence of commercial non-viability of these activities when compared to alternatives available within the economy. By providing these incentives, one is therefore reducing the returns to investment in the economy. By eliminating these incentives, the distortions to investment decisions resulting from these incentives will be eliminated and hence investment would be more productive and could in turn attract more investment.

v. Rationalising of the rates of tax in the new regime, with some commodities/ activities benefiting from lower rates of tax compared to the earlier regime, is expected to stimulate economic activity in these sectors. In the earlier regime, the manufacturing sector faced higher taxes when compared to agriculture and services. With rationalisation of the rates of tax, these differences should be reduced, thereby providing a level playing field and possibly attracting more investment into manufacturing.

vi. Apart from the effects that stimulate economic activity, GST could bring in business from the informal sector to the formal sector. These could be activities which are not reporting their transactions for taxes in the present regime.

While conceptually, all of the above factors could be at work in the economy subsequent to the introduction of GST, it would be useful to temper our expectations by examining the likelihood of each of these channels playing out.

While the first channel focuses primarily on the demand side, the other channels work through the supply side. The demand side channel depends on the prices being lowered to pass on the benefits from lower cascading to the consumer. This process could be realised with or without the government's intervention in the course of a few months. Experience in other countries suggests that the initial spurt in prices with an introduction of a VAT regime dissipates within a few months. In other words, given time, this channel should be realised.

Turning to the other three channels, these are all based on supply side. At the present juncture in India, these channels might be difficult to activate immediately for a number of reasons. First, from available information, it appears that many sectors in the economy are operating at excess capacity, suggesting that expansion in capacity might not be high on priorities. Further, the mounting non-performing assets (NPAs) and the stress on the balance sheets of corporate India too might suggest that finding resources for investment in the short run might be a problem for the potentially large investors. And finally, turning to the supply chain re-engineering, it is likely that efforts on this front might be related to the perceived quality of infrastructure on the alternative designs. For instance, if a company chooses to locate a central warehouse in central India, would it find adequate road infrastructure to connect with the markets it intends to supply to. Further, if warehousing requires refrigeration, the choice of location could be constrained by the availability of adequate, reliable power supply. In other words, the benefits from the supply channels might not be stimulated immediately upon the introduction of GST. These benefits might be realised a few years into the introduction of the new regime.

The effect of rates of tax on the economy is not expected to be realised in the short run, since the proposed structure of taxes is being designed to closely mimic the rates that exist at present. The rationale for this choice of rate structures is to ensure that there is no major clamour for changes in the rates of tax thereby delaying the implementation of the new regime. This, however, means that boost to the economy from rate rationalisation too might have to wait until the rationalisation which can be undertaken after the taxpayers and the governments settle into the GST system.

Turning to the impact of elimination of industrial incentives, it may be mentioned that governments might choose to replace the existing tax-based incentives with incentives through other fiscal instruments such as explicit subsidies or transfers. In this case, these benefits might not be realised.

Finally, the formalisation of the informal sector is an effect that is widely expected to be realised rather quickly. This effect depends on the agents in the informal sector perceiving costs to remaining informal and benefits to moving to the formal sector. Invoice-wise data capture is one of the features that is expected to induce such a movement. Informal sector could be viewed in two ways: first, those agents who would like to be part of the formal value added networks and, second, those who operate only within the informal segment – buying from and selling to the informal economy. The former would benefit from moving to the formal sector while the latter might need more persuasion.

Revenue Performance under GST

The trends of revenue in the last ten months with respect to GST are summarised in Figure 9.1. The total revenue collections (including revenue from CGST, SGST, IGST and cess) has been fluctuating somewhat recording a maximum of over Rs 1 lakh crore in April 2018 and a minimum of a little over Rs 83,000 crore in November 2017. The shares of the four components in total revenue on average are about 51 per cent contributed by IGST, 23 per cent by SGST, 8 per cent by cess and the balance by CGST.

It is useful to understand what IGST is and why it contributes the maximum amount to revenue collections. IGST is applicable on inter-state transactions as well as on imports into the country. These transactions include those between

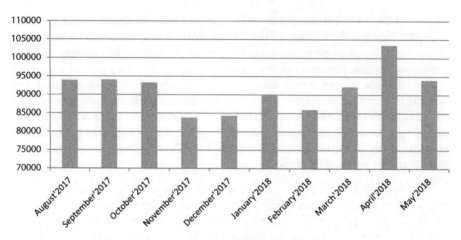

Figure 9.1   Monthly GST Revenue Collection (Rs Crore)
Source: Compiled by author from the press releases of GOI.

two registered entities as well as supplies to unregistered purchasers. In case the purchaser is a registered GST dealer, she can claim credit for the IGST paid against subsequent taxes collected. In cases where the purchaser is not registered under GST, there would be no claim for input tax credit and such balances would be distributed between the centre and states on a formulaic basis. In other words, IGST represents the value of supplies in transit as well as a fraction of supplies to final users. It is therefore possible that the IGST would contribute a larger share of the total revenue collections, especially in the initial period of the introduction of GST.

IGST, unlike CGST and SGST, is not a head under which revenue can be booked permanently. Revenue reported under IGST needs to be allocated to union and state governments at a suitable time. In other words, as and when the revenues are disbursed from this head, the balances should drop to zero in principle. IGST can be levied on two kinds of transactions:

1. B-to-C transactions: In the case of supplies where the identity and location of the purchaser needs to be ascertained by the supplier in the normal course of business, the transaction will be considered an inter-state transactions and be subject to IGST. The revenues from such transactions will be distributed between the centre and the states.

2. B-to-B transactions: In such transactions the revenue under IGST is akin to a bank balance which will be withdrawn subsequently. In cases where the credit is claimed within the financial year, the balances within the IGST collections would be depleted to the extent of credit claimed and transferred to the respective governments. For the remaining balances, there are two ways of viewing the accumulating balances: first, the tax rates have been set up with CGST = SGST for all commodities, the balances can be divided equally between the union and state governments. Any differences in the shares that arise when the credit is claimed

can be adjusted in subsequent periods. Second, since the union government is administering the IGST and is therefore answerable for the credit to be provided, the revenue can be appropriated by the union government and the states can be assigned their shares when the credit is claimed.

The union government has chosen to follow the second approach at the end of the financial year 2017–18. This approach helped the union government to balance its budget but it can have some implications for the revenue accrual in the next financial year. As discussed, the IGST is the amount of unutilised credit in the system. With the balances at the end of the financial year being credited to the union government, the temporal assignment of the revenue between the union and the states has been altered, implying thereby that in 2018–19, the union government would need to pay out more to the states than it receives by way of IGST revenue. This would be an important concern if the revenues from IGST in 2018–19 do turn out to be less than the balances at the end of 2017–18, as budgeted in 2018–19.

An important question is whether the revenues generated within GST are adequate to replace the taxes subsumed into GST. To begin with the union government, Figure 9.2 shows the monthly revenue from indirect taxes.[1] Since revenue tends

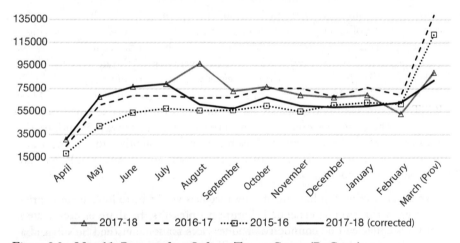

Figure 9.2   Monthly Revenue from Indirect Taxes – Centre (Rs Crore)
Source: Based on Monthly Accounts of the Controller General of Accounts (CGA).

---

[1] The revenue reported here includes Union Excise Duty, Service Tax and Customs Duty for the period before introduction of GST and for the period after the introduction of GST, revenues from CGST, UTGST and IGST. Revenue from GST compensation cess have not been added since the revenue is to be used for compensating the states for any loss of revenue and is ring-fenced. The revenues reported under CGST relate the revenues that finally accrue to the union government and not just collections under CGST. Similarly, since the union government has chosen to report all residual IGST revenue as its revenue, this too is added.

to fluctuate across months in any tax jurisdiction, attempting month-on-month comparisons would yield incorrect implications. Therefore in the graph, the monthly comparisons have been presented. In addition, a series called 2017–18 (corrected) is presented – since IGST would in principle accrue equally to the union and the states, only half of the collections are added to the union.

The graph suggests that the revenue collections after the introduction of GST did pick up in August but have not maintained the tempo since. In most of the months since, the revenue attributable to the union government has been lower than that in the preceding year. In February, the collections are in fact lower than those in 2015–16 owing to a net drawing down of the balances in IGST. These would suggest that the revenue from GST has not kept pace with the nominal growth in GDP.

The trends in the corrected series is more disturbing – for almost the entire period, the revenues for 2017–18 have remained below those for 2016–17. This constructed series provides the counterfactual scenario – one where the IGST revenue is divided equally between the union and the states. This series suggests that the revenue performance of GST has been less than par at least for the union government.

Turning to the states, details of revenue subsumed into GST as compared to the revenue from GST are not available as yet. However, given that the union government has underwritten any losses to states, where loss has been defined as a rate of growth of revenue less than 14 per cent per annum, one way of looking at revenue performance for states would be to see whether 14 per cent growth would be adequate for all states. Figure 9.3 shows the average growth rate over the period 2010–11 to 2015–16 for some of the states as well as the revenue reported for the reference year 2015–16. The figure suggests that a rate of growth of revenue of 14 per cent per annum would be generous and higher than the historical growth rate for any states. There are, however, a few exceptions – from this graph, it appears that Andhra Pradesh,[2] West Bengal and Tamil Nadu consistently had higher rates of growth. In other words, the assurance by the union government might not have been comforting enough.

An alternative way of looking at state revenues would be to look at the share of the states in the revenue generated. Figure 9.4 presents the share of each state in total taxes collected on commodities and services for some of the states in India.[3] In order to infer about the impact of GST on state revenues, the figure provides shares for 2016–17 and 2017–18. Bihar, Gujarat, Haryana, Jharkhand, Maharashtra, Punjab and Telangana show an increase in shares while Assam, Karnataka, Madhya Pradesh, Tamil Nadu, Uttar Pradesh and West Bengal show a decline in shares.[4]

---

[2] Here Andhra Pradesh refers to the erstwhile Andhra Pradesh.

[3] The data for Arunachal Pradesh, Manipur, Meghalaya, Sikkim and Tripura were not available at the time of completion of the draft.

[4] This analysis based on revised estimates from budget data of state governments.

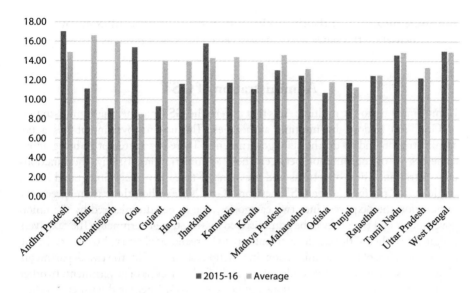

Figure 9.3   Rate of Growth of Revenue for State VAT
Source: Compiled from Finance Accounts of respective State Governments.

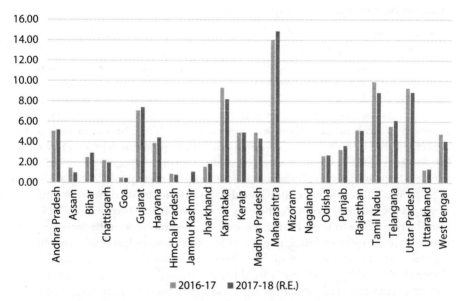

Figure 9.4   Change in Share of Total Taxes on Commodities and Services
Source: Based on budget documents of state governments.

The figure suggests that the change has not affected all states uniformly in spite of the compensation the states would have received for loss of revenue.

Administration of GST

Complementary to the multiple Acts that govern the GST regime, the administration of GST too is done by multiple authorities. The union government has a tax administration and so do the state governments. There is an attempt to bring about some degree of coordination between these administrations. Briefly, the functions of registration, filing of returns and payment of taxes have been integrated into a single online platform – the GST network (GSTN). Further, there is an agreement to partition the taxpayers into two categories, one to be administered by the union government and the other to be administered by the state government. The taxpayers assigned to either of the tax departments are to be reallocated every three years. In the actual operation of tax administration, in functions such as audit, the two departments plan to work separately, while undertaking audit for both levels of government. In other words, while the tax administrations are not completely integrated with each other, there are a number of elements of cooperation or coordination, especially keeping the taxpayer's interest in mind – so as to reduce the need for interface with two tax departments.

Number of Taxpayers – Filing of Returns

With the introduction of GST, the number of taxpayers has increased significantly from 66 lakh to over 1 crore. This could be for a few different reasons. To begin with, the expected impact of GST would be an increase in formalisation in the economy, resulting in more businesses choosing to register for GST. Quite apart from this, the design of GST itself would have brought in more registrations – GST is organised by states as the jurisdiction. Businesses in the country which proposed to work in more than one state needed to be registered in each of the concerned states. In the case of sale of goods, this regime existed even prior to the introduction of GST, but in services, there was a change in regime. Services in the earlier regime were taxed by the union government and required a single national registration. This could have contributed to an immediate increase in the number of taxpayers. A third reason for increase in the number of taxpayers could be the introduction of the 'reverse charge mechanism'. The mechanism by increasing the cost of purchasing from unregistered entities could have induced such suppliers to register with the tax department. This, however, is not the same as formalisation since value added by the tax payer would have been reflected in the turnover of the purchaser (since no credit would have been available for such purchases). Therefore, while there has been a significant increase in the number of taxpayers registered with the tax regime it is not yet clear how much of this contributes to or is a result of the formalisation of the economy.

Table 9.1   State of Filing GST Returns

	Number of taxpayers	Returns filed by due date (%)	Total returns filed (%)
July '17	6,647,581	57.69	96.10
Aug '17	7,370,102	36.98	92.97
Sep '17	7,823,806	50.29	90.87
Oct '17	7,721,075	56.58	87.78
Nov '17	7,957,204	61.74	85.02
Dec '17	81,22,425	66.81	83.08
Jan '18	83,22,611	64.81	80.44
Feb '18	85,27,127	63.93	76.96
Mar '18	87,15,163	62.63	64.61

Source: http://pib.nic.in/newsite/PrintRelease.aspx?relid=178962 (last accessed on 15 January 2019).

Moving forward from the number of returns filed, Table 9.1 shows that there is an increase in the average number of returns filed before due date, but the number continues to be less than 70 per cent of the returns due to be filed. The highest level achieved was 66.8 per cent in December 2017. It is, however, reassuring that if one includes the returns filed after the due date, the compliance level for the first three months is over 90 per cent. This suggests two things: one, the process of return filing is perhaps somewhat cumbersome leading to difficulties in filing returns and, second, the process of learning to comply with the requirements of the tax regime has resulted in improvements in the level of compliance.

It is interesting to explore whether the increase in the number of taxpayers is reasonably uniform across states or not. Information available for the month of January 2018 suggests that there is considerable variation across states in the percentage increase in the number of registered taxpayers.[5] The percentage increase in the number of taxpayers varies from 21 per cent to 66 per cent of the number of taxpayers who were migrated into the GSTN. Special category states seem to have had a higher increase in the number of taxpayers on average when compared to the general category states. Even within the general category states, there are a few which experienced an increase of over 40 per cent – Gujarat, Uttar Pradesh, West Bengal, Jharkhand and Bihar. This suggests that the GST regime did bring in considerable change in the taxpayer base in many states across the country. Turning to the aspect of compliance, the number of returns filed too varies considerably across states from a minimum 31 per cent to a maximum of 83 per cent of the total numbers required to be filed in the month.

Figure 9.5 presents the relation between registration and filing of returns. The figure suggests that across states, there appears to be a negative relation between

---

[5] Documentation of the taxpayers and returns filed by states are taken from the annexure to the following press release about revenue realised during the month of February 2018. See http://pib.nic.in/newsite/PrintRelease.aspx?relid=176823 (last accessed on 15 January 2019).

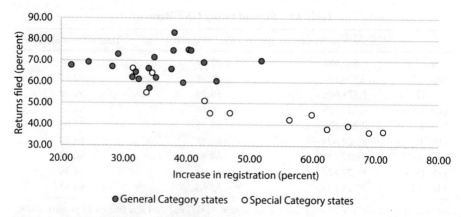

Figure 9.5   Registration and Filing of Returns
Source: Based on press releases of GST Council.

increase in the number of taxpayers and the percentage of taxpayers who filed returns to comply with the GST regime. In other words, states which experienced relatively higher increase in the number of registered taxpayers did not see an equally high share of returns filed. This seems to be the case more for special category states than for general category states.

To ask whether the number of taxpayers has effectively increased under GST, one can look into the ratio of returns filed to the number of taxpayers brought in from the earlier regime. Here too one can find considerable variation as shown in Figure 9.6. Punjab, Gujarat, Haryana, Delhi, West Bengal and Jharkhand have received more returns than the taxpayers they entered into the GST regime with. The number of returns in the case of Chhattisgarh, Assam and Nagaland, on the other hand, is barely

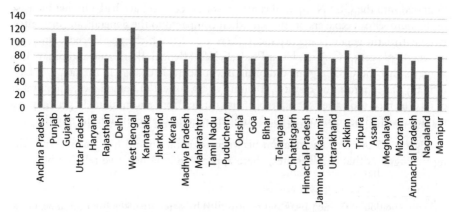

Figure 9.6   Returns Filed as Proportion of Pre-existing Taxpayers
Source: Based on press releases of GST Council.

60 per cent of the number of taxpayers they brought into the GST regime. Since the administrations as well as taxpayers are just settling into the GST regime, clearly one should not be attributing the differences to differences in tax administration, and so on. It is, therefore, important to ask what causes these differences and whether there are factors beyond the control of taxpayers which could be contributing to the differences in compliance, such as stable access to internet for instance.

Here it is important to discuss briefly about the compliance strategies built into the GST regime and what role they might play in improving compliance in the regime. The following sub-section explores this aspect.

Compliance and Its Impact

The GST regime is expected to encourage voluntary self-compliance for a number of reasons. Under the GST regime, as under previous VAT and CenVAT regimes, the taxpayer is allowed to claim credit for any input taxes paid. This in effect means that the tax paid by a taxpayer is a fraction of the tax she collects on her sales and this is expected to encourage the taxpayers to seek compliance. In comparison to the earlier regime, the GST regime is expected to be more effective in encouraging self-compliance since both for central taxes and for state taxes, the range of activities/transactions for which the taxpayer can claim credit has been expanded as a result of the expansion in base. In addition to this feature, the GST regime has sought to augment the inbuilt incentives of the VAT regime with three specific measures:

1. Transaction-wise reporting on purchases and sales: The system of compliance under GST has been set up to collect information on all sales and purchases by registered GST taxpayers. Registered GST taxpayers are required to file a documentation of all transactions of supply of goods and services along with details of the purchaser. The purchaser can claim input tax credit only for transactions which the supplier has uploaded. This system has been modified over the course of the last one year since the introduction of GST without changing the basic essence of it. One of the implications of this system is effectively transforming the GST regime from one which encouraged voluntary compliance to that which enforced compliance. This initiative can have a perverse consequence as well – taxpayers might be encouraged to have a discussion (supplier and purchaser) – to ensure that they are on the same page so far as compliance is concerned. In other words, it is possible, that the tax regime would reduce the unorganised tax evasion but encourage more organised evasion which would not get reflected in the returns and documentation filed by the taxpayers.

2. Reverse charge mechanism: taxpayers in the GST regime are of two kinds – the registered GST taxpayer and a taxpayer who follows the compounding scheme. While a registered tax payer can claim input tax credit, the latter cannot. If the registered taxpayer chooses to source supplies from an unregistered entity or from a taxpayer following the compounding scheme, the law requires the purchaser

to record the transaction and assess and pay tax on it before claiming input tax credit. In other words, instead of the seller charging tax on supply, the buyer is expected to pay tax. This provision has been introduced with two potential objectives: first, it would help identify suppliers who have not yet registered as GST taxpayers and check whether they have crossed the threshold for registration by cumulating information on sales across different buyers. Second, for the buyers, increasing cost of compliance for purchases from the informal or unorganised sector would disincentivise these purchases and therefore encourage hitherto unregistered entities to become part of the tax system by registering. It could also result in the delinking of some of the links between the formal and the informal economy.

3. E-way bill system: prior to the introduction of the GST, transportation of goods from one premise to another required accompanying documentation called waybills. In addition to these, in the case of inter-state transactions, the transactions needed to be backed by a c-form or an f-form to comply with the CST Act. With the introduction of GST, since CST has been replaced with IGST, the documentation of these transactions too underwent a change. The GST laws/rules require that any goods of value more than Rs 50,000 for a distance exceeding 10 kilometres, the transporter needs to carry an 'e-waybill' or an electronic waybill. The e-waybill can be generated by the supplier, purchaser or the transporter from the designated website upon providing information about the goods being transported, the details of the supplier, the purchaser as well as those of the transporter/vehicle. This compliance process was introduced to create documentation which could be monitored while the goods were being transported, so as to prevent undocumented sales of goods from taking place. Effective implementation of an e-waybill, however, would require monitoring of goods being transported on road. This could then create a significant interface between the tax department and the taxpayer, which could result in a subversion in the system of compliance.

The intensity of compliance requirements can have differential effects on the taxpayers. The formal sector in the economy is expected to gain from the regime with a reduction in the interface with tax administration – online filing of documentation and the elimination of need for documents to be issued by tax departments would aid this segment of the economy in growing or benefiting from the tax regime. On the other hand, for those who operate in the informal sector, the effect can be mixed. In the informal sector, there could be agents with smaller scale of operations, including those who supply to the formal sector as a part of the supply chain or who procure from the formal sector or finally those who procure from other informal units and supply to unregistered purchasers and consumers. While the former two would be encouraged to become a part of the formal economy, the latter set, that is, those who procure from the formal sector but sell to informal sector, might continue to remain in the informal sector. In the absence of formalisation, agents who hitherto supplied to the formal sector might actually be worse off and might be replaced by supplies from other players in the formal sector. In other words, while the GST regime seeks to increase formalisation in the economy, it might discourage linkages between the formal and informal economy. For instance, a supplier to the formal sector who has turnover less than the threshold required for registration under GST might be required to register and comply with GST if her business model is to remain unaltered. If the cost of compliance is perceived to be high, these units might have to move out of the formal chain. In adopting this strategy, therefore, two different forces have been set in motion, one pushing for formalisation and the other pushing for informalisation. It is far from clear which force would dominate.

Conclusion

Impact of GST and What Might Happen

R. Kavita Rao *and* Sacchidananda Mukherjee

The goods and services tax (GST) has been presented as the major tax reform for the Indian economy. It is therefore of importance to examine the impact it has had on the economy, as well as on the citizens of the economy. There are three broad categories of evidence to look at:

1. The economy
2. Tax administration/compliance
3. Revenues of various governments

The impact on revenues of various governments has been examined at some length in Chapter 9. Hence this chapter will look into some of the remaining aspects and present some concluding observations.

Impact of GST on Economic Growth and Inflation

One of the long-term objectives of introducing GST is that it will reduce the extent of hidden and embedded taxes in the system and thereby create opportunities for investment in order to capitalise on the altered tax regime. The change to GST as a predominant indirect tax was expected to increase gross domestic product (GDP) and reduce inflation. International experience shows that GDP growth falls after introduction of GST but it recovers after two—three quarters and, conversely, inflation rises in the initial quarters before it declines (The Treasury, Australian Government 2003). While it is barely four quarters since the introduction of GST in

India and hence the evidence of the reversal of the initial trends might not be visible yet, it would be interesting to identify the trends so far.

Impact on Overall Growth

Year-to-year growth rate of gross value added (GVA) at basic prices (2011–12 series, at constant prices) shows that growth rate was falling since Q4 of 2015–16 and it was 5.6 per cent at Q1 of 2017–18. The introduction of GST on 1 July 2017 lifts the growth rate of GVA as evident in Figure C.1. However, the average growth rate during 2017–18 (6.4 per cent) is lower than that achieved in 2015–16 (8.1 per cent) and 2016–17 (7.1 per cent). In drawing conclusions about the impact of GST on GVA from these numbers, it should be borne in mind that seven months prior to the introduction of GST, the economy received a shock in the form of withdrawal of high denomination notes. This shock is seen to have reduced the growth rate of the economy at least in the two quarters prior to the date of introduction of GST, resulting in a lower base and possibly a higher rate of growth in the period since. It can, however, be stated with full confidence that with the introduction of GST, the rate of growth of the economy has not recorded a sharp decline. In fact, it perhaps continued its recovery from the shock of withdrawal of high value currency notes.

Decomposing Impact by Components of Demand

The largest component of GDP when computed from the expenditure side is private final consumption expenditure (PFCE). It accounts for over 50 per cent of GDP in any given year – average share of PFCE in GDP was 56 per cent during 2012–18. This component seems to have been adversely affected after the introduction of GST: the average (year-to-year) rate of growth has gone down after

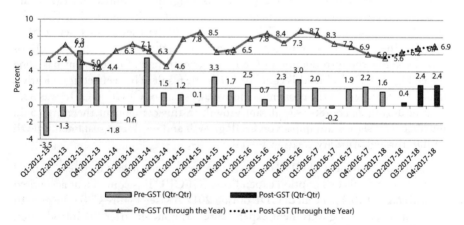

Figure C.1   Growth Rate of GVA at Basic Prices (2011–12 Series, Constant Prices)
Source: Based on the Economic and Political Weekly Research Foundation (EPWRF) India time series database.

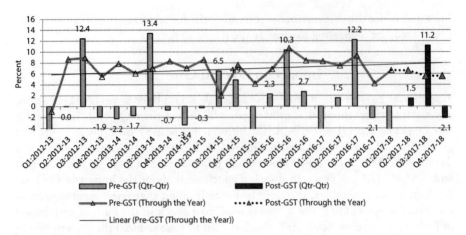

Figure C.2   Growth Rate of Private Final Consumption Expenditure (2011–12 Series, Constant Prices)
Source: Based on the EPWRF India time series database.

the introduction of GST (see Figure C.2). In other words, the pre-GST average growth rate was higher than the post-GST average growth rate. This observation has two implications: first, it was not private consumption expenditure which lifted the growth rate of GVA and, second, the increase in demand is not directly contributing to incomes earned for consumers in the economy. The lower growth in PFCE when compared to GDP is reflected in the marginal decline in share of PFCE in GDP from 61.4 per cent during Q3 (2016–17) to Q1 (2017–18) to 61.1 per cent during Q2 (2017–18) to Q4 (2017–18).

The second component of GDP which has a significant impact on the future growth in the economy is investment or gross fixed capital formation (GFCF). Growth rate (year-to-year) of GFCF reached the highest level (15.9 per cent) in Q1 of 2016–17. Thereafter it kept falling and reached 1.6 per cent in Q1 of 2017–18. After the introduction of GST, the growth rate of investment has gone up (see Figure C.3). While this could be partly the result of base effect, it is clearly a sign of a turnaround in the economy. The average share of GFCF in GDP was 32.2 per cent during 2012–18; a significant growth in this component therefore could contribute to a significant impact on GDP growth and result in a sustained growth in GDP through capacity creation as well.

The third component of GDP over which governments have a degree of control is government final consumption expenditure (GFCE). This component accounted for an average of 10.4 per cent of GDP during 2012–18 (see Figure C.4). The growth rate (year-to-year) of government expenditure has gone up after the introduction of GST. While GFCE is a useful instrument to support growth in the economy, increase in the growth of GFCE is constrained by commitments to fiscal correction and by the government's ability to raise additional resources by way of tax or non-tax

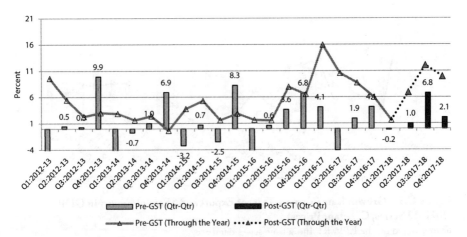

Figure C.3 Growth Rate of Gross Fixed Capital Formation (2011–12 Series, Constant Prices)
Source: Based on the EPWRF India time series database.

revenue. The growth in this component therefore cannot be attributed to corrections to the economy as a result of introduction of GST.

Another component of GDP is export of goods and services. This component contributes to the demand for Indian products while at the same time, since exports are zero-rated under GST, an increase in demand does not contribute to revenues. On the contrary, with the introduction of GST, if the system of input tax credit gets more streamlined, then this sector is expected to get more relief from embedded taxes and therefore could become more competitive. In other words, a well-designed GST should result in an increase in the growth of exports. The evidence here suggests that

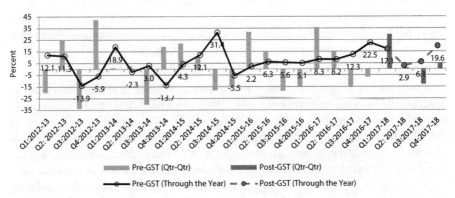

Figure C.4 Growth Rate of Government Final Consumption Expenditure (2011–12 Series, Constant Prices)
Source: Based on the EPWRF India time series database.

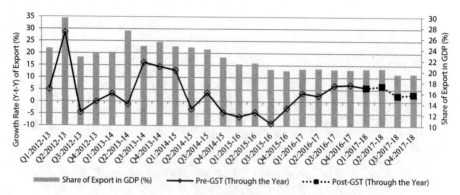

Figure C.5   Growth Rate (Year-to-Year) of Export and Share of Export in GDP (2011–12 Series, Constant Prices)
Source: Based on the EPWRF India time series database.

immediately after the introduction of GST, export improved marginally and thereafter it fell and remained stagnant (Figure C.5). This could be a result of non-domestic factors such as a weak international demand. The trends do suggest that so far, exports have not been the source of expanded demand for Indian goods and services and therefore for the higher growth in GDP post introduction of GST in India.

Finally, imports provide an alternative mechanism to satisfy domestic demand and therefore faster growth in imports implicitly results in slower growth of GDP. With the introduction of GST, a consistent countervailing duty on imports is being imposed which is equivalent to the tax faced by domestic suppliers. This should have resulted for most sectors in better protection from competition from imports and hence a decline in imports. Evidence suggests that this is actually observed – growth rate (year-to-year) of import fell immediately after the introduction of GST (in Q2 of 2017–18). Since Q3 of 2017–18, there is a marginal increase in the growth rate of import. The ratio of import to GDP has been hovering around 20–25 per cent since Q4 of 2015–16 (see Figure C.6). The increase in growth in imports could be a result of rising crude petroleum prices in the world markets. This trend, however, does neutralise some of the gains evident since the introduction of GST.

Inventory has a significant impact on revenue collections in the economy: tax departments in value-added tax regimes collect taxes not just on final consumption but in the interim on stocks held as well. Higher level of stocks held therefore results in higher tax collections. Further, higher stocks can also be considered an indication of confidence in the economy. In the context of a change from the earlier regime to GST, the incentives to hold stocks might have been altered. For instance, in a regime where taxes on intermediate goods are kept low so as to reduce the possibility of a refund in taxes, the embedded taxes in stocks too would be low. On the other hand, stocks face higher tax liability under GST - because Central Sales Tax (CST) on inter-state transactions has been replaced by integrated GST (IGST), where IGST

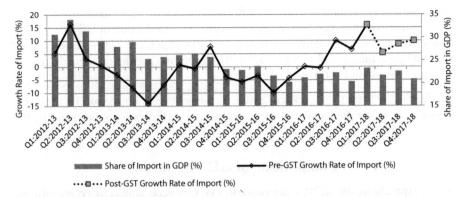

Figure C.6 Growth Rate (Year-to-Year) of Import and Share of Import in GDP (2011–12 Series, Constant Prices)
Source: Based on the EPWRF India time series database.

rates are higher than CST rate.[1] To examine whether this change resulting from the introduction of GST has had the expected impact, one can look at the trends in changes in stocks (Figure C.7). The figure shows that a dramatic fall in inventory has happened since the beginning of financial year 2016–17. The difference in average quarterly stock between 2014–16 and 2016–18 is Rs 39,865 crores or 1.57 per cent of GDP. While the decline in stocks pre-dates introduction of GST, it is possibly one of the factors that contributed to the decline. In anticipation of the introduction of GST, there was a considerable discussion on decisions to destock, given the uncertainties regarding transitional provisions. Other factors too could have contributed to the significant realignment in the stock holding patterns, especially noting the fact that

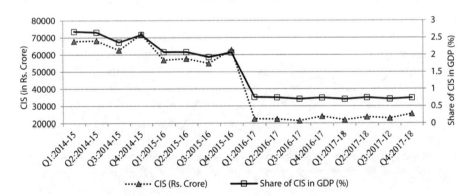

Figure C.7 Change in Stock (CIS) (2011–12 Series, Constant Prices)
Source: Based on the EPWRF India time series database.

---

[1] Moreover, in the CST regime inter-state consignment/ branch transfers were exempted from CST liability. In the GST regime, these transactions attract IGST.

the pattern has not changed in any significant manner subsequent to the introduction of GST. For instance, changes in tax rates after the introduction of GST could also result in uneasiness in holding stocks, especially in high taxed commodities, since a decline in the rates could result in difficulties in recovering the taxes paid through the input tax credit (ITC) mechanism.

The fall in inventory level will result in a level (scale) correction in the GST revenue collection. Perhaps this aspect of revenue shortfall was not perceived by the policy makers earlier.

Composition of GDP by Sectors

From expenditure on GDP, if we move to GVA by economic activity, we will see that the growth rates of manufacturing and trade, hotels, transport, and others have stabilised from the earlier trend of a systemic decline. For manufacturing, the growth rate was falling since Q3 of 2015–16 and for trade and others the growth rate was falling since Q4 of 2015–16 (see Figure C.8). In the period after the introduction of GST, the growth rates have stabilised above 8 per cent for trade and over 6 per cent for manufacturing.

Impact on Inflation

After the introduction of GST, inflation based on the wholesale price index (2011–12 = 100) remained stable (see Figure C.9). Even inflation based on the consumer price index (2012=100) (rural and urban combined) also remained stable, after an immediate jump from 2.2 per cent in Q1 of 2017–18 to 3 per cent in Q2 of 2017–18 (see Figure C.10). In fact, in comparison to the earlier trends, the volatility in prices is markedly lower in the period since the introduction of GST.

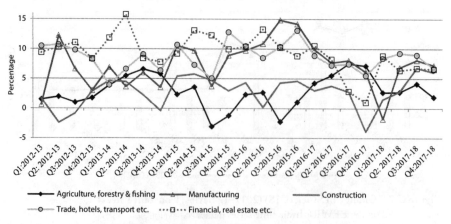

Figure C.8   Growth Rate (Year-to-Year) of Major Sectors of the Economy*
Source: Based on the EPWRF India time series database.
Note: *by their share in GDP.

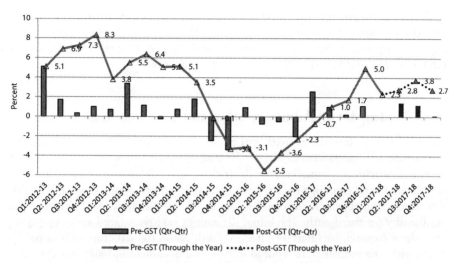

Figure C.9   Inflation Based on Wholesale Price Index (WPI) (Base 2011–12 = 100)
Source: Based on the EPWRF India time series database.

CPI inflation increased from 2.2 per cent in Q1 of 2017–18 to 3 per cent in Q2 of 2017–18 and 4.6 per cent in Q3 of 2017–18, and thereafter it remains stable at 4.6 per cent (Figure C.10).

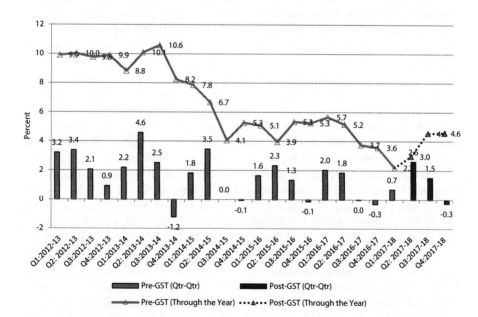

Figure C.10   Inflation Based on Consumer Price Index–Combined (Base 2012 = 100)
Source: Based on the EPWRF India time series database.

The trends in growth and inflation in India seem to be somewhat different from the observed general international experience. While it would be still early to read anything substantial into these trends, it would appear that the introduction of GST has not caused a major disruption in the economy.

Impact on Administration and Tax Compliance

The regime was introduced with rather onerous compliance requirements. All registered GST dealers were required to file three returns every month – one declaring details of individual transactions of sale, the second, which would be partially auto-populated, would contain a declaration of the transactions of purchase and, finally, a third document which summarises the sales and purchases and declared the tax liability for the month. The initial difficulties taxpayers faced with complying with these requirements have resulted in a rethink on the structure of returns. To begin with, the returns were reduced to two, one documenting sales and the other summarising all transactions to arrive at the tax liability due. It was proposed that this format was temporary and would undergo some more changes in times to come. There were a series of changes in the requirements to file returns and in the input tax credit rules as well. In addition, some provisions have been added while others have been discontinued. For instance, the law had provision for reverse-charge mechanism for purchases made by registered sellers from unregistered entities. This provision has been deferred till 30 September 2018. On the other hand, a provision for mandatory generation of e-way bills for transport of goods beyond a distance of 10 kilometres was introduced to monitor movement of goods and the corresponding payment of tax. These changes reflect the efforts to streamline the procedures taking into account the concerns of both taxpayers and the tax administration. This evolutionary process also means that the regime would take some more time to stabilise, in turn suggesting that the taxpayers would continue to face changes in forms of compliance. In this evolving scenario, to understand the impact of the regime on taxpayers, one can look at some of the evidence available. Apart from the level of compliance as reflected in the number of taxpayers as discussed in the last chapter, it is possible to look at the mirror image of this statistic, that is, the number of late filers and the cost they paid via late fee. The following table presents available information on late filing and late fees. In the initial months after the introduction of GST, late fee was waived as a mechanism for taxpayers to acclimatise with the new regime. In the subsequent months however, late filing was to be associated with a late fee. Looking at the numbers in Table C.1, it appears that the number of late filers per month has reduced, and the amount they were paying in the form of late fee has increased. The average late fee has increased from Rs 100 in September 2017 to over Rs 800 in February 2018. This does suggest that while compliance is picking up, the percentage of returns which are filed late has declined from over 60 per cent in August 2017 to a little over 16 per cent in February 2018 – there are perhaps some difficulties with complying with the system resulting in people paying late fees.

Table C.1 Compliance Cost of GST as Reflected in Late Fee Paid

Return Period	Required to File	Returns Filed on Time (A)	Cumulative Returns (B)	Late Returns Filed (B-A)	Late Fee and Interest Paid for Late Filing of Return (Rs lakh)	Late Fee and Interest Paid for Each Late Return (Rs)	Late Fee for Late Filing of Return (Rs lakh)	Late Fee Per Late Return Filed (Rs)
July '17	66,47,581	38,34,877	63,88,549	25,53,672	0.97	0.04	0.2	0.01
Aug '17	73,70,102	27,25,183	68,51,732	41,26,549	648.81	15.72	432.2	10.47
Sep '17	78,23,806	39,34,256	71,09,143	31,74,887	4,457.16	140.39	3,472.4	109.37
Oct '17	77,21,075	43,68,711	67,77,440	24,08,729	16,171.03	671.35	14,868.5	617.28
Nov '17	79,57,204	49,13,065	67,65,603	18,52,538	4,666.90	251.92	3,127.4	168.82
Dec '17	81,22,425	54,26,278	67,47,887	13,21,609	8,258.41	624.88	5,252.8	397.46
Jan '18	83,22,611	53,94,018	66,94,387	13,00,369	13,085.25	1,006.27	9,246.8	711.09
Feb '18	85,27,127	54,51,304	65,62,362	11,11,358	12,682.25	1,141.15	9,046.47	814.00

Sources: http://pib.nic.in/newsite/PrintRelease.aspx?relid=178962 (last accessed on 25 June 2018); https://taxguru.in/goods-and-service-tax/important-aspects-rti-reply-received-cbic-rs-900-crores-collected-gst-late-fees.html (last accessed on 25 June 1018).

In a recent document International Monetary Fund (IMF) mentions:

> While evidence on GST compliance costs in India are scanty, anecdotal evidence suggests that for large firms, the cost has increased from negligible shares to 0.2 percent of total costs (excluding switch-over costs which are estimated to be around the same level), though there are economies from switching to a simpler tax structure particularly for inter-state commerce. It is also taken as well established in the literature that compliance costs are regressive. Another important benefit of a simpler rate structure is that it would reduce opportunities to lobby for lower rates among firms. (IMF 2018)

Cases Undertaken under Anti-Profiteering Clause

In order to pre-empt unfair gains by suppliers in the changeover from the existing regime to GST, an anti-profiteering clause has been incorporated into the GST law. As per this clause, a taxpayer is expected to pass on benefits accruing as a result of lower taxes or additional credit through the input tax credit mechanism. An anti-profiteering authority has been constituted to monitor any issues raised on this front and deliver adjudication. While a number of cases have been flagged for the authority to look at, so far the authority seems to have delivered only four orders, and all four of them conclude that there is no evidence of undue profiteering by the concerned firm. There are a number of ongoing high-profile cases under review with the authority. The issues under review and the orders issued by the authority can be viewed as a mechanism for the government to portray concern for the consumer by reining in unfair gains by suppliers. The nature of analysis required to establish unfair gains in many of the cases, however, can be beyond the scope of a legal body and can potentially be contested in a court of law. In other words, this provision, while optically very interesting, might lead to more disputes, a matter which needs to be addressed carefully by the authority.

Cases of Disputes under GST

One indicator of the compliance friendliness of a tax regime is the extent of disputes arising from the regime. While there is little information about the nature of disputes being raised with reference to the GST regime, Table C.2 summarises the information available for disputes as on 16 March 2018. The table suggests that within the first eight months of the introduction of GST, there are 14 cases that have escalated to the Supreme Court. While it is difficult to judge from the number of cases whether the GST regime is more prone to disputes than other tax regimes that the country has had, what the table does indicate is that the cases seem to be disproportionately associated with certain regions/high courts. This could be read as a relatively high acceptability of the regime in the other regions of the country – a positive indicator given the magnitude of change involved. More recent figures on the number of disputes registered is, however, not available.

**Table C.2   Cases Filed due to Disputes Arising out of GST
(as on 16 March 2018)**

Forum	No. of Cases
Supreme Court	14
Various High Courts	179
- Allahabad	7
- Bombay	23
- Bombay (Nagpur Bench)	2
- Bombay High Court (Aurangabad Bench)	1
- Calcutta	2
- Chhattisgarh	5
- Delhi	53
- Guwahati (Itanagar Bench)	1
- Guwahati (Kohima Bench)	1
- Gujarat	9
- Hyderabad	8
- Jharkhand	19
- Karnataka	4
- Kerala	10
- Madhya Pradesh	1
- Madhya Pradesh (Indore Bench)	1
- Madras	2
- Madras (Madurai Bench)	3
- Orissa	3
- Punjab and Haryana	12
- Rajasthan	4
- Rajasthan (Jodhpur Bench)	4
- Shimla	1
- Sikkim	3

Source: Rajya Sabha unstarred question NO-3595, answered on 27 March 2018.

To deal with the possibility of disputes especially resulting from differences in classification of goods and/or services, the GST regime has a mechanism for advance ruling. The Authority for Advance Ruling is expected to provide written clarification to the taxpayer seeking such clarification regarding supply of goods and services. The clarification is sought and provided prior to the commencement of the business activity. The introduction of an advance ruling arrangement can work towards reducing some of the disputes that might arise in the regime. So far, the Authority of Advance Ruling has provided 111 rulings. Table C.3 shows the distribution of these rulings across states. The distribution appears to suggest that taxpayers in some states seem more keen to use the Advance Ruling Route rather than the dispute route – though the two may relate to different kinds of issues.

Table C.3   Advance Rulings Issued (as on 8 August 2018)

State	No. of Advance Rulings
Andhra Pradesh	8
Chhattisgarh	2
Delhi	6
Gujarat	18
Haryana	10
Karnataka	12
Kerala	7
Maharashtra	16
Odisha	1
Rajasthan	6
Telangana	7
Uttarakhand	7
West Bengal	10
Total	110

Source: http://gstcouncil.gov.in/rulings-by-advance-authority?field_state_ut_
tid=All&field_year_tid=All&page=11 (last accessed on 8 August 2018).

Revenue Performance of States

With limited information in the public domain about the details of revenue collections across states, it is difficult to infer about the likely impact on state finances. In the short run, however, the assurance of the Union government of 14 per cent year-on-year growth in revenue as compared to the reference year of 2015–16 ensured that states are protected from fluctuations in revenues due to the introduction of GST. Further still, it allows for the GST council to experiment with policy changes without immediate concerns of state revenues. The assured rate of growth of revenue is rather generous given the fact that inflation in India is now mandated to remain at an average of 4 per cent as per the mandate assigned to the Reserve Bank of India. A low rate of inflation and growth in GDP of 7 per cent would imply a growth in nominal GDP of only about 11–12 per cent. With 14 per cent assurance, the states in effect get a tax buoyancy of at least 1.17.

In the medium term, looking beyond the period of assured compensation, the revenue profile can be different for different states, just as it was in the period prior to the introduction of GST. Table C.4 presents the revenue collection for four states with a comparison of revenues prior to the introduction of GST. The table highlights the fact that the revenue performance had a remarkable difference across the four states considered, with Maharashtra reporting 29 per cent growth on one side and Odisha reporting a decline in revenue collections. Interestingly, both Tamil Nadu and Kerala display rates of growth that are less than 14 per cent. While this picture might undergo considerable change with the evolution of the GST regime and with

Table C.4 GST for a Few Selected States

	Tamil Nadu (Rs Crore)			Odisha (Rs Crore)			Maharashtra (Rs Crore)			Kerala (Rs Crore)		
	2016–17	2017–18	% increase/ decrease	2016–17	2017–18	% increase/ decrease	2016–17	2017–18	% increase/ decrease	2016–17	2017–18	% increase/ decrease
GST		16201.70			3766.47			36418.30			11467.62	
IGST		8706.99			2377.33			14480.25			7103.71	
VAT (on GST Goods)	26127.51	9375.91		5859.98	226.55		61742.21	35332.78		17854.37		
CST (on GST Goods)	5125.20	1737.17		727.54	– 18.77		6502.43	3061.29				
Sales Tax	188.65	168.44		11.91	4.09							
Entry Tax	2528.24	899.51		1219.37	336.34		369.96	149.72				
Entertainment Tax	85.81	36.48		18.50	12.28							
Luxury Tax	379.01	137.18					538.23	190.69				
Others	7.86	2.03					99.03	49.73				
Total State Tax Revenue under GST and Subsumed Act (A)	**34442.28**	**37265.41**	**8.20**	**7837.29**	**6741.83**	**–13.98**	**69251.86**	**89682.76**	**29.50**	**17854.37**	**18571.33**	**4.02**
Non-VAT (on Non-GST Goods)	33134.49	35928.35		3696.81	4448.26		18977.42	22652.28		16183.99	16997.87	
CST (on Non-GST Goods)				0.68	0.83							
Total State Tax Revenue Outside GST (B)	33134.49	35928.35	8.43	3697.49	4449.09	20.33	18977.42	22652.28	19.36	16183.99	16997.87	5.03
Total (A+B)	**67576.77**	**73193.76**	**8.31**	**11534.78**	**11190.92**	**–2.98**	**88229.28**	**112335.04**	**27.32**	**34038.36**	**35569.20**	**4.50**

Sources: Tamil Nadu: https://ctd.tn.gov.in/documents/10184/20741/ADMINISTRATIVE+REPORT+2017-2018/748773c3-2f25-4192-a416-268eb4931cd9?version=1.1 (last accessed on 23 July 2018).

Odisha: https://odishatax.gov.in/sites/default/files/inline-files/Comparative%20Analysis%20of%20collection%20of%20Tax%20revenue%28net%20of%20refund%29%20from%20aug%202017%20to%20March%202018.pdf (last accessed on 23 July 2018).

Maharashtra: https://mahagst.gov.in/en/act-wise-sales-tax-revenue-gross-receipts-years-1996-97-2017-18 (last accessed on 23 July 2018).

Kerala: http://keralataxes.gov.in/2018/05/24/tax-collection-2018-19/ and http://keralataxes.gov.in/2018/01/06/details-of-collection-and-budget-estimate-for-the-year-2016-17-and-2017-18-rs-in-crore/ (last accessed on 23 July 2018).

the anticipated positive economic response kicking in, in its present state the picture suggests that some states might face considerable handicap within the new regime. This is an aspect that the GST Council would perhaps monitor closely.

The Way Forward

The GST regime is evolving in many different ways – it is evolving in structure as well as in the associated compliance and administrative regimes. The evolution is desirable and helpful inasmuch as it addresses the concerns faced by the taxpayers. However, the evolution also implies a long transition before the regime achieves stability, which in turn introduces an element of uncertainty into the regime. The positive gains from GST would be associated partly with the structure of the new regime and partly with stability in the regime. In other words, the timeline for the economy to experience the gains from GST might be extended beyond the initial years.

What is, however, very interesting is that the graduated transition to the 'ideal' GST regime seems to have resulted in the Indian economy bypassing some of the anticipated shocks in the form of an increase in inflation or a reduction in growth rate. The overall context of the economy, however. is beset with a number of potential problems – increase in the international price of crude oil and stress in the Indian banking system, to name a few. These too could contribute to a delay in the speed with which the economy can extract gains from the GST regime. Any analysis of the impact of GST should therefore be suitably nuanced to take these factors into account.

References

International Monetary Fund (IMF) (2018). 'India: Selected Issues', IMF Country Report No. 18/255, August 2018, Washington, D.C.: International Monetary Fund.

The Treasury, Australian Government (2003). 'Preliminary Assessment of the Impact of the New Tax System', Economic Roundup AUTUMN 2003. Available at: http://archive. treasury.gov.au/documents/580/HTML/docshell.asp?URL=New_Tax_System.asp (last accessed on 13 August 2018).

Index